DAS REICH

DAS REICH

THE MILITARY ROLE OF THE
2ND SS DIVISION

JAMES LUCAS

CASSELL

This book is dedicated to those men, living and dead, who fought in the ranks of the 2nd SS Panzer Division 'Das Reich' or in any of the formations of the SS 'V', 'Deutschland', or 'Reich' Division, out of which it evolved.

Cassell Military Paperbacks

Cassell & Co
Wellington House, 125 Strand
London WC2R 0BB

First published by Arms and Armour 1991
This Cassell Military Paperbacks edition 1999
Reprinted 2001 (twice), 2002

British Library Cataloguing-in-Publication Data
A catalogue record for this book is available from the British Library.

ISBN 0-304-35199-7

Designed and edited by DAG Publications Ltd
Edited by Michael Boxall; designed by David Gibbons

Printed and bound in Great Britain by
Cox & Wyman Ltd., Reading, Berks.

Contents

Maps

Acknowledgements

Those of us who write the histories of units that fought in recent wars are fortunate because modern methods of communication make it easy to contact men who soldiered with those units. Thus, even before research began on this book, I knew that there were still living a great number of those who had served in 'Das Reich' Division. In addition to those living witnesses I had also learned that an unofficial archive existed which held official reports, personal accounts and letters. It is upon the spoken and written testimony of former members of the Division and its constituent regiments that my text is based. The words of veteran soldiers project images of brilliant colour and dramatic action which imprint themselves indelibly upon the mind. These are not inherited memories but are the true and lively words of men who fought, suffered and survived the terrible battles which they so vividly describe.

While carrying out research on this book I was very fortunate in making the acquaintance of two very special men: Otto Weidinger, the last commander of 'Der Führer' Regiment and Mark Yerger, the American historian and author. Through Otto Weidinger's influence I was invited to the 'DF' regimental reunion, where I met a great many former officers and men of 'Das Reich' Division. Mark Yerger, whom I also met there, gave and has continued to give selfless encouragement and has supplied me with invaluable advice on the history of the Division, its personalities and organization.

I acknowledge, with grateful thanks, my debt to those two gentlemen in particular, as well as to the former soldiers of 'DR' Division, in general. They all helped in the preparation of the text and many supplied personal photographs. The names of those whose stories illuminate my text are given at the end of this book, but there are some contributors to whom I must offer a more personal expression of gratitude. These are: Her Highness, Ingeborg Alix, Princess Stephanie of Schaumberg-Lippe; Colonel Ernst Deutsch; Colonel Hans Garn; Major Hans Hauser; Oberstudienrat Heid Ruehl and Hans Werner Woltersdorf.

Thanks also go to the several libraries, archives and institutions, both in Germany and in the United Kingdom, whose officers were, as always, courteous, helpful and efficient.

Finally, to my dear wife, Traude, go my thanks and love for her unfailing support and encouragement.

James Lucas

11

Preface

There was a time, in this country, when a writer presenting an objective history of a German division that fought in the Second World War faced the accusation of showing leniency to one of Britain's former enemies. To present an objective history of an SS division attracted violent criticism because the general public accepted, without question, that the whole SS organization was criminal and, thus by inference, each man who had served in it was a felon.

More recently we have come to admit that the German soldier had the same qualities as the soldiers of other armies and those who esteem the military virtues of loyalty, courage and duty recognize that the Germanic SS divisions, of which 'Das Reich' was one, had those virtues in great measure. Its officers and men were, as a consequence, exceptionally skilled warriors.

Enlistment into the ranks of the Waffen SS in the pre-war years, was voluntary and the physical, mental and moral standards were set so high that only a minority of those who volunteered were accepted. During the war, despite strenuous efforts to maintain it as an all-volunteer force, it became common, from mid-1944 onwards, to cover the terrible losses which the Waffen SS suffered, to transfer groups of men *en bloc* from the Luftwaffe or the Kriegsmarine into the SS. Once in its ranks those men were quick to absorb that elusive mystique which imbues volunteer élite units, that indescribable and intangible yet potent force which keeps such formations fighting long after others have given up the struggle. The élite know they are the best and repeatedly prove that claim in bloody and wasteful battle.

In the case of 'Das Reich' Division, bloody battle, particularly on the Eastern Front, was carried out at close quarters or even hand to hand. All front-line military units, at some time in their active service lives, fight such battles. For the Germanic SS and, particularly for the Division whose history is recounted here, fighting at close quarters or hand to hand was the rule and not the exception. It fought a hard and uncompromising war whose nature is difficult to comprehend by those who have not experienced it. Hand-to-hand fighting often meant grappling with an enemy soldier as you tried to kill him with chopping blows of an entrenching tool or with a bayonet's thrusting blade. Close-quarter fighting meant, in some cases, trotting alongside the steel colossus of a tank in order to place a high-explosive charge on its outside. That was the infantryman's war as the Grenadiers of 'Das Reich' experienced it. The battlefield of the panzermen was a cramped steel box filled with deafening noise and action. Always present was the knowledge that a direct hit might fill the vehicle's fighting compartment with a whirling, solid-shot projectile whose velocity could, within seconds, mash the crew into bloody gobbets of flesh or whose careering course might start a fire and cremate the crew, turning the panzer into a funeral pyre. All these battlefield incidents as well as other, more terrible things, the reader must experience through my words and see these in his own mind's eye as he follows the men of 'Das Reich' Division in their campaigns. Despite the frequent mentions of close-quarter and hand-to-hand combat the reader will find no braggadocio attitudes among the accounts, reports and anecdotes which are recorded here. Those who fight and bleed in battle have no need to dramatise their exploits with extravagant emphasis. If anything, the actions in which they fought are understated and their own part in them played down.

Readers familiar with the British Army's method of rotating units on active service will be surprised to learn from this history that the men of 'DR' often spent weeks and months in the line without relief, taking casualties at a rate that would have destroyed a lesser unit. The response of Obersturmbann-führer Kumm when asked the strength of his unit, was to point through the window to 35 men standing in the Russian snow; the survivors of his regiment which had gone into battle three battalions strong. Georg Vilzmann's battle account of the fighting in the Ardennes, concluded with the chilling statement, '...That night No. 5 Company, with a total strength of one officer, three NCOs and eight men took part in a counter-attack ...'

The leadership qualities of SS NCOs and officers were encapsulated into the slogan 'Follow me, men.' In attack the commanders led from the front as the story of Obersturmbannführer Harmel in the fighting along the River Donets during March 1943, demonstrates. And in withdrawal, such men were the last to leave, as is shown by the account of Obersturmführer Wagner of the Division's Replacement Battalion in Prague during May 1945. Inevitably, casualty lists were long and filled with the names of the most adventurous, the most willing and most self-sacrificing. As the German Army song proclaims, 'We buried so many of our best in foreign soil.'

Paradoxically, the losses suffered by 'Das Reich' and the other SS Divisions helped maintain the warrior reputation which had been gained. The constant infusion of fresh blood, of trained, dedicated young men, was one factor which kept the fighting edge sharp. Another was the unique bond of comradeship between all ranks of the SS, the product of their training, the SS ethic and the shared experiences of the battlefield. The longer the war lasted the stronger became that bond and in the bitterness of defeat it transcended the privations and humiliations of prison camps and remains today as firm as ever, despite the passing of more than half a century.

Those who fought in the ranks of 'Das Reich' helped to create, in the short period of the six years of the Second World War, a military reputation that was worthy of its position as the premier Division of the Waffen SS. Although it was the first SS Division to be raised, it was numbered two in the order of precedence of those divisions because Adolf Hitler's bodyguard formation, the Leibstandarte, could be second to none. It is, however, a fact that from SS

'V: Division or its successors, came the commanders who led other SS divisions and inspired them with the ethos they themselves had acquired under Steiner, Hausser and the other innovators of the Waffen SS.

Organization and Recruitment

The defence squads of the National Socialist Workers Party; its Schutz Staffeln or SS, were created in the 1920s, specifically to protect the fledgling Party's orators against the violence of their opponents. The Nazi Party grew in size and developed from being a minor and provincial Munich-based organization into a national, political force. One consequence of that development was the need to increase the size of part-time SS defence squads and to raise others in many of Germany's principal cities. Eventually, the Party was able to employ its defence squads on a permanent, full-time basis and to quarter them in quasi-barrack accommodation. By this time the SS formations, whose name was changed, temporarily, to 'Politische Bereitschaften' (Political Stand-by detachments), had the unofficial status of special police detachments.

In addition to the 'Defence Squads', there was another SS grouping, the Allgemeine or General branch, whose tasks were chiefly administrative. Although the first Politische Bereitschaften were formed from the Allgemeine SS, 'Das Reich' Division, the subject of this book, developed separately from the Allgemeine and became one of the first units of the Waffen SS (SS Under Arms).

The Nazi Party became the national government of Germany on 30 January 1933. The leaders of the Party, considering theirs to be a revolutionary body and their assumption of power to be an act of revolution, took steps to ensure that there could be no counter-revolution to depose them. The easiest ways of ensuring this were to use the Allgemeine SS to penetrate every aspect of German life and to increase the dominance of the Politische Bereitschaften by stationing large detachments of them in all the principal cities of Germany.

The miscellany of units which constituted the Politische Bereitschaften then needed to be regularized, placed on an official footing and centrally administered. Measures to accomplish this began as early as 14 December 1934, when Himmler, the Reichsführer SS, issued a memorandum: ' . . . with immediate effect the former Politische Bereitschaften, including the "Leibstandarte SS Adolf Hitler", will become units of the Verfügungs Truppe'. Then came in succession the amalgamation of sub-units into battalions and eventually into three Standarten (regiments): 'Adolf Hitler', 'Deutschland' and 'Germania'. Because of its role as the Führer's own guard regiment, 'Adolf Hitler' left the mainstream Verfügungs Truppe or V-T organization and in 1938 was replaced by 'Der Führer' Standarte. In October 1939, at the conclusion of the Army's victorious campaign in Poland, those regiments and miscellaneous V-T units which had not yet been grouped within a Standarte, were all amalgamated into a Verfügungs or SS 'V' Division.

But long before that step was taken the role foreseen for the full-time SS regiments had undergone a change. They were no longer considered as armed police but as a para-military body. This acorded with Hitler's statement made to the Reichstag in 1935, when he proclaimed the reintroduction of conscription. He foresaw a peace-time army of 36 divisions, one of which would be an SS formation. That division would not be on the establishment of the police or army but would be a permanent body of troops to be used as he ordered. He did concede that in the event of mobilization the SS 'V' Division, whose strength he limited to 20,000 men, would be subordinated to the Army High Command. In order that the SS men should become proficient in military tactics and the use of weapons, groups of them were temporarily posted to infantry regiments of the regular army and, as an outward sign of the military role which it was foreseen that they would play, army badges of rank were introduced. These were worn on the shoulder-straps, but standard SS badges of rank were retained on the jacket lapels. Permanent barracks were built to house the SS regiments and, so as to accord more closely to the structure of army battalions, certain SS rifle companies were converted to such specialist roles as motor cyclist, anti-tank and pioneer companies, and in 1939 the lack of heavy weapons was overcome by the creation of an artillery' regiment.

The V-T formations underwent another change of name when a memorandum dated 2 November 1939, issued by the Reichsführer SS, ordered: ' ... with effect from ... [1. 12. 39], the whole replacement organization of the SS and Police will be renamed and known as the "Replacement Department of the Waffen SS". ... The Head of that Department will be known as Chief of the Replacement Department of the Waffen SS, i.e., the armed units of the SS.' In his book *Die Waffen SS – Eine Dokumentation,* Klietmann asserts it to be possible that the term, 'Waffen SS' was in use at an earlier date than that of Himmler's memorandum.

This book deals with the men and units of the original Waffen SS 'V' Division, and follows them and their successors through the series of organizational and name changes, the end product of which was 2nd SS Panzer Division 'Das Reich'.

As the following pages will show, 'Deutschland' and 'Germania' regiments, two of the first three organized V-T formations, were the principal sources out of which many of the 38 Divisions of the Waffen SS were to be created during the Second World War. Throughout the war a stream of senior and subaltern officers, NCOs and men were posted away from their parent Standarten or from 'V' Division, to train the soldiers of newly raised SS units. The attitudes and training which those instructors had themselves undergone were passed down to the soldiers whom they led in battle, producing an élan and combat efficiency that is generally acknowledged to be the hallmark of the Germanic Waffen SS formations.

Because of its special position within the divisional structure 'Deutschland' Regiment together with its constituent battalions will be described at length; the other battalions and regiments of the Division less so.

Regiment 'Deutschland'

1st Battalion. In October 1933, the 1st Battalion of what was to become Regiment 'Deutschland' or 'D' was created around a cadre of about 35 specially selected men, one from each Standarte of the Allgemeine SS, and who had been posted to the 'Munich Regiment', of the Bavarian provincial police. The first cadets were selected for training as future officers of the SS and graduates from that first course went on to the SS Officers' Academy at Bad Tölz in Bavaria. The course for officers was succeeded by one for other ranks, the volunteers for which were drawn chiefly from the Allgemeine SS and kept together so as to form SS platoons within the police companies. Out of those platoons there evolved, in July 1934, a 'Politische Bereitschaft München', made up of three infantry companies, a machine-gun company and an infantry gun company. The commander of the Politische Bereitschaft, Ritter von Hengl, transferred from the police to the SS and took with him police officers to command the new body. The rank and file required to bring the companies up to establishment were all volunteers from the SS and chiefly southern Germans.

On 1 October 1934, that 'Politische Bereitschaft' amalgamated with two others to form a Standarte or Regiment and it was retitled, 1st Battalion of Standarte 1 of the SS Verfügungs Truppe [abbreviated to 1/SS 1. V-T]. Following certain administrative changes, the SS V-T organization ceased to be a Party body and became instead a national one organized along the lines of, and having the structure of a unit of, the regular army. Although the 1st Standarte V-T was not yet considered to be a component of the armed forces, its battalions and regimental units were under the nominal command of the army's 7th Infantry Division. During the Reichsparteitag celebrations the regiment was named 'Deutschland' and had colours presented to it and to its constituent battalions. Regimental armbands were issued in November.

The battalions took up quarters in barracks, the 1st Battalion entering the newly constructed Munich Freimann Barracks in 1936, where the regimental headquarters was established in the early summer of 1939. The emphasis in training was not only upon practical subjects, such as field training, but also included long periods of foot and arms drill, necessary instruction for units which were called upon, as 1st Battalion was, to perform ceremonial duties.

The organization of V-T formations followed that of standard infantry units, with the companies in the rifle battalions as well as in the heavy weapons companies numbered serially. A cadre was created during October 1934, around which No. 13 Infantry Gun Company was built and taken on charge of 1st Battalion. With the expansion of the battalion to regimental strength, No. 13 Company was transferred on to regimental establishment. The anti-tank gun company, No. 14, was raised in 1937 and No. 15, the motor cycle company in January 1935. The latter, like the infantry gun company, at first formed part of 1st Battalion but reverted to regimental control.

2nd Battalion. The predominant national group within 2nd Battalion was Austrian, its men being members of the Austrian SA and SS who had fled from their own country into southern Germany. The title of the first unit into which these men were grouped was 'The Austrian Legion' but the group underwent a change of name to 'Hilfswerk Osterreich' and then to 'Hilfswerk Schleissheim' before it became 2nd Battalion of 'D' Regiment. Pay and rations for the 'Legion' were poor and the priority given to their needs so low that many recruits carried out duties while still dressed in their civilian clothes. Indeed, no proper uniforms were issued until March 1934. During that year, Mussolini, as the more powerful of the two Fascist states, and at the instigation of the Austrian government, demanded that all Austrian Nazi units stationed in Germany be disbanded. To avoid this, German citizenship was granted to all members of the 'Austrian Legion'. Himmler, the Reichsführer SS, proposed that the 'Legion' be taken on to the strength of 'D' Regiment as its 2nd Battalion and on 1 April 1935, Carl-Maria Demelhuber took over command. Under him the battalion expanded to full strength and was quartered in the barracks in the Ingolstadt Landstrasse.

3rd Battalion. On 1 July 1936, a third battalion was raised in the Munich-Freimann barracks around a cadre drawn from 1st and 4th Battalions of the regiment. Company commanders for the new unit were supplied by 4th Battalion. Volunteers to bring the battalion up to full strength came from Bavaria and from Württemberg and such was the enthusiasm of all ranks that the battalion was raised and its men fully trained within a year.

4th Battalion. During May 1935 volunteers from the south-western region of Germany were formed into the 'Politische Bereitschaft Württemberg' and quartered in Ellwangen barracks. Although volunteers came in from all parts of Germany, the greatest number came from the Württemberg area. An initial shortage of NCOs was overcome by seconding these from army units, and relations with the army were strengthened when junior NCOs of the SS were temporarily attached to military units to be instructed in man-management.

The 'Politische Bereitschaft', became 4th Battalion of the regiment on 1 October 1934, and passed under the authority of 5th Infantry Division in Ulm. During the late summer of 1935, Felix Steiner succeeded Major Boye as battalion commander and assumed commander of Regiment 'Deutschland' on 1 July 1936, in the rank of Standartenführer. It was on 1 November 1938 that 4th Battalion left the regiment upon conversion to a motor-cycle battalion.

Let us here consider those men who came forward to serve in the SS.

Volunteers for the V-T came from every part of Germany and from every social class. Recruits were accepted only after the most stringent tests and after meeting the most demanding requirements. What the recruiting officers were looking for chiefly was idealism and enthusiasm. Political attitudes, in the pre-war days, were not considered important, nor did volunteers need to be Party members or to have served in the Hitler Youth, although many had. Those who came forward felt themselves to be, as did so many German lads of the time, the standard-bearers of a finer and better Fatherland. They were keen to become soldiers for they saw themselves as following in the footsteps of their fathers, the men who had fought in the Great War. And they wanted to serve in the SS because it was an honour to be accepted for an élite unit — the equivalent in the Third Reich of the old Imperial Guard regiments. So many volunteers came in that an exceptionally high standard could be demanded, and most of those who volunteered were rejected.

Karl Pichler and Walter Schminke were two men who volunteered and were accepted; Pichler before the war and Schminke in the early years of the war.

'We were three Austrians from the province of Steiermark, Hans Loibner, Rudi Zottler and I,' wrote Pichler. 'It was about 20 September 1937, and we were in Munich hoping to enlist into the SS Verfügungs Truppe, a unit of which we knew nothing other than that it was an élite formation. At the recruiting office there were about fifty young Bavarian boys waiting to join up. Yet every time the door to the office opened and a candidate came out our hopes dropped. From all the men who had gone in no more than one or two had been accepted for the SS.

'The first of our trio, Hans, went in and we waited anxiously for him to come out. When he did words were not necessary; his smile stretched from ear to ear. Then it was my turn. After giving my personal details to an officer I underwent a complete medical examination from the soles of my feet to the crown of my head. I passed and was declared fit for the SS. Rudi Zottler then went in and he too was accepted. We caught a bus to Freimann where "Deutschland" had its barracks and we were very impressed with these. We had never seen anything like them in our lives. Four huge buildings, several storeys high formed a quadrangle around a vast parade-ground. There were hundreds of soldiers drilling there and my first impression was that this could not be the unit into which we had enlisted. The instructors shouted at the men as if they were all deaf. Some recruits were crawling on their bellies, others hopped like rabbits, ran backwards and forwards, flung themselves to the ground, jumped up again and carried out such mad movements that I was sure we were in a madhouse. We did not stay long at Freimann and a couple of days later went by truck to a new barracks, a series of single-storey buildings.

'We waited in the hall of the administration block and a couple of minutes later a young officer came out. I learned later that this was Obersturmbann-führer Deutsch, the commanding officer. He asked who we were and then said, "So, you want to be soldiers?" Remembering what I had seen in the Freimann barracks I replied, "No, I want to join the SS." To this he remarked that it was one and the same thing. My comrades and I were now in "N" battalion of the SS.'

Walter Schminke's fascinating booklet, *Errinerungen an meine Dienstzeit in der Waffen SS (Memories of my time in the Waffen SS)* recalls how he enlisted and describes the initial training he underwent:

'When the war with Russia broke out in 1941, I was one of those who rushed to join the Colours. It was really not that simple because I was in a reserved occupation working in a department designing secret equipment. In those days masses of men flocked to the recruiting offices, a situation which is unimaginable today. They volunteered, not because it was the "in" thing to do, but because of something else, the results of education, tradition, inherited feelings, etc. Totally unmodern today.

'I decided to volunteer for the SS, which was rather like reaching for the stars. I filled in the forms and returned a week later to join a crowd of men all about 1.76m tall and each of them classified as Al. Most had a military bearing and some were in the uniform of the Hitler Youth. Once again we were medically examined and I was afraid that a small scar on my forehead might disqualify me. Then came the racial inspection, where the skull was measured, the distance between the eyes checked, length and width of the nose, the shape and size of the ears, shoulder width and a great many other things measured. The NCO carrying out these tests looked at me for a long time, like a cattle dealer, before telling me that I was accepted . . . The inspecting officers looked pleased with their work. So few had passed. There had been a good weeding out – Himmler, the Reichsführer would be well pleased with them.

'When I joined my unit there was a series of quick selections; the result of being ordered to move to the right or to the left. I was one of the final "left" group and found out that I was now one of the mortar platoon. Then we were allocated to our rooms and shown how to fill matresses with straw, how we were to wash our feet, in which trouser pocket we were to carry our handkerchief and how to make up our beds. Days passed and then we were issued with uniforms. We were then instructed in marching, running, lying down, saluting, standing up, how to keep a straight face, how to keep your trap shut, how to shout loudly and a number of other useful things. Then we received our rifles, equipment and service dress. The black parade uniforms were kept in a cupboard and were not to be issued until we had won the war.

'The daily round started with reveille at 06.00 hours, wash, shave (even with our bum fluff), dress, drink coffee, make up the beds, clean the room, collect the heavy weapons. Then we paraded, listened to a few words from the company commander and marched off to the tram stop. Because of the weight of our heavy weapons we actually travelled by tram to the training ground. There we spent the whole morning in field training; setting up the mortar, breaking down the mortar, changing position, setting up the mortar, etc., etc. Sometimes we spent the time digging in, flinging practice handgrenades, camouflage and gas training before returning by tram to the barracks. Wash, finger-nail inspection and off to lunch. The meals were excellent, filling and well cooked. Then other types of training; musketry, marching, saluting drill, etc. At 17.00 hours back to our rooms to clean weapons, polish equipment, carry out darning, etc., and then a cold evening meal. At 19.00 hours orders for the next day were issued followed by instruction in the lecture hall on ballistics, the different ranks, weapons, history and political matters. Some lectures, especially those by the Spiess on architecture, art and the history of Prague (where we were stationed) were very educational. Then at 22.00 hours lights out and the pleasure of lying on our straw sacks, listening to Lala Andersen singing "Lili Marlene" and to the murmuring conversation of our mates. It was a very nice feeling.'

Karl Pichler recalled one training ground known to all recruits of the pre-war "N" Battalion as 'Paradise':

'One of our platoon officers loved that piece of ground so we were often "in Paradise". One autumn day we marched out through a steady drizzle of rain to "Paradise". We arrived just as the farmer had finished spreading the area with manure. There was a terrible stink of cows and pigs in the air. The prayer, "Lord let this cup pass from me", was not granted and on our officer's lips was a satisfied smile as he explained the tactical situation. He waved his hand across the dung-covered "Paradise" and pointed to a small wood. There, he explained, were the enemy trenches and went on to say that it was our task to carry out an attack and to drive him from those positions.

'The machine-guns opened up and we fired our blanks at the imaginary enemy. Then we had to rush forward and fling ourselves flat. Some recruits tried to find a nice place on which to lie down. This caused our officer to order a new movement. "The enemy barrage is too heavy. As we cannot pass through it we will roll over and over on the ground in order to reach a new assault position. Follow me," and he flung himself on to that dung covered field and rolled over and over. With rifles pressed between our knees and tight to our chests we, too, rolled over and over, cursing and swearing.

'We returned to barracks stinking from the filth which encrusted our uniforms. But our officer marched at our head as proud as a Spaniard, as if we had just won a battle. Before he dismissed us he spoke a few words. "Lads, think of this. If we were under fire you would not have time to find a nice place to fling yourself down. You would hit the deck quickly, irrespective of whether it was a field of flowers or a pile of shit." He was right, of course.'

The strenuous training in the open air sharpened already large, youthful appetites and there is no armed force in the world in which rations are not a subject for discussion or complaint. In the summer of 1938, Himmler, the Reichsführer SS, carried out a tour of inspection of V-T units and his visit to 'N' Battalion was recalled by Hans Riedl: 'As usual the unit officers were issued the same meal as the men. Before we were marched to the dining-hall our hands and finger-nails were given a more thorough going over than usual. Then we marched off, singing, to the dining-hall. When we were all assembled the Reichsführer, his aides and our own unit officers entered. Himmler stopped at a number of tables, putting a question here and a question there. At our table he asked Perzel of No. 3 Company, if it were usual to be given three dumplings with the meal. Quick as a flash Perzel replied, "No, Reichsführer. Only because you have come." There was dead silence among the embarrassed officers accompanying the Reichsführer, but Himmler had already moved away to the next table.

Karl Wolff of the same battalion recalled that meal of roast pork, sauerkraut and dumplings, but for a different reason. 'We young recruits all had healthy appetites. Paul Hahn of No. 2 Company was celebrated for his capacity. When the meal was ended and the officers had left – they did not seem to have very healthy appetites – there were several terrines of food left on their table. Our Paul, lightning fast, had been waiting for just such an opportunity and pretty soon two terrines full of dumplings were on our table. Paul broke the battalion record by eating twelve of them.'

The introduction of the grey Service dress during 1935, was an indication that the V-T was being trained for a military role. An extract from a memorandum issued by the Supreme Commander of the Army on 1 August 1938, reads: ' . . . The Führer has given instruction to the Army Supreme Command concerning the employment of the SS Verfügungs Truppe in the Field Army . . . The "Leibstandarte SS Adolf Hitler", is to be organized like a motorized infantry regiment. SS Standarte "Germania" . . . like an infantry regiment, SS Standarte "Deutschland" like a four-battalion infantry regiment . . . '

At this point and before the other V-T formations are described, it is appropriate to mention Felix Steiner and his influence upon the training of the units under his command. It was as commander of 4th Battalion of 'Deutschland' Regiment in Ellwangen that Steiner was able to develop his theories on the employment of infantry on the battlefield. The success which his battle drills achieved, at first on peace-time manoeuvres and then under active service conditions, ensured that they were taken up enthusiastically by the whole SS organization and there is no doubt that these drills played an important part in producing the spirit of moral superiority which enabled the Germanic divisions of the SS to achieve their spectacular victories. Steiner broke completely with the standard methods of training and devoted his considerable energy and powerful personality to instructing and educating his men along lines which he himself had formulated. In place of barrack-square drill which produced a soldier only able to operate as part of a military formation, Steiner aimed to train an individual who combined the fieldcraft of a skilled hunter and the fitness of a trained athlete. Steiner intended that this new-model soldier should be able to operate in any type of terrain or climate. Further, his warrior would be so physically fit that even at the end of a long and strenuous march his reserves of energy would be sufficient for him to carry out an attack upon the enemy's positions. Steiner believed that through a combination of warrior skills battlefield losses could be kept to a minimum, accepting wholeheartedly the concept that sweat in training saves blood in battle.

But it was not enough to bring the individual up to a high physical standard. He must also be competent to meet the psychological pressures of command and Steiner insisted that all his men, irrespective of rank, were to be trained to take over the duties of their immediate superior so that if he were killed a given task could be brought to a successful conclusion. Developing from the individual to the unit, Steiner considered that the conventional military organization was not flexible enough to use his highly trained men to their best advantage. He replaced traditional and rigid military groups with small assault detachments which, when grouped, created a powerful fighting formation similar to the German storm battalions of the Great War.

An example of the physical fitness of Steiner's battalion can be gauged by the fact that in 1937, at the conclusion of a long-distance marching competition, the 450-man strong group of 4th Battalion, not only covered the 25 kilometres at an average speed of 7 kilometres per hour carrying full pack and equipment, but they completed the course marching past the saluting base at the exhausting goose step. Steiner's interest was not limited to physical fitness but extended to matters of equipment. The most important of the developments he fostered, and one whose influence can be seen today in every major army of the world, was the issue of camouflage-pattern clothing.

One of the disadvantages of an élite unit is that demands to carry out ceremonial duties interfere with the purely military training and this led to the V-T detachments being mocked as 'Ashphalt soldiers'. Despite the demands which ceremonial duties made upon the SS formations, Steiner was able to train his regiment to such a pitch that a demonstration of their battle techniques during the 1938 spring manoeuvres, caused a sensation. The assault detachment carried out the task of demonstrating the closing stages of an attack upon a fortified position by capturing the enemy trenches using the tactics of fire and movement which Steiner had developed.

The same combat skills were demonstrated to Hitler during May 1939. The Führer, informed of the new battle drills, wished to see for himself how effective these were when infantry and field artillery collaborated in their use. The task of Steiner's 'Deutschland' Regiment was to open an attack after limited reconnaissance, overrun the enemy outpost line and drive its defenders back to the main line trenches. Artillery supporting the attack would then open fire upon the field defences and under the barrage the storm troops were to break through strong barbed wire barricades using 'Bangalore torpedoes' and go on to capture the enemy's positions.

For this demonstration 'Deutschland' had two of its battalions up and a third in reserve. Hitler arrived and spent some twenty minutes looking over the battlefield. He then asked with some asperity when the demonstration would begin, only to be told that it had been under way for some twenty minutes. The Führer then noticed individual soldiers, who were visible for only a matter of seconds, moving swiftly across the ground towards the objective. The artillery and machine-guns opened fire but Hitler refused to take cover despite artillery shells falling upon the trenches only 300 metres distant from the observers and watched the assault unfold from a position in front of a blockhouse. As the barrage crashed down, light machine-gun fire kept the enemy defenders inactive while a special storm troops detachment blew breaches in the barbed wire entanglements with explosive charges. Through these gaps the assault infantry charged to take out the trench system and destroy the enemy with hand-grenades, machine-pistols and flame-throwers. One positive result of this demonstration was that Hitler ordered an artillery regiment to be added to the V-T establishment. Gunners for the new arm of service were drawn from existing infantry gun companies and heavy machine-gun companies. Slowly, the components of a complete division were coming together.

Regiment 'Germania'

The other infantry regiment on the V-T establishment at the beginning of 1938, was 'Germania'. When, on 1 October 1936, the units on the 'Germania' establishment were grouped regimentally, the Standarte consisted of three infantry battalions and three heavy weapons companies: infantry gun, anti-tank gun and motor cycle.

During the 1936 Reichsparteitag ceremonies in Nuremberg Standards were presented to the regiment as well as to its battalions and the unit name was officially bestowed. Although the regimental units were linked for administrative purposes, a variety of reasons prevented the battalions from serving together, a situation which created difficulties in standardizing training. An attempt to surmount these difficulties by the senior commanders meeting for a three-day seminar each quarter, failed to overcome those difficulties. In common with the other Standarten of the V-T 'Germania' supplied drafts of men to raise fresh SS formations. New barracks were built in Hamburg and were occupied by 1st Battalion and the heavy weapons companies. In 1940, 'Germania' left SS 'V' Division to become one of the regiments making up the newly created 5th SS 'Viking' Division.

Regiment 'Der Führer'

It was at the end of March 1938, shortly after his return from Austria, that Obersturmbannführer George Keppler received orders to raise a new V-T regiment. It was plannned that Regimental HQ and the 1st Battalion would be stationed in Vienna, with 2nd Battalion in Graz and 3rd Battalion in Klagenfurt. New barracks were constructed in those towns to quarter the battalions.

The 2nd Battalion of 'Deutschland' Regiment, whose national composition was predominantly Austrian, was taken from its parent unit to become 1st Battalion of 'Der Führer' Regiment. The other two 'DF' battalions were only a cadre of officers and men posted from 'Leibstandarte' and 'Germania', but soon sufficient Austrian volunteers had come in to fill the ranks of the battalions. During the 1938 Reichsparteitag celebrations the regiment received its official title and was presented with regimental and battalion Standards. The regiment had the experience of being 'shot over' when it took part in manoeuvres with live ammunition in Pomerania in May 1939, and then returned to Prague to take up guard duties again until the outbreak of war. As one of the formations selected for the Western Front, 'DF' was posted to the Black Forest area, but returned to Pilsen when the 'V' Division was formed.

There were other, individual, V-T battalions. These were:

Sturmbann 'N' (Nuremberg). Obersturmbannführer Deutsch's 'N' Battalion was one of those V-T units which it was proposed would be independent and remain outside regimental attachment. The battalion was stationed in Nuremburg where its role was to carry out ceremonial duties during Reichsparteitag and other celebrations. 'N' was created in the autumn of 1936, around a cadre of officers and NCOs drawn from both 'Leibstandarte' and 'Deutschland' and the unit was designated an independent infantry battalion (horsed). The establishment was for three rifle companies and a machine-gun company, a headquarters detachment, signals section and a band. There was also a motorized column. At first, the slow flow of recruits meant that only Nos. 2 and 4 Companies could be brought up to establishment and even by the end of 1936 the battalion was still only at 60 per cent of its proposed establishment. Battalion strength was further reduced by having to supply detachments, albeit on a temporary basis, to 'Deutschland' Regiment when that unit entered Austria. Recruits from Austria finally brought the under-strength companies up to full establishment. Then followed two conversions. 'N' Battalion became first the Motor-Cycle Battalion 'N' and then, on 10 July 1939, the anti-tank battalion of the V-T organization.

Signals Battalion. Towards the end of 1934, the first candidates were selected for what was to become the V-T Signals Battalion. Recruits came in chiefly from the eastern provinces of Germany: Silesia, Pomerania and East Prussia. Graduates from the army-run signals courses ensured a flow of trained signallers to the embryo SS battalion whose companies were made up of a motorized platoon and two horsed platoons. The battalion band was a mounted one. Shortly after the occupation of the Sudetenland the battalion was converted to fully motorized status. In July 1939 it went by sea to Königsberg in East Prussia, was incorporated into the Panzer Division 'Kempf' and took part in the campaign in Poland.

Pioneer Battalion 'Dresden'. During February 1935 a cadre of 24 men was assembled and around them a pioneer detachment had been formed by the beginning of March. In April the battalion became a motorized one within the V-T establishment. Volunteers were drawn chiefly from Saxony, Thuringia and central Germany, and men from all the V-T units were sent for training in the Pioneer School.

In addition to the units detailed above, the V-T organization raised in 1939, either through conversion of existing units or by new creation, three battalions, reconnaissance, anti-tank gun and Flak machine-gun, as well as an artillery regiment.

Thus, as early as 1938 an SS division was being created with three infantry regiments as well as artillery and other divisional units. A division on active service fielding that number of infantry regiments had very great transport difficulties to overcome. Despite the logistic and tactical disadvantages which did face the division on active service, when 'Germania' left the Division in 1940, its vacant place on the war establishment was filled by 11th 'Totenkopf' Regiment. Losses to that regiment caused it to be broken up and its survivors were posted to 'Deutschland' and 'Der Führer' Regiments.

But before the outbreak of the Second World War the SS 'V-T' regiments and battalions gained valuable experience in unit movement. They were employed during the crises of 1938; the entry into Austria in March, the occupation of the Sudetenland in September and of the rump of Czechoslovakia during March 1939. As a result of experience gained in these operations and in line with a general move towards complete motorization of the field army, there were a number of improvements in the equipment issued to V-T units including the replacement of horses by lorries. In those last months of peace in the world, it seemed to be only a matter of time before Hitler's intention to raise an SS Division was finally realized.

1939

Axis territory and general strategic movements ■

'Das Reich':
1 Invasion of Poland, September
(See sketch maps overleaf)

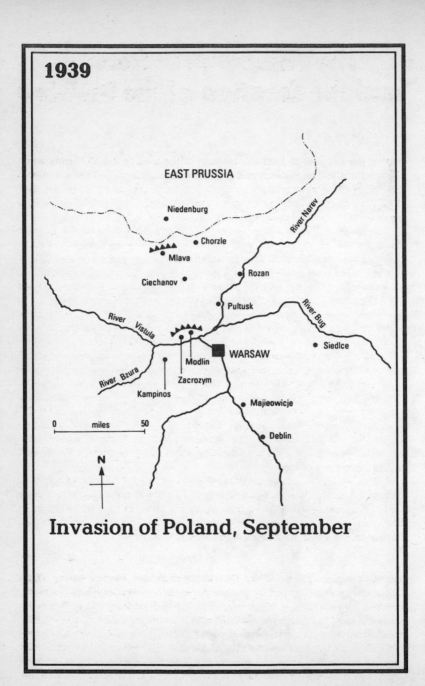

1939

Invasion of Poland, September

The Campaign in Poland and the Creation of the Division

In the summer of 1939 the feelings of the men in the V-T units were optimistic. The Sudeten crisis of the previous autumn had been resolved by the four most powerful states in Europe and it was felt generally that the present differences between the Third Reich and Poland could also be peacefully resolved by diplomatic means.

In the last summer of peace the V-T detachments were carrying out the usual round of duties familiar to professional soldiers in peace-time. 'Deutschland' Regiment in East Prussia on field firing exercises, also had a role to play in the parades commemorating the 25th anniversary of the Battle of Tannenberg. Thousands of former soldiers had begun to arrive in East Prussia and preparations to feed and quarter these veterans and organize the commemorative parades were well advanced. Then, towards the middle week of August, the Polish-German crisis worsened and the first rumours of war began to circulate. Unless the Führer could produce another diplomatic *coup* to reduce the tension, hostilities between the two countries seemed inevitable. Acting upon contingency plans which had been drawn up the V-T units moved to their battle stations. 'Der Führer' Regiment was posted to the Black Forest area while 'Germania' Regiment and the pioneer battalion formed part of the forces facing southern Poland; 'Germania' as a unit of VIII Corps and the pioneer battalion serving with XV Corps. 'Deutschland' Regiment was incorporated into Panzer Division 'Kempf', one of the formations on the strength of I Corps, in Third Army, serving in Fedor von Bock's Army Group North.

Thus, for the first campaign of the new war, the V-T were not combined to form a single major SS fighting unit but were dispersed, each operating under army command. This 'splintering' was a situation with which the men and units were to become increasingly familiar, not just for that first campaign, but throughout much of the Second World War.

The battle plan produced by Oberkommando des Heeres (Army High Command) was influenced by the geographical advantages which Germany enjoyed *vis-à-vis* Poland. These were that German territory – East Prussia in the north and Slovakia in the south – outflanked the industrial western half of Poland as well as the capital city, Warsaw. The most important sentence in the OKH campaign orders was that the German forces were: ' . . . to cut off the mass of the Polish Army . . . west of the Vistula–Narev line by concentric attacks from Silesia on one side and from Pomerania and East Prussia on the other . . . ' General von Bock's Army Group was to thrust for Warsaw and, in conjunction with Army Group South, was also to encircle and destroy the enemy east of the River Vistula. The Polish Army was, thus, to be trapped and destroyed in a double encirclement, one to the west, and one to the east of Warsaw.

The campaign opened unusually. The code-word had been given for hostilities to commence at 06.00 hours on 26 August, and units had already begun to move into their concentration areas. The signing of the Anglo–Polish Agreement offered the possibility that concessions might be won from the Polish government and Hitler cancelled the order to march, but so great a movement of troops could not be halted immediately nor could the German deployment be hidden from the Poles. The Polish government issued orders for general mobilization on 30 August, demonstrating that it would not compromise, and in response to that move Hitler re-issued the order for the German Army to march. The war which opened in eastern Europe on 1 September eventually spread to become the Second World War.

Political events in Europe leading to the outbreak of war had relegated to a very low priority the creation of a Verfügungstruppe Division and hostilities opened before it could be completely raised. Thus it was that for their baptism of fire the SS units fought not within the framework of an SS division but as part of Army formations. 'Deutschland', as stated above, together with the artillery regiment, the Flak machine-gun battalion, the reconnaissance and the signals battalions all served with Panzer Division 'Kempf', an experimental unit set up to establish whether a panzer division with a single infantry regiment instead of the standard two, could be effective in modern warfare. In this chapter I have selected only those operations undertaken by 'Deutschland' Regiment to represent all the divisional formations that fought in the Polish campaign. The missions undertaken by 'Deutschland' covered every aspect of infantry warfare, from attacking enemy's field fortifications, through co-operation with panzers and up to assault against massive fortresses.

The Polish road network was not well developed and there were few all-weather highways. Most other roads were often little more than tracks in the predominantly sandy soil, tracks in which vehicles sank up to their wheel hubs in good weather and up to their axles in the clinging mud which a downpour of rain could produce. The sand of Poland scoured and ruined pistons, clogged up weapons and quickly wore out the infantry who had to march through it for mile after exhausting mile. The autumn of 1939 was recalled by many contributors to this book as being particularly hot and sunny – they called it 'Führer's weather'. When it rained it was chiefly at night. In the daytime's searing heat the infantry battalions of 'Deutschland' marched long distances because already, there was a shortage of fuel, a shortage which was to grow into a famine and which was to affect dramatically the outcome of German military operations in the latter part of the war. Small wonder then that the OKH order for Operation 'White', the battle plan for the campaign against Poland, laid stress upon '. . . strong blows leading to a quick decision . . . '

Panzer Division 'Kempf' moved into the frontier region of East Prussia, near Neidenburg, where it was confronted by the permanent fortifications of the Mlava Line. The task of 'Deutschland' in Kempf's Division was to force a way through Polish positions screening the town of Mlava; the SS attack to be supported by a barrage fired by the whole of the divisional artillery. For this first operation Steiner, the regimental commander, had two battalions 'up'. The 3rd Battalion on the right had the village of Dvierznis as its first objective. The left flank attack was to be carried out by 1st Battalion which would have the village of Zavadski as its first objective. Both battalions would be striking southwards to Mlava down the road from the East Prussian frontier. Once they had gained their first objectives the battalions were then to go on to capture the high ground around a hill, Point 192. Georg Prell, who served with No. 3 Company, recalled the fighting around Zavadski. 'We have been at war for six hours now. No. 3 Company reached the village of Zavadski on the road up which we were advancing. On the enemy side of the village there were barbed wire barricades and beyond that high ground from which the Poles had good observation. The tempo of our attack could not be slowed down. Unterscharführer Luk Krieger worked his way through the barbed wire and stormed up the heavily defended ridge. In the murderous enemy fire Luk was mortally wounded and we could not at first recover the body of this, the first comrade of our Company to be killed in action. So we shifted the attack to a different sector and had soon forced a way through.'

Within fifteen minutes of moving over their start-lines the leading companies had crossed the German/Polish frontier. Soon they were advancing down the Mlava road, meeting little resistance from Polish infantry or artillery, and the SS men were surprised to find that the enemy's outpost positions along a secondary road some 2 kilometres to the west of Bialuty were empty. This uncontested advance came to an end when the attacking battalions reached the foot of a steep and completely open slope upon whose crest were sited the Mlava defences. The SS companies were completely exposed to the Polish fire which struck them as soon as they began their uphill advance. In that murderous hail of shot the attack stopped. First attempts to revive it failed and orders came from Division that the SS were to send out reconnaissance patrols to probe the Polish line for weak spots. Before these patrols could go out Corps had produced a new battle plan. Its divisions were to open a combined assault at 15.00 hours. 'Deutschland' was to carry out a frontal assault on Point 192, striking at the hill from two sides. Artillery support would be given and panzers would accompany the attacking battalions.

The promised armoured support turned out to be less effective than the SS had expected: the vehicles of Kempf's 1st Panzer Battalion had barely crossed the start-line when they found the way barred by anti-tank obstacles made of sections of railway lines fixed in cement. These were too heavy for the light vehicles of the panzer battalion to push aside and Polish artillery fire then concentrated upon those panzers that had sought to manoeuvre past the obstruction. One after another the German vehicles were knocked out and to avoid further loss the commander of the panzer regiment broke off the attack and ordered his units to withdraw. Corps, agreeing with that decision, issued orders within an hour for the Panzer attacks to be aborted. Polish opposition was far too strong. The SS grenadiers, of course, stayed in position enduring the shelling and sniping. The pace of their attack, which had gone in at 15.00 hours, had been so swift that one group from 1st Battalion reached a point only 150 metres short of the first line of bunkers before being halted. At that point the grenadier attack had died and the survivors were pulled back during the night to the regiment's main defence line. Thus ended the first day of the War for 'Deutschland' Regiment

On 2 September, Division Kempf was taken from its position in front of the Mlava Line and switched eastwards to Chorzele where the neighbouring Corps had broken through the Polish defences. Infantry battle groups, from 'Deutschland' under Steiner and Kleinheisterkamp, together with 7th Panzer Regiment, then opened a battle of pursuit which stormed as far as Rozan on the River Narev where the regiment ran up against a complex of forts built in the time of the Tsars. The first assaults of the regimental battle groups made no progress against the frontal and enfilade fire of the Polish defenders who then followed up the repulse of the SS attacks by launching a series of cavalry charges. These forced the SS temporarily on to the defensive, but with the fall of Rozan enemy resistance began to lessen. The SS advance flowed again from Rozan to Loriza: then on to Czervin and as far as Hadbory the fighting pursuit continued through a succession of hot and dust-filled days and rainy nights. On 10 September, the Division crossed the River Bug at Brok with orders to drive southwards to cut the retreat of the Polish armies moving to reinforce the garrison defending the capital. These new orders to the SS regiment proved to be no easy task to fulfill. The Poles, with a major force now concentrated, were neither demoralized nor weak but were of high morale, strong and willing to fight. Although lacking tanks, their infantry and cavalry attacks against Kempf's Division were well led and strongly supported. By this stage of the campaign the Division was no longer a single cohesive force, but was split up into a number of widely separated battle groups, unable to support one another and frequently fighting in isolation.

Polish resistance, no matter how determined, could not withstand the overwhelming German pressure and by 15 September, opposition east of Warsaw had been broken and the city itself had been encircled. 'Deutschland' reached Siedlice and then turned towards Majieowicje on the Vistula. The great battle in the bend of the River Bzura had already destroyed the Polish armies but that defeat alone could not bring about the end of the campaign. Warsaw itself had to be captured and this could only be accomplished once the forts of Modlin, to the north-west of the city had been taken. Kempf's Division retraced its footsteps, swinging back behind Warsaw and then driving south-west to Naczpolsk, moving into position for what was certain to be a bloody and protracted battle to take out Modlin's Nos. 1 and 2 Forts. These lay, respectively, to the west and to the north-east of the town. It was the task of the army divisions to co-operate in the attack and to capture the remaining forts in the complex.

The investment of the Modlin forts lasted from 19 to 28 September. Preparations to storm them were not completed until the 22nd and patrols were sent out to determine enemy strengths and to probe weak spots in the defence. The first SS reconnaissance groups returned having suffered heavy casualties. Preparations began to soften up the enemy. Under cover of Stuka bombing the pioneers of 'Deutschland' blew a gap in the barbed wire defences around the objectives and then a second series of Stuka attacks went in, preparing the ground for an all-out assault which was to be launched on 29 September. On the evening of the 27th an officer of 1st Battalion reported to 'Deutschland' 's commander that the garrison of Zacrozym Fort seemed to be weak and that it might be possible to capture it by a sudden, storming assault. Standartenführer Steiner carried out his own reconnaissance, agreed with the Obersturmführer's appreciation of the situation and issued the appropriate orders. At 15.30 hours on 29 September the regiment was ready to attack Zacrozym and Modlin. By 05.20 hours the companies which were to make the assault had worked their way forward through the Polish outer defences and stood ready to open the main attack. An order came for this to be postponed by an hour as it was believed the Polish garrison might surrender. No offer was made by the enemy and at 06.15 hours the German artillery opened upon the first two objectives, Zacrozym and No. 1 Fort. Punctually, at 06.30 hours the companies crossed their start-lines. Flame-throwing detachments spearheading the infantry attack had soon forced a passage into Zacrozym and the small town was captured within an hour and a half. There was then a period of confusion with some Polish soldiers obeying an order to surrender and others, perhaps not knowing of that order, fighting on. A fierce bombardment of No. 1 Fort from which firing was still coming, forced the enemy garrison to surrender and by 14.00 hours 'Deutschland' could report that its battalions had captured their objectives.

With the fall of the Modlin forts the campaign in Poland came to an end so far as 'Deutschland' Regiment was concerned. Together with other V-T units, it was then posted to Pilsen where, on 19 October, the miscellaneous groups were formed into the SS 'V' Division. The composition of the newly raised formation was, 'Deutschland', 'Germania' and 'Der Führer' Grenadier Regiments, an artillery regiment and battalions of signals, reconnaissance, pioneers, anti-tank and anti-aircraft machine-gunners.

1940

Axis territory and general strategic movements

'Das Reich':
1 Central Netherlands, May
2 Walcheren, May
3 Dunkirk perimeter, May
4 Conquest of France, May–June
(See sketch maps overleaf)

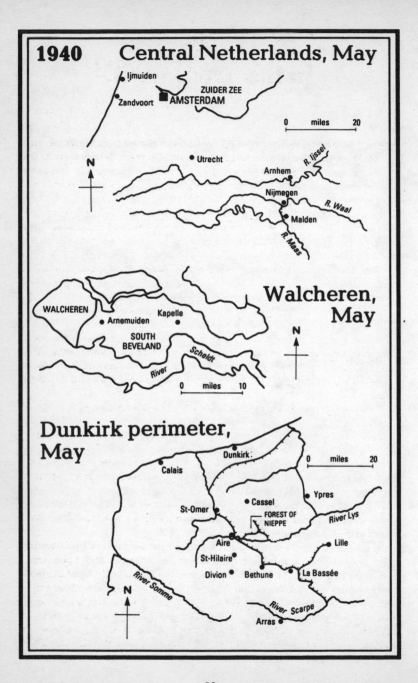

1940 **Central Netherlands, May**

Ijmuiden

Zandvoort

ZUIDER ZEE
■ AMSTERDAM

0   miles   20

Utrecht

Arnhem   R. Ijssel

Nijmegen

Malden   R. Waal

R. Maas

**Walcheren,
May**

WALCHEREN

Arnemuiden   Kapelle

SOUTH
BEVELAND

Scheldt

River

N

0   miles   10

**Dunkirk perimeter,
May**

Dunkirk

Calais

0   miles   20

Cassel   Ypres

St-Omer

FOREST OF
NIEPPE   River Lys

Aire   Lille

St-Hilaire

Divion   Bethune   La Bassée

River Somme

River Scarpe

N

Arras

SS 'V' Division
in the West, 1940

During November 1939 SS 'V' Division moved from the Pilsen area of Czechoslovakia and into western Germany where it spent the next six months carrying out intensive training at company, battalion and regimental level. During April 1940 a number of sub-units were raised and added to the divisional establishment. Such increases in strength together with such intensive training could have only one purpose; a new campaign was imminent and one in which the 'Verfügungs' Division would play a prominent part. The enemies to be attacked were certain to be the armies of the Western Allies.

The War in the west which opened on 10 May, had two parts, the first of which, Operation 'Yellow', was an attack upon Holland, Belgium and northern France. When this was successfully concluded Operation 'Red', the battle for France, opened. Although SS 'V' took part in both these operations it did not do so as a complete division. As early as December 1939, 'Der Führer' Regiment, together with 2nd Battalion of the artillery regiment, a pioneer company and a vehicle column were detached to serve with 207th Infantry Division and the divisional reconnaissance battalion together with an armoured car platoon of 'Deutschland' Regiment was attached to 254th Infantry Division.

The opening move of Operation 'Yellow' called for Eighteenth Army, of which 'V' Division was a component, to thrust into Holland and by rapid advance to break through the succession of defensive lines which the Dutch had set up along their rivers and canals. These defences were, principally, the Ijssel – Maas river line, the Grebbe Line in the north and the Peel Line in the south, extending from the Zuider Zee almost to Maastricht. The third set of defences was around 'Fortress Holland', extending from Zudzee to Dordrecht and from Utrecht to the sea. To strengthen the lines of pillbox defences the Dutch were prepared to open the dikes and let in the sea water to form a barrier to the German advance.

Eighteenth Army's battle plan depended for its success upon seizing intact the bridges across Holland's rivers and canals, and upon rapid movement to overrun the Netherlands before the Dutch could flood the land. It was to carry out such tasks that 'V' Division had undergone such intensive training and it was put to good use by 'Der Führer' and the recce battalion, both of which went into action with their respective divisions at H-Hour on D-Day, 05.35 hours on 10 May. Some idea of the size and complexity of the opening stages of Operation 'Yellow' can be gained from the fact that when the recce battalion and 'Der Führer' crossed their start-lines at dawn on the

10th, the remainder of the Division was a long way east of the Rhine in one of the numerous columns of lorried, armoured and horsed transports heading westwards. Herbert Christiansen recalled that the vehicle columns of the Train had orders to reach a stated destination by 03.00 hours on 10 May. 'I had to drive my own truck and so the task of map-reading was left to an Obersturmführer. My questions, are we on the right road, were always answered with "Yes", but eventually it was very obvious that we were lost in a pitch-black night and that we stood no chance of reaching the objective on time. A junior officer of 2nd Battalion then gave me directions on how to get to Holland. Shortly before reaching the objective I saw a group of officers at a road junction and recognized our General, Hausser. We had to wait a long time before the 'Germania' Regimental column arrived with Standartenführer Demelhuber at its head. When Demelhuber went over to report to Hausser the divisional commander's first words were, "I thought you intended to open operations with the Train. They've been here for some time." '

Let us at this point consider the actions fought by the detached units. The reconnaissance battalion, an army machine-gun battalion and an artillery battalion, formed the 'Grave Group'. This was sub-divided into five assault detachments with orders to seize the bridge across the Waal at Nijmegen and the canal bridges at Neerbosch, Hatert, Malden and Heuman. Only that at Heuman could be taken intact and at Hatert, although every man of the assault detachment was either killed or wounded, Untersturmführer Vogt captured the damaged bridge with only four men and soon had it in operation. Tenacious Dutch resistance had everywhere caused the attacking SS men a great many casualties. With its first missions completed the recce battalion returned to the control of 'V' Division on 11 May. 'Der Führer', serving with 207th Infantry Division in X Corps, struck forward at H-Hour and within two hours 3rd Battalion had carried the advance to the eastern bank of the River Ijssel near Arnhem. All the bridges across the river had been destroyed, but by 13.00 hours 2nd Battalion had carried out a successful assault crossing and had set up a bridgehead. The heavily fortified and strongly defended complex of strongpoints at Westervoort were captured and by midday Arnhem had fallen to the storming advance of 3rd Battalion. The Ijssel positions, which the Dutch had expected to hold for at least three days, had been taken within four hours. Both the recce battalion and 'Der Führer' had undergone their baptism of fire. 'Der Führer' concentrated that night in the Renkum area. Ahead lay the fighting for the Grebbe Line. Within a day the regiment, in a classic example of fire and movement, smashed a gap through that second line of Dutch defences.

The OKW communiqué of 14 May reported that the breach in the Grebbe Line had been extended, that the Peel positions had been penetrated and that ground had been gained on the Utrecht sector. On the following day the commander of X Corps declared that 'Der Führer', which had broken through the Ijssel and the Grebbe Lines, would have the honour of carrying the advance into the heart of Holland. The fighting attack which the regiment then spearheaded carried it past Utrecht and into Amsterdam, finishing at Ijmuiden and Zandvoort where the Regiment reached the North Sea. Two days later it moved back through Holland and rejoined the mass of 'Verfügungs' Division in Marienbourg.

While the two detached units of the Division had been in action from D-Day onwards, the main body of SS 'V' had spent the first days moving forward in two motorized columns towards Hilvarenbek, north of Antwerp. OKW had anticipated that strong Allied forces in northern Belgium would strike into the left flank of Eighteenth Army. It was to meet that eventuality that the 'Verfügungs' Division had been placed on that sensitive flank and Hausser had been given orders that his Division must hold any Allied assaults until the slower-moving infantry formations had come forward to relieve it and take over its task. When the expected Allied attack did not transpire the 'Verfügungs' Division was free for other duties and was ordered to change the direction of its advance and to swing southwards so as to confront the Anglo-French formations in northern Belgium. The move was to be made with best possible speed, but this was an order which it was soon discovered could not be executed quickly. The press of military traffic on the main roads was too great and in an effort to bypass the jams which had built up Division sent out recce patrols to find alternative routes along less crowded country roads. Objectives were set for each battalion and it was the task of each commanding officer to bring his unit to the stated place by the stated time.

The units arrived, SS 'V' Division regrouped and began its advance to battle. Then came fresh orders which changed the direction of the divisional advance yet again. Hausser's Division was now ordered to thrust towards Antwerp with the principal task of guarding the flank of a force which was threatened by French Seventh Army. Within the framework of these new orders 'Verfügungs' Division was ordered to capture the islands of Walcheren and Beveland and to interdict shipping in the Westerschelde.

In order to capture those islands an attacker has first to pass through a narrow neck of land across which lies the South Beveland Canal. Beyond the village of Kapelle the ground opens out into South Beveland, and in May 1940 the greatest part of that area was flooded. At Arnemuiden the island narrows again and leads into Walcheren by way of a strong dam on which there was just enough room for a road and a single track railway. By this stage of the campaign the Dutch troops, outnumbered and facing Luftwaffe attack and the furious assaults of the better trained German Army, began to show the strain of fighting against that double assault. The Army of the Netherlands was being overwhelmed by a force it had not been trained to meet and on 14 May it capitulated. The Allied garrison on Walcheren was determined to fight on and rejected surrender demands, despite the threat of bombardment by twenty-one battalions of heavy artillery and air assault by six Stuka and five heavy bomber squadrons. The Allies were determined to make the Germans fight for Walcheren and the Scheldt.

For its attack upon Walcheren 'V' Division formed two battle groups. The

3rd Battalion 'Deutschland' Regiment under Kleinheisterkamp, and Witt's 1st Battalion. For the opening stages of the assault 1st Battalion would have to follow 3rd Battalion because its own thrust line was made impassable by flood water. Shortly before midday on 16 May, the Kleinheisterkamp battle group reached the area of Westerdijk and came under intensive fire from defenders holding well-sited permanent defences along the embanked road. The ground on both sides of the road as well as its surface were covered by barbed wire and sown with mines which killed sixteen men during the advance. The Allied defenders were well supported by heavy artillery fire from Antwerp as well as from ships of the Royal Navy out at sea. The two SS battalions shook out into the attack across the flooded fields of South Beveland and fought their way towards the Walcheren Dam. It was a bitterly fought operation; in every sense an infantryman's war in which the grenadiers waded under fire across flooded ground, advanced over fields of mines set to explode under the lightest pressure and engaged a resolute enemy holding well-prepared positions. The story of the fierce battle to cross the killing ground of the Walcheren Dam was recorded by Paul Schuermann who fought with No. 9 Company in 3rd Battalion of 'Deutschland' Regiment.

'We wait . . . for the order to open the attack . . . Now, on your feet . . . and we charge into the hell that the enemy has prepared for us. As our first comrades leap on to the dike roadway they are met with murderous fire from machine-guns, anti-tank guns and artillery. Each step we take brings us closer to the enemy. What are 800 metres? One thing we all know; the company must get to grips with the enemy. We must get him within range of our hand-grenades. As we storm forward I see one man fall, then two on the right and then another comrade who lies crumpled, face down. Some men are using their teeth to tear open field dressings to bandage their shattered arms or chests.

'The first rank of our comrades lies in front of that damned concrete dike, behind which the enemy pours fire into our ranks. That fire tears the weapons for ever out of the hands of those who are killed in action. More and more of our machine-guns cease firing with their crews silent, bloody and pale behind the weapons . . . The attack halts. We must dig in as best we can into the ground, alongside the ashphalt road, between the railway sleepers or else crouch in the craters which enemy shells have created . . . A comrade passes me. His shirt is torn from this shoulders. There is a gaping wound in his back and I can see the pumping movement of his lungs. To the left of me another comrade goes back, almost marching, erect, ignoring the bullets flying through the air . . . paying no attention to death. His throat and chest, covered in field dressings, are blood soaked. His untocused eyes are wide open, his face is grey and he looks straight past me . . . A shouted order "Bring a machine-gun forward." Horn, my No. 2, leaps up and then falls back with a cry of pain. I go to bandage him but it is too late. He has been shot through the stomach. To my right a comrade is lying on his back. His twitching fingers claw at the air. It is Unterscharführer Vonscheidt. The sun picks out the coloured ribbon on his tunic, that of the Iron Cross he won in Poland. Our No. 9 Company is pulled out of the fight. We go back, slowly, some walking erect. Others are carrying bloody burdens. Slowly feelings return and I am conscious of the fact that I am both hungry and thirsty. A wild fury boils up in us. Half an hour later the enemy behind the concrete dike pulls out . . . That action cost us seventeen men killed and thirty wounded. The bloody 17 May comes to an end as night falls . . . '

While the SS 'V' Division had been fighting in Holland as part of Eighteenth Army in von Bock's Army Group 'B', the mass of the German Army in the west had captured Brussels and had cut its way through southern Belgium and northern France striking towards the Channel coast. That thrust had created a salient separating the Allied armies in northern France from those which had been flung back to the River Somme. The Dutch surrender allowed the bulk of Eighteenth Army to be redeployed and, leaving only a token force in the Netherlands, it turned south to help in the task of stiffening the walls of the salient with motorized and infantry divisions. To carry out its part in this 'stiffening' operation, XIL Corps issued an order on 22 May for the 6th and 8th Panzer Divisions, together with SS 'V' Division, to drive without halt via St-Omer to Calais. Let us consider what that order meant to the fighting troops who had, it will be remembered, been fighting for weeks without relief. Almost every order they had been given had urged them to move fast so as to fulfil High Command's strategic plans. Despite their exhaustion the soldiers were inspired by the realization that when they gained the Channel coast not only would the Allied armies in northern France and Flanders have been separated from those south of the Somme, but the encircled Allied formations in the Dunkirk region would be ripe for destruction. The promise of a splendid military victory spurred on the exhausted grenadiers. To carry out its part in the fighting between Calais and Ypres, SS 'V' Division was deflected northwards towards the La Bassée Canal to stop the enemy attempting to break out across that waterway. The Division was further ordered to establish bridgeheads across the canal and to drive the British out of the forest of Nieppe. Although the Allies in Flanders were encircled and had their backs to the sea they were not impotent and in staunch defence as well as in spirited attack produced several unpleasant shocks for the German units surrounding them.

At 18.58 hours on 22 May, XIL Corps ordered SS 'V' Division to protect Corps right flank against enemy assaults and to occupy the area Divion – St-Hilaire. Division intended to reach the area around Aire where its units could concentrate and once his Division's right flank was on the Canal d'Aire, Hausser could feel that that wing was secure. Later that same evening Army issued an order halting the advance of its panzer divisions towards the coast. Obedient to the orders they had received the SS regiments halted where they were along the sides of the roads. There they took up defensive positions and settled down for the night waiting until fresh orders came for them to resume their advance. Compliance with this unexpected and peremptory halt order meant that SS 'V' was not concentrated but was dispersed in small groups all around the Divion–St-Hilaire area. 'DF' was in the area of Blessy – St-Hilaire, the divisional advance guard and 2nd Battalion 'DF' were at Aire and 3rd Battalion on the banks of the canal. In the fast movement of modern warfare firm battle lines cannot be maintained; there was confusion regarding unit boundaries in the area where they were bivouacked. To add to the confusion on that dark night of 22/23 May, many SS units were struck by detachments of French infantry and armour probing for weak spots in the German perimeter through which they might escape.

In the very early hours of the new day 'Der Führer' Regiment came under attack. No. 9 Company was overrolled by a French battalion of tanks and Nos. 10 and 11 Companies were surrounded. The French assault then struck Nos. 5 and 7 Companies at about 04.00 hours and at about the same time enemy forces penetrated the area at Blessy where the TAC HQs of 2nd Battalion 'Der Führer' and of the artillery regiment's 2nd Battalion together with an artillery battery had pulled off the road into a field and had settled down. It was a night of confused fighting. Schulze's platoon of No. 7 Company of 'Der Führer' was called to arms when the alarm was sounded. He moved his vehicles and anti-tank guns to join what he thought was a column of panzers. The NCO found to his horror that the vehicles before and behind him were enemy ones. Swinging his group out of the column he unlimbered the guns and put them into action against the surprised French. Schulze's little group destroyed between fifteen and twenty enemy vehicles.

Another incident in the confusion of that night was recorded by Hauptscharführer Roeske, serving in the signals detachment of the artillery.

'During the evening of 22 May 1940, the TAC HQ of 2nd Artillery Battalion reached Blessy. The regimental wireless group which was also with us went into position under a large tree in the middle of a meadow surrounded by hedges. The CO of our battalion, Sturmbannführer Erpsen-mueller, had the vehicles driven up close to the hedges and ordered tents to be put up. Then the Spiess came along with canteen goods.

'Not far from where TAC HQ was set up there was an inn where the unit First Aid Post had been set up. We put out sentries and I lay down in the cabin of the wireless truck and went off to sleep immediately. The wireless detachment leader and one of the signallers wrapped themselves in blankets and lay down in the hedge. Shortly before dawn, at about 04.00 hours, I was wakened by a sentry shouting, "Stabsscharführer, the French are here." To collect my rifle and roll out of the truck was a single action and then came the cry from a number of sentries, "Alarm! alarm!" and the sound of firing.

'By this time the light had improved and we could pick out details. I flung myself down into cover and landed near an Obersturmführer to whom a motor-cycle dispatch rider had just brought the message that we were surrounded. The DR was about to drive away when there was a flurry of shots which killed him and wounded the officer in both thighs. I carried him to the Aid Post and found there were already ten wounded comrades in the room. As

I left the room I heard someone call out that the regimental wireless group should sent out a message for help. That meant me. I crept and crawled to the wireless truck. As I reached it a French soldier came towards me with raised hands. I gesticulated that he should lie down but it was too late. A burst of MG fire killed him on the spot. As I opened the door of the truck a group of several French soldiers stormed from the hedge towards the lorry but they did not reach it. Another burst of fire, this one from a different direction, mowed them down. I learned later this fire was from a group of men from 'Der Führer' who were in the farmyard.

'I climbed into the wireless truck, called up Regiment and got through immediately. Then I realized to my horror that the voice from Regiment was becoming fainter and fainter. The batteries on my set were running out. To obtain fresh ones meant I would have to leave the truck and go round to the back. That was a risky thing to do as the French were firing from positions all along the hedge. Thanks to the covering fire of my comrades in the farmyard and others in the supply truck I obtained and fitted a new battery. I passed the message that we were surrounded and needed infantry support. Hauptsturm-führer Kreutz called for a signal pistol to let our comrades know where we were but there were no signal flares to hand. The CO shouted out "German soldiers here!" and he must have been heard because no more fire came from the "DF" men. Shortly afterwards a heavy battery from 2nd Battalion came up and, firing over open sights, they and the "DF" group soon cleared up the situation. That day we lost sixteen men killed in action.'

Karl Kreutz recalled the death in action of Sturmbannführer Erpsen-mueller.

'He told us quite calmly that he would not survive the campaign. The NCO who raised the alarm in the early hours of the morning opened fire on the French troops marching along the road in closed formation. It was clear that they had no idea where the front actually was. I took my carbine and fired across the top of the hedge on the French whom I identified through the crests on their helmets. Suddenly I saw Erpsenmueller was standing beside me smoking a cigarette. He asked, "Kreutz, aren't you firing on prisoners of war?" The next second, while I was reloading I saw him fall, shot through the head. He lay face downwards with the cigarette still burning in his left hand. I shall never forget it. In that engagement we captured the standard of an Alsatian regiment which we later presented to our regimental commander, Peter Hansen. I also recall that HQ did not believe what was happening "so far behind the line" and Hansen sent someone to find out what was going on. That man was very promptly wounded. Now regiment knew the form and sent the infantry to relieve us very quickly.'

The French assaults in the 'Der Führer' area were absorbed and then halted in St-Hilaire, south of the canal, when the regimental anti-tank guns came into action. A situation which had seemed to be critical was soon mastered as gunners and grenadiers collaborated in destroying the enemy tanks. During the morning of 23 May the actions carried out by 'Der Führer' changed the course of the battle as the regiment swung from a defensive to an offensive posture. The 3rd Battalion alone, destroyed thirteen enemy armoured fighting vehicles, many of them knocked out by grenadiers using explosive charges. Five hundred French soldiers were also taken prisoner and the enemy was flung back across the La Bassée Canal. Fighting then became general along the entire front of the SS Division. In one action Untersturmführer Vogt, who had already distinguished himself in Holland, led his motorcycle reconnaissance patrol into a small but intense fire-fight against overwhelming odds. He saw a column of enemy troops and vehicles heading eastwards towards Mazinghem, ordered the anti-tank guns of his detachment to be unlimbered and to open fire upon the soft-skinned vehicles at the tail of the column. Then the gun barrels swung towards the tanks at its head. The action ended with the surrender of a whole enemy battalion to the thirty men of the recce patrol.

The French tank thrusts – which were the first 'Der Führer' Regiment had had to face – demonstrated in a most frightening way that the standard German anti-tank gun lacked the power to penetrate enemy armour. The Renault 35 tank, in particular, could only be knocked out at very close range and there was one action during that day when an enemy tank reached to within 5 metres of the barrel of an anti-tank gun before it was destroyed. By 24 May, the Division had crossed the La Bassée Canal and had forced bridgeheads against bitter opposition put up by the British defenders. While still engaged in fighting off the attacks of 2nd British Infantry Division, orders issued on 26 May presented the Division with its most difficult task yet. Its two grenadier regiments and the recce battalion were directed to clear the British out of the forest of Nieppe. The attack opened at 08.30 hours on 27 May, with 'Germania' on the right wing, 'Der Führer' on the left and the recce battalion taking post between the 1st and 3rd Battalions of 'Der Führer' Regiment. Only slow progress could be made against the well-constructed British field fortifications in the forest which were defended vigorously. 'Germania' was held by the Queen's Own Royal West Kent Regiment and the excellent marksmanship of these British soldiers was acknowledged in post-battle reports. But the SS pressure was too strong to be held indefinitely and by the evening 'Germania' had advanced as far as Haverskerque. On its sector 'Der Führer' had passed through the Bois d'Amont and its right wing companies had reached the banks of the Canal de Nieppe. The strong British resistance worried Corps who were aware that its role in the second part of the war in the west, Operation 'Red', would be jeopardized by a long-drawn-out battle. All loose ends had to be tied up before Corps could be redeployed, and the most important of these loose ends was the capture of the forest. On 28 May, the day on which the Belgian forces capitulated, Corps directed that the Nieppe was to be cleared speedily and thoroughly. This proved to be a less difficult task than formerly for the Belgian surrender had laid open the British flank and further resistance in the forest of Nieppe no longer served any purpose. The Queen's Own, together with the rest of the BEF, pulled back in a fighting retreat to the beaches.

Corps, aware of how much the strain of the fighting had exhausted its formations, ordered SS 'V' Division to rest but the respite from battle was brief. On 31 May, 'Germania' on the Mont des Cats and 'Der Führer' around Cassel were close in pursuit of the retreating British troops. 'Der Führer' detachments on the hill at Cassel had a panoramic view of the whole Allied perimeter, dominated by the pall of black smoke rising from burning oil tanks into a cloudless blue sky. A welcome addition to divisional strength came on 1 June when more than 2,000 officers and men arrived to replace those who had been lost in the campaign. These reinforcements were welcome, not so much because companies making an attack would be up to strength again, but because the onerous and tiring round of sentry duty now being shared among a greater number of men came round less frequently. A soldier's life centres on such trivial details.

Late in the evening of 1 June the Division marched to Bapaume, being no longer needed in the contracting perimeter at Dunkirk. When the last survivors of that Allied garrison surrendered on 4 June, the SS 'V' Division was resting as part of Army Group reserve, ready to move into the next phase of the war in the west: the battle for France. The German Army High Command envisaged a threefold campaign. In quick succession three Army Groups would roll up the French battle line in an operation vaster than anything seen in warfare hitherto. The opening blows would be struck by Army Group 'B' on 5 June, along a line extending from the Channel to the Aisne, north of Reims. The intention was to force a breakthrough on the lower Seine.

Only four days after Army Group 'B' had opened the offensive it would be the task of Army Group 'A' to start the main attack between the Aisne and the Franco-German frontier. This move would strike into the back of the French divisions holding the Maginot Line. While the attention of the French Army of the East was concentrated on warding off the assault of Army Group 'A', Army Group 'C' would cross the Rhine and assault the Maginot Line from the east. If the campaign in Flanders had been a terrible blow to the French Army, the assaults which began to rain upon it in the first week of June, were disastrous. Although it deployed more than sixty divisions south of the Somme, these formations were facing an enemy superior not only in number, but also one which had mastery of the air and who held the military initiative. The blows of the German Army were, heavy, sustained and mortal.

Within days the French defences along the Somme, extravagantly named the Weygand Line, had been broken and on 9 June the Aisne was crossed. The following weeks saw one river line after another carried with ease. On 14 June, the same day as that on which the Marne was crossed, Paris fell and with the surrender of the capital French morale plummeted and military efficiency suffered. This does not imply either that the French Army did not continue to fight well or that SS 'V' Division saw no action of any importance. Many French divisions struggled heroically, but by the evening of 17 June the Army of the East was breaking up and by the 22nd it had surrendered. This forced the French government to ask for an armistice which was signed on the 25th. An account of that pell-mell advance southwards from the Somme, was given by Ernst Schuelke who was on a course for unit leaders in Sennelager when the campaign in the west opened.

'We all wanted to get back quickly to our units, but we had to stay and finish the course. It was, therefore, not until the middle of May that the RTO in Cologne could send me back to my unit, 3rd Battalion of the Artillery Regiment. Our army's advance had been so rapid that I did not catch up with the Division until it was positioned on the east bank of the River Somme.

'The enemy had blown the bridges and was defending the west bank. The guns of our battalion, together with the heavy weapons companies of 'Deutschland' Regiment, were to support the crossing by that regiment's infantry. On the night before the crossing was made the enemy artillery fired without pause but caused little damage. The artillery survey group, to which I belonged, together with 'D' Regimental HQ crossed the river at dawn. The artillery shoot was faultless. The infantry then went into action along the whole length of the Somme and as we of the artillery survey group were with them we could quickly bring down enfilade fire to good effect. Resistance was soon broken and with the enemy defeated on the Somme the great pursuit battle began. We thrust past Orléans, Tours and Poitiers and south of that place were given a short rest. The CO gave me orders that on the following day I was to go out and survey good artillery positions south of Poitiers. I left at dawn heading west and noticed that many of the villages had similar names, differentiated only by the name of a river. Soon I was hopelessly lost. Then we heard the sound of BMW motor cycles. It was the lads of No. 15 Company of 'Deutschland' Regiment. In the middle of the column rode Steiner and his officers. I reported to him and he told me to join the group. We were still heading westwards in the direction of Angoulême and there was not another German soldier on the road, but we did see columns of French soldiers who mistook us for British troops, probably because of our camouflage jackets. As we rushed past them we could hear their shouts of "Lay down your arms!" Angoulême came in sight. At the side of the road stood a French machine-gun mounted on a tripod, but before the soldiers manning it could grasp what was happening they had been disarmed and we drove towards the railway station. The roads leading off the station were guarded by platoons of No. 15 Company. Standartenführer Steiner then reported over the wireless that we had penetrated more than 60 kilometres through the French lines.

'He then ordered me to take my five men and a motor-cyle combination to fetch the mayor and arrange the surrender of the town. Outside the Town Hall there were about thirty heavily armed policemen. I jumped from my car and asked them in a friendly fashion where the mayor could be found. They were so surprised that none of them reacted aggressively. I was taken to a conference room while my men stood around our vehicle with their guns at the ready. The men in the hall jumped up, shocked, when I entered. I told them, through an interpreter, that the town was surrounded and that if the mayor did not present himself without delay at the railway station the town would be blown apart by artillery. I directed the mayor to take a seat in my car and to wave a white flag. If there were any resistance in the town he would not have long to live.

'In this fashion we drove back to the station and handed over our prize to the regimental commander. In the course of my report I remarked that we had seen a number of officers and soldiers in the town. Immediately Steiner told me to fetch the Town Major. I must admit that his order shook me, but we drove back into the centre of the town. It was now midday. People whom I questioned told me that it was lunch time and that I would find the officers and their ladies in the Mess. This was a large three-storey building located just outside the town. We reached it, and together with two signallers I raced up the stairs while the rest of my detachment stayed with the car. On my way to the first floor I noticed, with relief, that the officers had left their pistols in the cloakroom. We charged into the hall. In it was a horseshoe-shaped table set with food and lots of wine. Around the table sat a number of officers and their ladies.

'What sort of impression we three made I cannot say. There we were in our dirty, dusty camouflage jackets with weapons at the ready. A hubbub of noise broke out and I shouted above this, in French. "Gentlemen, you are my prisoners." The ladies reacted hysterically and again I shouted, "The ladies will please leave the room." They departed quickly and in response to my question whether any of those present spoke German an Alsatian lieutenant came forward. I asked him to point out the senior officer present. This was an elderly colonel, the commander of a tank regiment which was quartered in barracks just outside the town. The interpreter translated my message that resistance was useless, the town was surrounded and that any resistance would be met by an artillery barrage. The officers formed three ranks and marched behind my car with the colonel and the interpreter seated in the back and waving white flags. One hundred and sixteen officers marched behind my car while the motor-cycle combination brought up the rear with a machine-gun trained on them. Standartenführer Steiner was quite surprised with our little haul and gave me the order to return to the barracks with the colonel and bring in the tank regiment. A platoon of motor cyclists accompanied me. The colonel was told to parade his men on the barrack square without weapons and the prisoners were guarded by a small group of our SS motor cyclists until these were relieved by an infantry unit.'

One last anecdote from the fighting on the Western Front is that of Hermann Busch of No. 15 Company of 'Deutschland' Regiment. He was one of a team chosen to test the British Boys anti-tank rifle, numbers of which had been captured during the fighting in the Nieppe forest. 'An armoured plate was set up but the first shot did not hit the target. We did notice, however, that a stallion grazing in a field to the right of the target had suddenly dropped down. Inspection showed that it had been killed by the bullet fired by the anti-tank rifle. We then found out that the Tommies had slightly bent the barrel of every one of the guns before they took ship at Dunkirk.'

With the signing of the Franco-German armistice, hostilities in western Europe came to an end. There was a short break in the South of France before SS 'V' moved into Holland at the beginning of July where chief among its duties was the supervision of the Dutch army's demobilization. Life had returned to an almost peace-time level and the local population, if not overly friendly, was certainly not hostile. The colour of the uniforms worn by the soldiers in the streets, the army of occupation, was field grey and not the familiar khaki of the Royal Netherlands Army, but the men of SS 'V' Division were young, smart and willing to be friendly.

During the stay in the Low Countries men and sub-units were posted away to 'Leibstandarte', as cadres for units which that formation was raising. There was expansion in 'V' Division when the number of battalions in the artillery regiment was increased. A new SS Division 'Viking' was being created at this time and drafts were supplied from 'V' Divisional Head-quarters, from 'Germania' Regiment, the 2nd Battalions of the artillery and of the reconnaissance regiments as well as No. 3 Company of the anti-tank battalion. The biggest loss to 'V' Division was that of Brigadeführer Steiner, commander of 'Deutschland' Regiment, who went off to lead 'Viking' Division. He was replaced as regimental commander by Willi Bittrich.

From Holland SS 'V' marched to Visoul in southern France where on 3 December an order from Reichsführer HQ changed the title to SS Division 'Deutschland', a distinction which was held for only a brief time.

1941

Axis territory and general strategic movements ■

'Das Reich':
1 Yugoslavia, April
2 Eastern Front, June–September
3 Yelnya, July–August
4 Kiev encirclement, September
5 Operation 'Typhoon',
October–December
(See sketch maps overleaf)

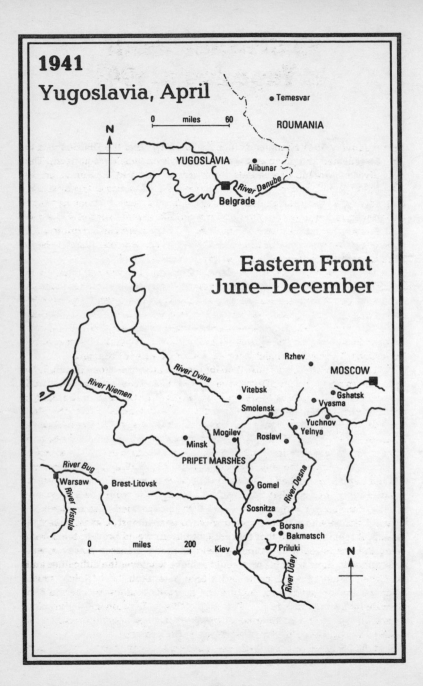

1941
Yugoslavia, April

0 — miles — 60

ROUMANIA

• Temesvar

N

YUGOSLAVIA
• Alibunar

River Danube
Belgrade

Eastern Front
June–December

River Dvina

Rzhev •

MOSCOW

River Niemen

Vitebsk •

Gshatsk •
Vyasma •

Smolensk •

Yuchnov •
Yelnya

Mogilev •
Minsk •

Roslavl •

River Desna

PRIPET MARSHES

River Bug
Warsaw
Brest-Litovsk •

River Vistula

Gomel •

Sosnitza •

Borsna •
Bakmatsch •

0 — miles — 200

Kiev •
Priluki •

River Uday

N

SS Division 'Reich' in Yugoslavia, 1941

In January 1941 Himmler's office issued orders that the Division was to be renamed and given a new role – SS Division 'Reich' (Motorized). The divisional infantry regiments were restructured and new units, an SP battery and a motor-cycle battalion, were raised. It was at this time, too, that a divisional tactical sign was designed and introduced. Manoeuvres were undertaken to improve co-operation between the several arms of service as well as intensive training at personnel level. These were carried out to such good effect that by the end of March 1941 the Division was considered to be in all respects ready for active service in its new motorized role.

Only a few days later orders came for 'Reich' to drive to Temesvar in Roumania to join XII. Corps in List's Twelfth Army. The wildest rumours circulated and bets were laid as to the Division's destination. Speculation ended when it was learned that on 6 April, during the time that the SS units were undertaking the eight-day land journey from southern France to western Roumania, Germany had begun hostilities against both Greece and Yugoslavia. The next battlefields would, therefore, be in the Balkans.

At Temesvar there was little time for rest after the tiring road march. Late in the morning of 9 April, Division was ordered to send armoured car and motor-cycle battle groups to find a route across the Danube so that Corps could advance with best possible speed towards Belgrade. It was accepted that the capture of their capital city would destroy the will of the Yugoslavs to resist and Corps stressed that every effort was to be made to take the city by a *coup de main*. But in order to reach Belgrade the bridges across the Danube had first to be captured and crossed and the all-weather main road from Alibunar to the capital had to be reached. At a briefing the Corps commander promised that the unit that first reached the highway would have absolute priority in the matter of road traffic. Such a promise seemed to be academic to 'Reich' Division whose route forward was across an almost roadless stretch of swamp. It seemed certain that this difficult terrain would prevent them from being the first to reach the Alibunar–Belgrade road. Hausser, however, was determined to show what his men could achieve whatever the difficulties and his Order, dated 11 April, contained a final paragraph. ' . . . "Reich" must, whatever the circumstances, capture the Belgrade bridges and be the first German troops into the city . . . ' The story of 'Reich' Division in the Yugoslav campaign is that of a fighting advance across the rain-sodden marsh and a daring drive by a handful of men who captured the capital.

At 09.05 hours on the 11th the divisional attack began to roll and although a great many vehicles were held fast in the clinging mud the remainder pressed the advance forward. Determinedly, the motor-cycle battalion forged ahead along its thrust-line, avoiding much of the swampy ground by driving along railway embankments and the tops of dikes. By an equally determined effort 'Deutschland' Regiment had brought all its battalions to Alibunar by 17.30 hours. The SS were the first of the Corps formations to gain the objective, thereby ensuring that the road was now free for them.

Aware that the day's operations had shattered the Yugoslav forces in front of it, Corps determined to give the enemy no chance to regroup but to pursue him closely and issued fresh objectives which SS 'Reich' Division was to gain. These orders could not be met. The grenadier regiments were exhausted by the strain of battle and of the march through mud which was often knee deep and frequently thigh deep. Corps then cancelled its pursuit orders and directed instead that units that had reached the banks of the Danube were not to cross but halt and rest on its northern bank. It was clear that this order did not reach Hauptsturmführer Klingenberg, commanding No. 2 Company of the motor-cycle battalion, for he ferried ten men of his company across the river in a captured motor boat. By 16.30 hours he and his group had landed and grouped on the southern bank and had begun their drive towards and into the capital. Near the War Ministry in the centre of Belgrade, as Klingenberg halted to set up two machine-gun posts, an employee of the German Embassy approached him and pleaded that the SS protect the building and the ambassadorial staff.

From officials in the Embassy Klingenberg became aware of the unique opportunity he had to gain a victory through bluff. The German Military Attaché ordered the mayor of Belgrade to present himself at the Embassy and upon his arrival Klingenberg was introduced as the commander of a very large military formation. The Hauptsturmführer then issued the ultimatum that unless the city capitulated he would order the Luftwaffe to launch a major bombing raid. The bluff worked and by 18.45 hours the mayor had formally surrendered Belgrade to the Hauptsturmführer and his ten men. During the night that small garrison was strengthened by the arrival of the advance guard of 11th Panzer Division. In the early hours of Sunday 13 April, a member from Klingenberg's group arrived at Hausser's HQ, bearing a dispatch from the German Military Attaché, advising Hausser that the motor-cycle patrol had captured Belgrade. His orders had been carried out.

On 18 April, Yugoslavia capitulated and with the campaign now at an end the Division returned to Temesvar before moving on to the Salzburg area for leave and retraining. When the Greek army, too, capitulated there was no more fighting on the European mainland and many soldiers in 'Reich' Division wondered whether their future battlefield might be in the deserts of Africa where Rommel seemed to be winning the war against the British.

However, it was not to be Africa where the Division was to see its next action but Russia where Operation 'Barbarossa', the attack upon the Soviet Union, was only weeks away.

The First Campaign
on the Eastern Front, 1941–1942

I t is not possible within the framework of this book, to cover in detail each
of the actions and battles fought by SS Division 'Reich' during its years of
service on the Eastern Front. What I have done is select and describe
closely a small number of major operations linking these with a less
detailed narrative to cover other offensives. The causes of and the strategy
behind the war against Russia, and the composition of the forces which fought
it are well known, and it is only necessary to say that the Division served in
Operation 'Barbarossa', the opening campaign against Russia, as part of
Panzer Group 2 in von Bock's Army Group Centre.

It was during the fighting on the Eastern Front that 'Reich' grew to stature
and maturity, as did all the Germanic Divisions. Indeed, it was during that
war that the entire Waffen SS organization erupted from being just three
divisions strong, about 60,000 men, into a force numbering thirty-eight
divisions and having a strength of nearly one million men. As 'Reich' Division
grew in experience so did the demands upon its fighting qualities grow. As
we have seen from the accounts of past campaigns the division was never
employed as a single formation and its component units were frequently
given such unexciting roles as guarding the flank in an advance. For the
opening stages of 'Barbarossa' the division, once again, had a militarily
unimportant task to fulfil, but within four months had created a fighting
reputation which caused it to be given the task of spearheading military
operations, a role which it was never to lay down. The Eastern Front was a
forge whose fire produced the steel-hard officers and men of 'Reich' Division,
while lesser units were turned into dross by that same fierce flame of battle.

The whole of that war was a matter of superlatives, the longest battle
line, extending north to south over 1,600 kilometres at the opening of the war
and unfolding to nearly twice that length as the three German Army Groups,
North, Centre and South, advanced eastwards. The German Army which
invaded Russia numbered three million men; 3,580 panzers and 600,000 other
vehicles accompanied them. Those Army Groups went in under a barrage
fired by 7,184 guns and 1,830 aircraft covered the opening assaults. On no
other front did such masses of men and *matériel* move across so great an area
of ground.

Certain factors influence military planning and among these are terrain
and climate. At OKW level the weather consideration was disregarded. The
campaign would be swift and would be concluded before the onset of winter.
Thus, there would be no need of special cold-weather clothing. One
consequence of this faulty appreciation was that the grenadiers who had

crossed the frontier in the high summer of June were still wearing the same uniforms when the bitter blasts of winter struck them and temperatures dropped often to 40 degrees below freezing.

One terrain factor in the area across which SS Division 'Reich' first advanced was the great Pripet Marsh. Away from the marsh where there was firm going grit from the predominantly sandy soil scoured and ruined vehicle engines. The Division's trucks were often forced to drive across country because there were so few roads. The Chief of Staff of Twelfth Army, von Greiffenburg, wrote in his appreciation when planning the new campaign ' . . . east of the Bug – San Line in Poland . . . the shortage of roads restricts movement . . . The rivers often overflow and cause widespread flooding. This disadvantage becomes more prominent the farther east one penetrates, particularly in the marshy, heavily forested regions of the Pripet marshes and the River Beresina . . . '

Thus, the German Army, designed for warfare in western Europe with its vast network of good roads backed by extensive railway systems, found itself committed to fight in the east, in a vast country where there were few all-weather roads and where the main railway lines could be counted on the fingers of a single hand. It is, therefore, obvious that railway lines and junctions as well as main roads assumed a great importance in military operations and why much of the Division's hardest fighting was made to capture or defend those strategically important objectives. Nor was it only the division's vehicles which were forced to move across country. The few highways of the western provinces of the Soviet Union had to be reserved for the panzer divisions and their follow-up motorized infantry. The roads were too few in number and too narrow to carry the huge volume of traffic that the German Army put into its first assaults. Units with a low priority were relegated to minor roads or, where these did not exist, to long, cross-country foot marches. It was not uncommon for the infantry to cover up to 70 kilometres each day on foot and then to finish that day's exertion with a fire-fight against a determined Red Army rearguard, or having to withstand a Soviet attack.

And so it continued for day after long day for weeks on end. Nothing within the experience of the German soldiers had prepared them for the size of the country through whose vastness they were marching. They passed fields of sunflowers or maize extending from one horizon to another; mile after boring mile of golden-yellow monotony – a monotony broken only when sniper fire came from the jungle of green stalks below those golden heads. The march snaked its way past woods of such dimension and of so primeval a growth that only token incursions could be made in pursuit of Red Army units who fled into them. The Army crossed unembanked rivers often half a mile in width and always fighting against an implacable, cunning enemy who might strike out of nowhere and then vanish completely or else would marshal thousands of troops into an attack to defend a village of little or no tactical or strategic importance. How the Red Army obtained the masses it required was shown in a report written after the 1943 Kursk offensive, ' . . . we found out how those numbers were obtained. Apparently, as we withdraw the Red Army re-occupies the area and rounds up all adult civilians, men and women alike. These are then formed into makeshift workers' battalions and then sent into attacks to make up weight and numbers. It does not matter that these conscripts are untrained . . . and that most of them are sent in without arms. Prisoners . . . told us that those without weapons are expected to take up those from the fallen. These unarmed civilians, forced to accompany the assaults, had been suspected of collaboration with us and were paying, in many cases quite literally with their lives, because of this suspicion . . . '

Gruppenführer Simon wrote nothing less than the truth in his report: ' . . . At the beginning of the campaign . . . we German soldiers generally speaking, knew little about our adversary . . . ' Thus it was, that the German Army went into a war in a country of immense size, against unimagined difficulties of terrain, forced to carry out weeks and months of foot marches in a country almost without roads, across marsh and waterless steppe, burned by the glaring heat of summer or wading thigh-deep through the snows of deep winter. Let us follow that Army in its operations on the Eastern Front and, specifically, its representatives in this book, the grenadiers and officers of SS Division 'Reich'. The milestones on the bloody road of advance and retreat which they trod in the first months of the campaign are the crossing of the River Beresina on 6 July and then of the Dnieper, leading into the defensive battles at Yelnya. That month-long agony of terrible losses and unbelievable privation was transmuted into a black joke when Guenther d'Alquen, the editor of the SS newspaper, *Schwarze Korps*, visited the Division. It was resting, at that time, in France and at tea one afternoon Hausser asked d'Alquen whether he would like a piece of Yelnya gateau. Accepting, in the belief that he was about to eat a splendid cake of a type previously unknown to him, d'Alquen was astonished when he was presented with a piece of unbuttered black bread sprinkled with a few grains of granulated sugar It was a subtle, or perhaps not so subtle hint of the gulf which existed between privations endured by the Waffen SS in the field and the comfortable life enjoyed by the Allgemeine SS in the Homeland.

From Yelnya the Division moved southwards to take part in the encirclement battle at Kiev and then changed direction to drive northwards again, to break through the defensive positions guarding Moscow, reaching Borodino on 13 October. Then came the thrust to take out the cathedral city of Istra, where the Division lacked the strength to push forward into the Soviet capital. Operation 'Typhoon', the offensive to capture Moscow died when the grenadiers could no longer bring the advance forward through the numbing cold of that first terrible winter, and the year ended for the Division with defensive battles fought, first in the Istra and then in the Rusa positions before moving northwards again to hold the line of the Volga in the Rzhev sector. In March 1942, part of the Division returned to Germany leaving 'Battle Group Ostendorff' to fight on until it, too, rejoined the mass of the Division during

June 1942. Thus there were soldiers of 'Reich' Division who had been almost continuously in action for nearly a year.

Let us return now to the time when there was still peace along the Russo–German frontier and when the Division was resting in the Salzburg area of Austria. A member of the divisional artillery regiment recalls the situation.

'At the beginning of May 1941, the peace-time atmosphere in which we had been living suddenly changed. All unit commanders in the Division were called to a conference at Gmunden am Traunsee, to be briefed on the coming war against Soviet Russia. There were no enthusiastic cries of "Sieg Heil!" at this announcement for there was none of us who did not have some concern at the size of the landmass in which we were soon to operate. The rank and file were not put in the picture at that time so that when the eastward movement began in June the wildest rumours spread – including one about a march through Russia and into India. We unloaded in Lublin, passed through the vast Polish forests and arrived at last in the area of the River Bug. There we bivouacked but were not allowed to light fires. Some very good friends brought us beer instead.

'Untersturmführer Kindl and a few men of Battery HQ, moved into deserted farmers' huts on the River Bug from where they could carry out observation of the eastern bank. They could see men laying mines and other soldiers keeping watch through binoculars on us on the western bank of the river. The Battery Survey Troop began to mark out the gun positions near the river bank and target maps were distributed. In the night of 21 June, the Battery, in common with every unit on the Eastern Front, took up its battle positions and at 04.15 hours thousands of guns opened a mighty barrage. Our battery commander and his HQ group crossed the river with the infantry and set up the first OP on the far bank. Enemy resistance was weak. It was clear that the attack had taken the Soviets completely by surprise. Huge fires showed that the artillery fire had been effective – a good beginning, but as we advanced it became clear why the Russian defences did not need to be strong on this sector. Before us lay a huge marsh.'

The transmission of the code-word 'Dortmund' at 12.05 hours on 21 June had advised units that Operation 'Barbarossa' was to begin on the following day. The bombardment mentioned above was the first blow in the new campaign and the initial task of 24th (Motorized) Corps, of which SS Division 'Reich' was a component, was to regulate traffic along the thrust-line of 2nd Panzer Group's advance between the Vistula and the Bug. When the order finally came for the Division to move up towards the battle zone no space was allocated to it on the highway and as a result a long foot march faced the grenadier formations. A number of enterprising companies hitched rides on vehicles driving up to the front and thus avoided the foot slog undertaken by the less adventurous detachments. Not until the 28th was the Division given its first military objective when Corps ordered it to force a river crossing between Citva and Dukora. While the mass of the Division was employed on that operation a battle group consisting of the motor-cycle battalion, the recce battalion, Flak and pioneers was to drive up the No. 1 Highway and reach the area of Sluck. The latter operation did not go as planned and a rescue mission had to be mounted for which Division used its newly created SP detachment for the first time. Three SP guns, 'Yorck', 'Ziethen' and 'Schill', were put in against the village of Starzyca and the unit's post-battle report on the operation described how the Russians had been driven out of the village during the 29th, but had then filtered back past the SS sentries so that by dawn the motor-cycle battalion was surrounded and cut off. Already, and as early as this, the unusual, perhaps unique character of the war in the east was manifesting itself, as a grenadier of 'Deutschland' Regiment wrote ' . . . even the wounded take up arms again and fire into our backs. We have to be damned careful – it is another type of fighting to the one we knew in the West.' The SP detachment's post-battle report began:

'Deutschland' Regiment's 3rd Battalion was ordered to advance on Starzyca, supported by the SP gun "Yorck", and to help the encircled detachments. The enemy was barring the way with tanks and strong infantry forces were positioned on both sides of the road. "Yorck", at the head of the battle group, first of all opened fire on the two Russian tanks. The first was hit and caught fire and the second was abandoned by its crew. To assist our own infantry advance fire was opened on the enemy occupying positions in a wood on either side of the road forcing them to retire. The village was reached and contact made with the motor-cycle battalion. During that time three more Russian tanks came in from an easterly direction. "Yorck" rolled forward and opened fire. After a short engagement all three had been immobilized. Anti-tank guns opened fire from the edge of the wood and the SP had a length of spare track and a right wheel-guard shot away. Hardly had these tanks been destroyed when "Yorck" engaged the anti-tank guns and had soon knocked out four of them. The SP pulled back to take on board fresh supplies of ammunition and returned to engage and to destroy another enemy tank advancing from the north-west. "Yorck" then moved with a recce group to seize a bridge. This had been blown but "Yorck" supported by "Lützow", dominated the enemy on the far side of the river until the divisional pioneers had made good the damage. Both vehicles then moved forward to guard the bridge and were joined by "Schill" and "Ziethen". "Schill" was ordered forward to support 'Deutschland' 1st Battalion in its attack on Serhioyevicza. The bridge at that place was blown as the divisional advance guard reached it, but "Schill" opened fire on the enemy's retreating columns and destroyed four enemy tanks.' The report concluded ' . . . at a distance of 800m enemy movement was observed, but targets could not be accurately identified because of the onset of darkness. Despite this 20 rounds were fired . . . next morning it was discovered that an additional eight smaller tanks had been hit and abandoned in the woods . . . '

That action by 'Yorck' began a close and enduring collaboration between the grenadiers and the mobile artillery. Another gun of the divisional battery smashed its way through the Russians at Brodez and on the heights outside that place opened a bombardment of the enemy's vehicles and soldiers striving to cross the 150-metre-long, wooden bridge across the Beresina. 'Lützow' then raced down from the high ground and rolled on to the bridge, thrusting its way through the crowds of fleeing Russians. As the German SP reached the centre of the bridge, Russian engineers blew it and the SP dropped into the river, leaving the crew wet and shaken but otherwise unhurt.

Heid Ruehl's report on the fighting of the first weeks mentioned the swamp into which the Division passed. This was the great Pripet Marsh; almost the size of England. It was to influence operations in a later stage of the opening campaign. He recorded the difficulties encountered in making one's way through the huge swamp.

'I went forward with the OC of No. 9 Battery, Hauptsturmführer Eichberger and his HQ group. Crossing the swamp was very difficult as we had to jump from one clump of grass to another and often had to put down our rifles and pull ourselves out of the swamp so that we did not get sucked under. That was not the only problem. We were also attacked by huge clouds of voracious mosquitoes. Using the radio we laid a barrage along the edge of a piece of woodland some 2 kilometres ahead of us where we calculated the Russian defence line would have been set. It was on rising ground from where the Russians would have excellent observation. Eichberger could not get through to his own battery and so the fire of both our units was co-ordinated and directed on to the target. We had little trouble from the Russians on that sector, after that.

'A few hundred metres behind the edge of the woods we reached a good road and the Battery had soon caught up with us. We rolled onwards towards Brest-Litovsk. The town and its citadel were defended by the Russians with the utmost tenacity against Army units. Our Division did not halt but drove on towards Minsk. At that time the divisional sign was changed to include the letter 'G' showing that we were part of Guderian's panzer group. The divisional task was to protect the flanks of the advancing Army panzer divisions as they drove along the highway. The enemy avoided being drawn into direct action and withdrew into the almost impenetrable woods and forests. That meant that we had frequent brushes with Russian units that had been by-passed. These fire-fights and the lack of proper roads both played their parts in slowing down our advance.

'We by-passed Mogilev, driving towards our next objective, Smolensk. No. 8 Battery was point unit and on the road forward we passed a German 15cm battery which had been attacked and destroyed, but we could see neither sight nor sound of the enemy. That night the light of the moon was bright enough to read by and our infantry had advanced so far ahead that we were completely isolated. The first vehicles of our column, the commander's car, the OP truck and Battery HQ truck, had just passed a small hollow when a single shot fired from an enemy anti-tank gun hit and destroyed our prized possession, a 5,000-litre petrol bowser. From all sides came the chilling cry "Ooohrah!" and then a storm of small-arms fire. Our iron discipline manifested itself; the intensity of our training and of the everlasting drill paid dividends. We needed no orders. Like a fire-spitting hedgehog we were soon in action laying down a heavy barrage and throwing hand-grenades just like infantry veterans. A Russian grenade came flying through the air and landed next to Kindl. I shouted a warning and he rolled over into the hollow. Luckily for him that it was a dud, otherwise he would never have made it. A gun team, crawling on their knees, brought their gun into the hollow and they opened fire at 100 metres' range which reduced the pressure a little. By this time the other gun teams and the Train personnel had come forward and had come into action. When the other sub-units saw our tanker go up in flames they thought that we had all been wiped out. A DR was sent with a message asking for help, but none came until the following morning when No. 7 Battery moved forward, by which time we no longer needed help.

The morning light showed us what had happened. The Russians had abandoned Mogilev and their line of retreat had cut right across our line of advance. Our recce patrols moved into the next village and came back with food which included Russian iron rations. These consisted of a piece of hard brown bread as large as a fist and a similarly sized piece of cane sugar. The two together produced a feeling of fullness which our own iron rations never achieved. In the evening we formed a "hedgehog" and No. Battery took up position near an abandoned cemetery. Some of the men found straw-covered bottles of vodka which proved to be too much even for hardened drinkers and which was undrinkable even when diluted with every sort of mix. I was thinking about how much I fancied a drop of spirits when there was a loud heel click, just like on a barrack square, and then a voice, "Oberscharführer Dressler reporting with four new prime movers and fifteen men from the replacement regiment in Munich." He had also brought with him ten bottles of three star brandy. Dressler took over his old No. 1 Troop and we all celebrated his return "home".

The next morning Division took over the task of protecting the northern flank of the advance along the Minsk–Smolensk highway towards Yelnya. We stormed Smolensk against really determined resistance. No. 8 Battery was seconded to support Klingenberg's motor-cycle battalion which was lying south of Yelnya in the area of Ushakova. Klingenberg briefed us and the battery then moved into positions some 500 metres from Ushakova. Battery HQ passed through the village during the evening and took up positions some 300 metres ahead of us, along the edge of a wood in cratered ground. In order to provoke a reaction from the enemy some sub-units changed positions and fired from different places in the woods but there was no response at that time. It was a different story next day. At first light a barrage of heavy calibre shells crashed down forcing us to pull the guns back and to set up our OP in the middle of the village. The battery fired a barrage on to those places in the woods where we thought the Russians would be concentrating. Through the scissors periscope we could see trainloads of their reinforcements being brought forward, obvious signs of an impending attack, but the railway line lay beyond the range of our guns.'

The Defensive Battle of Yelnya

On 22 July the Division, thrusting up the main Minsk–Moscow highway, opened an attack to take the high ground east of Yelnya. That operation was to lead into a four-week battle whose strain remains clearly impressed today upon the memory of all those who fought there. Yelnya itself, standing on the River Desna, was a typical small town in western Russian and its importance lay in the fact that not only was it a crossroads but the high ground to the east of it was strategically important. Whoever held it dominated the road to and from Moscow, 300 kilometres distant. Thus, for both sides possession of that high ground was vital; for the offensive or for the defence. The savagery of the fighting of that four-week battle and the number and fury of the Red Army's counter-attacks confronted the grenadiers with methods and styles of fighting previously unknown. Hour-long bombardments by shell and rocket, incessant infantry probes and massed tank thrusts were portents that the fighting would become increasingly more bitter the closer the German Army came to Moscow. The divisional attack opened with the principal effort made by 'Deutschland' on the right flank supported by the armour of 10th Panzer Division. 'Der Führer' was placed on the left and 11th Regiment formed the second wave, ready to reinforce any point at which a breakthrough was made. The attack opened at 09.15 hours when the leading files of the 1st and 2nd Battalions of 'Deutschland' Regiment moved over their start-lines without a covering barrage; not that the artillery regiment would have been able to offer much support; the failure of the ammunition trucks to reach the divisional dump had led to a rationing of shells.

The Russians, holding a well-sited and extensive trench system situated on the heights, poured down a hurricane of fire upon the thin line of grenadiers. The companies reeled, but then regrouped and resumed the advance, passing swiftly through the curtain of shells and bullets; not charging impetuously, but moving with the practised ease of veteran soldiers. Their smooth advance was a testimonial to the training they had received and moving with panache, beating down the Red Army's most determined resistance, by evening 'Deutschland's tired but exultant companies stood on the crest of the first ridge.

On its sector 'Der Führer' did not move off until late in the morning and its attack followed the same pattern of fighting as that experienced by the sister regiment. Again, by late evening the grenadiers had fought their way into the

Russian main defensive line. But it is one thing to capture ground and another to hold it with soldiers who are exhausted by the strain of daylong battle carried out in searing heat and on a water-less, shade-less upland. During the night the Russians brought forward fresh formations and at 06.00 hours on the 23rd opened a counter-attack along the whole length of the Division's front. The fighting raged for hours in the trenches and dug-outs and over the open high ground to the east of Yelnya. By midday the SS were masters of the situation and had driven the Russians downhill in panic flight. Corps, recognizing that 'Reich' was too weak to continue with offensive operations, ordered that it should go over to the defensive, but the fighting did not diminish in fury.

An example of the pitch at which the battle continued to be fought is shown by the post-action report of an anti-tank detachment. On the 24th a 5cm Pak was put into position on the road to Doregobush, at a point where the road became a steep-walled cutting. ' . . . eight Russian tanks appeared and the NCO in charge of the gun ordered fire to be held until the lead vehicle was within 50 metres. Unterscharführer Rossner used the familiar tactic; kill the first vehicle, then the last and, finally, destroy the trapped remainder, at leisure. The first Russian tank was hit and "killed", but the second was a flame-throwing vehicle which projected huge gouts of flame at the anti-tank gunners. The Russian crew then leapt from their machine and raced towards the gunners, who grabbed entrenching tools and grenades, doubling forward to meet the Russian charge. On that bright July morning a small knot of men, Germans and Russians, fought for their lives and when, at last, the Russian tankmen had been killed the SS gunners went back to their Pak and carried on firing until all the Russian tanks had been destroyed.' Heid Ruehl recalled that:

'The Russians around Yelnya attacked with tanks and penetrated as far as our artillery positions. One of our stretcher-bearers won the Iron Cross here by knocking out an enemy tank with a hand-grenade. He threw it into the open hatch. Finish! The gunners, working like fury, finally beat off the first Russian tank attacks, but these were then renewed in greater strength and then our motor-cycle battalion came under heavy pressure. We were smothered in a drum fire such as we had never before experienced. The courage of our soldiers and how well they fought is shown by the actions of Foerster Group of the motor-cycle battalion, who fought to the last man and whose determination destroyed the Russian attacks. Because of the severe losses which it had sustained motor-cycle battalion had to be taken out of the line and was replaced by an East Prusian engineer battalion. With the help of that formation we stemmed the Russian advance, albeit only temporarily, for soon ammunition for the guns began to run out and we were only allowed to fire against certain, specified targets.'

The fighting continued with Russian attacks mounted with clock-work regularity and across ground spread with the bodies of the fallen. Massed machine-gun fire from No. 4 Company of the motor-cycle battalion cut down one battalion assault and crisis followed crisis as the furious thrusts of the Red Army penetrated the front held by the SS regiment. To seal off one gap in the line at Ushakova the divisional pioneer battalion had to be committed in an infantry role and was backed by three SPs and a platoon of anti-tank guns. Heid Ruehl's account of operations included a description of the fighting for Ushakova, a small village which lies to the north-west of Yelnya.

'The small, typical Russian village was located on a ridge and ran roughly west to south-east. About 200 metres from the eastern end of the village there was a single, large and very prominent tree which marked Point 125. Near that tree we had an OP manned by Untersturmführer Kindl, a wireless operator and a telephone operator, and defended by a small infantry group. No. 8 Battery of the divisional artillery regiment was firing from positions some 2½ to 3 kilometres south-west of Ushakova, in support of Army units as well as of our own divisional infantry.

'We had been in position for two days, fighting off incessant Russian infantry attacks which eventually came so close to the OP that Kindl ordered our guns to lay a curtain barrage. The infantry group which was supposed to be defending the OP had so much to do fighting off the Russian infantry that they had scant time to defend the OP group. Obersturmführer Schuelke ordered me to take a machine-gun and go forward to support the OP. Hasenkopf, my No. 2, took a couple of boxes of ammunition with him and I carried the gun. The Russian artillery was firing the whole time but sheltered by the houses in the village Hasenkopf and I passed through the storm of shells and made our way towards the large tree. Untersturmführer Kindl waved to us indicating a place some 30 metres to his right where he wanted us to set up the machine-gun and go into action.

'A Russian heavy artillery gun, probably the 17.2, which we called the 'black sow' then opened fire aiming at the tree, firing a shell about every 3 to 4 minutes. The third one landed about 10 metres ahead of us and under that cover Russian infantry, crawling towards us through dead ground, finally reaching a point only 50 metres from our position. The sun was behind me so I could see them quite clearly and using short bursts of fire kept them at bay. Kindl decided he could no longer pass fire orders to the guns and left the OP together with the wireless operator. As he passed he shouted out to me to carry on firing the machine-gun. I heard another artillery round coming in. This landed on the spot where the Untersturmführer and the operator had had their OP. Then we, too, pulled back through the burning village, holding off the pursuing Russians with bursts of machine-gun fire and grenades. Our officer was busy organizing the evacuation of the wounded although he had lost a leg and, in fact, died on the way to the Dressing Station. The operator had been killed outright.

'Luckily, our right flank was secure. The ground there was swampy and covered with willow trees. We worked our way back towards the battery positions using the map which I had with me and keeping the Russians back with hand-grenades and bursts of machine-gun fire. Soon we had run out of hand-grenades. We fired a very long burst of fire which forced the Ivans to keep their heads down and raced towards our battery positions. We reached these just in time to see the last prime mover and gun pulling out in a cloud of dust. The battery had been ordered to pull back from its positions near Ushakova. We were not the only ones on the road. Motor cycles loaded with wounded and other comrades, either alone or in groups, were making their way out of the burning village, all of them completely exhausted, dusty and sweaty. The Russian advance had rolled over our thin infantry defensive lines and a lot of our lads did not get out. Ahead of us were some armoured reconnaissance vehicles, one of which was carrying the divisional commander's pennant. Obergruppenführer Hausser was standing in the turret. He asked me for a report and also inquired about survivors. He checked Ushakova with his binoculars and over the wireless ordered a Stuka attack upon the village. It was a relief to meet "Papa" Hausser and to see the Stukas go in about an hour later.

'By that time we had reached the battery position where we found the guns in action firing on the village. The Luftwaffe and artillery attacks brought us respite for what remained of the day and for that night. Our battery commander told us to have a good sleep – or at least as well as we were able under the circumstances. Ushakova was recaptured next day using panzers and assault guns.'

With its regiments fighting around Yelnya in the high summer of 1941, 'Reich' Division achieved the distinction of being the division of the Army which had advanced farthest eastwards. Against it were pitted élite units of Zhukov's armies with orders to halt any further German advance towards Moscow.

An incident in the fighting was recalled by Roman Geiger, serving with No. 8 Battery of the divisional artillery regiment.

'We were firing in support of Hauptsturmführer Klingenberg's motor-cycle battalion, to the right of Ushakova. We were told that because of the severity of the fighting and of the losses which Klingenberg's unit had suffered, every man of his battalion had been put into the line. To cover our own losses the Spiess, Hauptscharführer Bierleutgeb, went up to the OP which was situated on a rise left of Ushakova to replace the FOO who was forward with the men of the motor-cycle battalion. Numbers 3 and 4 guns of our battery faced NNW to support the infantry at Gredina, while the 1st and 2nd guns faced ENE, to support the motor cyclists. At the end of two days we were running low on ammunition and had orders to conserve it. One morning, about 04.00 hours, shortly after first light, I was crawling out of my slit trench when one of our drivers arrived on foot, wounded and exhausted. He told us that the OP had been overrun, that the Spiess was wounded and was lying in a ditch close to the Steyr truck. The driver then collapsed. The battery commander called for volunteers to rescue the Spiess and told me to bring both machine-guns and ammunition. Every man of the battery volunteered for the mission and we climbed on a six-wheeler lorry which had been brought up. Not all those who had volunteered could go. Someone had to be left behind to serve the guns.

'The officer and Sturmscharführer Dressler got into the cab. I mounted my MG on the roof of the cab, while the other together with another five men was inside the truck. In his quick briefing our commander had told us that he intended to drive as far forward as possible, certainly until we came under fire. Then we set out on the journey to Gredina, some 5 kilometres distant. The truck rolled into the village and had passed the first wooden houses before the enemy opened up. I returned fire with the machine-gun while the driver reversed the lorry to bring us back into cover. We had hardly covered 50 metres when our officer ordered, "All out! One machine-gun on the left of the road, the second on the right. The remainder, follow me." I noticed that the heaviest enemy fire was coming from the right of the road and from a small dip in the ground. I changed position so as to enfilade the enemy and my No. 2 on the gun, Hasenkopf, brought along two boxes of ammunition. I fired several short bursts and then we had a stoppage. Once it was cleared I stood up to see the enemy more clearly, intending to bring more effective fire upon them. That was not successful and so we moved back again to our original positions by the side of the road.

'There we found that two comrades had been killed and that Obersturmführer Schuelke was being carried off with a bullet through the jaw. Sturmscharführer Dressler had taken over command and told me to go across to a nearby fence which I could use as a support for the gun. He thought that from that position I would be able to fire more effectively into the dip in the ground. Eventually, he took the gun from me and resting it on my shoulder fired bursts into the enemy positions. After a time the enemy fire began to die down, probably because two Panzer IV from the 'Grossdeutschland' Division had moved into the area. We waved at them. They rolled over one fence and then swung round in the direction of the enemy. Dressler climbed on to one of the panzers and sat behind the turret issuing fire orders. Then from all sorts of hiding-places, but particularly from out of a haystack, Russian soldiers came out to surrender. By the time I returned to the road three dead comrades were being loaded on to the truck and the wounded were being taken back to the Dressing Station. I was just in time to shake the hand of the dying Gunner Stritzel but before he closed his eyes for ever he told me to take his last greetings to his comrades. We found our Spiess dead in a ditch, killed by a shot in the neck. The 'Grossdeutschland' Division sent a message to our Regiment commending us for the action which had cost us so dearly. The Russian penetration of this sensitive part of the line had gone unnoticed by Division. Unfortunately, our new Commander, Obersturmführer Schulze, was not of that opinion. He thought that the whole thing had been a pointless exercise.'

The defensive battle at Yelnya dragged on, but now without the participation of the survivors of the badly mauled 'Reich' Division who were rested for a few days away from the front line. One after another Army divisions were put into the fight and destroyed after only a few days of this fierce attritional warfare. The pace of battle had changed from that of *Blitzkrieg* to static warfare; like that of the Great War. Army Group's losses were so terrible that a point was fast approaching when there would be barely sufficient strength to maintain the battle at such an intensity and certainly not enough to advance the battle line farther eastwards. The blood-letting in the Red Army was at an even higher level than that suffered by the Germans, but the Russian manpower reserves were still able to make good the losses many times over. The finite human resources of the Reich were already showing signs of strain.

The men of 'Reich' Division, resting behind the line, speculated as soldiers do, on when they would next be committed to action. There were three options: a renewed drive for Moscow, a strike to take out Leningrad or participation in the giant battle of encirclement which was developing around Kiev. It was to take part in the last-named operation that, during the second week of September, 'Reich' moved southwards as the right flank unit of XXIV Panzer Corps.

The terrain factor of the Pripet marsh was responsible for the creation of a huge salient which projected between the inner wings of Army Groups Centre and South. By comparison, movement on the outer wings of these Army Groups had been rapid. The result was a salient with its western end around Kiev and its eastern exist some 150 kilometres beyond that city. Contained within the pocket were five or six Russian armies, a force of between fifty and sixty divisions. Hitler, faced with the choice of a strategic thrust to take out Moscow or a tactical victory which would destroy fifty Russian divisions, chose the tactical option. The battle plan was simple and classic. The Russian defenders at the western end of the salient were to be held fast by Sixth Army and with the defence thus committed a strong force would execute a double encirclement. German Second Army and Panzer Group 2 were to strike down from the north to meet the up-thrusting drive of Seventeenth Army and Panzer Group 1. The two infantry armies would form the inner pair of jaws while the two panzer groups, whose forces would meet some 180 kilometres to the east of Kiev, would compromise the outer pincers. The task of XXIV Panzer Corps, of which the SS Division was a component, was to strengthen the southerly drive of Guderian's panzer force.

The part played by SS 'Reich' in what was, to that date, the biggest encirclement battle in the history of warfare, in terms of numbers killed and captured, opened with a long drive by a battle group comprising 'Der Führer' Regiment, the motor-cycle battalion and supporting units. So urgent was the need for men in the line that the components of this battle group were put into action before the main body of the Division reached the battle zone. The given task was to strike south-westwards, to penetrate the Russian line and to swing behind the enemy forces to the front of and on the left wing of Second Army, thereby cutting off their retreat. The attack, mounted on 6 September, rolled well and had reached an important junction at Sosnitsa, when orders came for the motor-cycle battalion to undertake a swift raid to seize the undamaged railway bridge at Makoshim, there to create and hold a bridgehead on the south bank of the River Desna. Flexibility in operation was one of the keynotes in *Blitzkrieg* operations.

This particular mission did not open well. A Stuka attack to hold down the Russian defenders of the bridge while the SS motor-cyclists crossed it, was ordered for 13.30 hours. Over an hour later the dive-bombers had still not arrived and, unwilling to waste more time, Guderian, who had now reached the bridge, ordered the SS battalion to advance. The feelings of those committed to this enterprise can well be imagined. They were to cross this huge iron construction which had most certainly been prepared for demolition by enemy engineers. At any time during their careering ride – in German Army parlance 'A Hussar stroke' – the massive detonating charges might be set off and those who were not killed in the explosions would be flung into the river and drowned.

The motor-cycle assault opened. At full speed the machines were raced over the sleepers and before the Russians could react to this move, the leading SS groups, whose machine-gunners in the side-cars sprayed the area with bursts of fire, had smashed through the enemy barricades. Behind the SS battalion Army engineers moved slowly cutting detonating wires where they found them and taking away the high-explosive charges. The bridge was captured and an SS perimeter on the south bank of the Desna established and consolidated. Then, overhead, their wings shining in the bright afternoon sunlight, twenty-seven Stukas appeared, swooped, bombed and flew away. They left behind them ten dead and more than thirty wounded SS men, but the bridge itself was not badly damaged.

The whole Division then moved into the perimeter, burst out of its confines and struck south to the River Uday. 'Reich' Division crossed the river on the 16th with 'Der Führer' on the right wing at the Priluki bridge and with 11th SS Regiment to the east of Borsna. The bridges spanning the river were blown as the SS advanced guards reached the river bank. Enemy resistance on the south bank of the river was very determined and resulted in heavy losses to the infantry companies. With the crossing of the Uday and the setting up of a perimeter at Priluki the divisional task had been accomplished. It was one of the final actions in closing the ring around the trapped Russian armies. The closure finally came on the 14th and was followed on the 15th by a telegram from von Bock, the Army Group Commander, expressing his ' . . . recognition of the achievements of the commanders and men of the SS Division "Reich" . . . ' An encircling ring had certainly been flung around the Russians, but now its area had to be reduced against an enemy who would make the most determined efforts to smash a way out to freedom. The Russians flung in no fewer than three infantry divisions, two cavalry divisions and two tank brigades in one single effort, and on another sector of Corps front, at Putivl, the pupils of the Kharkov military academy, showing considerable courage and astonishing élan, charged, singing, into the fire of the SS machine-guns and died to the last man.

A précis of the Division's post-battle report covering operations from 11 to 18 September, recalls that after creating a bridgehead to the south of Makoschino, 'Deutschland' led the advance along the railway line to the junction at Bakmatsch. It was less the fanatical enemy resistance and more the terrible road conditions and appalling weather which affected the pace of the advance. On the 11th touch was gained with the left flank neighbour, 4th Panzer Division, and torrential rain washed away the roads resulting, on at least one occasion, in trucks being driven along railway embankments standing above a flooded countryside. Despite the delays the Division never lost contact with the enemy and continued to press towards the new objective, Priluki, where it was to create a perimeter around that important road network. The report laid great stress upon the extensive minefields which obstructed the advance and upon the intricate trench systems which the enemy was able to construct in a very short time. It concluded with the statement that with the creation of the Priluki bridgehead on 18 September, the divisional task had been accomplished. There was some fighting against Russian forces attempting to flee the Kiev encirclement but then 'Reich' Division was taken out of the line on 24 September and rested until 2 October.

In that encirclement battle five Russian armies were completely destroyed and a further two severely mauled. A million Russians had been killed, wounded or captured. More seriously, the road to the great industrial area of the Donets basin and to the oil producing region of the Caucasus lay open to a future German thrust. To conclude this account of the participation of 'Reich' Division in the Kiev encirclement, the following extracts from a soldier who fought there, provide a kaleidescope of impressions.

'06.15. 7 September. The rations which came up during the night are distributed. Two and three-quarter loaves between twelve men; that is four slices of bread for a day's ration. It isn't much but is better than nothing . . . 8 September. By 16.00 hours we march off towards the Desna . . . Later we debus and leave the trucks behind. We cross the river by a railway bridge which our motor-cycle battalion captured yesterday . . . 9 September. At 02.00 hours rations came up. At last something hot to eat and enough bread. We advance along the side of the railway line and the Russian shells sink into the swamp which we are crossing and do not usually explode . . . One shell which did go off fell between me and another man but did us no injury although my comrade has been affected by the blast. He will not go back for medical treatment, so I take over his machine-gun and using its sling, link him to me. Every time I let him go he walks around in circles. . . . 12 September. We march along a railway embankment. It is very tiring walking on the sleepers . . . Our feet are suffering from being continually wet from the rain and the swamp . . . A grenade explodes near our Section and shrapnel ignites the Very light pistol ammunition carried by the platoon runner. He is soon enveloped in flames and suffers not only burns but shrapnel wounds as well, from which he dies ... 14 September. The burning hot sun has dried the ground and our feet begin to hurt ... We come under fire ... everywhere there are calls for stretcher-bearers ... Our Company suffered 14 killed and 17 wounded ... The regimental commander, Bittrich arrives ... It is not the first time that I have seen him in the front line getting an idea of the true situation ... Our wounded comrade Gail died on the way back. His death depresses us very much because only two days ago he had received a telegram telling him he was the father of a healthy boy ... During the morning of 10 September, we brewed some tea and although our feet are very painful, we carry on ... We strain our eyes through the pouring rain looking for the first sign of 1st Panzer Division.' [When touch was gained with that formation the ring around the encircled Russian forces was sealed.]

' ... On roads that have been washed away, in pouring rain, carrying all our weapons and equipment, we fight our way against enemy resistance. We are at the end of our strength. We have been marching for days and with only poor rations. The supply trucks are stuck fast in the mud 30 or more kilometres away. Many of the comrades have only socks to cover their feet. Their boots have fallen to pieces. Others go bare-foot and their feet are torn as a result of the marches ... A rumour; we link up with 1st Panzer Division tonight ... Soaked to the skin we dig in and our slit trenches fill quickly with water. The rain continues to pour down ... We are lying in water and yet we are thirsty ... We are told that we are taking part in a gigantic, destructive battle ... 13 September. We work our way through one village after another. The enemy has abandoned great masses of vehicles and material ... On 21 September we reach Romny. Here for the first time we get a beer issue ... We are taken back to a village in the area of Chernigov ... After a meal we fall into a deep sleep. When we wake the civilians in the village, who were reserved to begin with, become more friendly. We give them tins of food and salt. They supply us with potatoes and warm milk.'

Even while the Battle of Kiev was being fought new plans were being prepared for an offensive which would capture Moscow. On 6 September, orders were issued for an operation that would trap the enemy in a double encirclement around Vyasma. When the Russian armies within that pocket had been destroyed the road to Moscow would be open and Army Group Centre could then open a battle of pursuit which would end with the capture of the Soviet seat of power. On 26 September Army Group issued orders to its subordinate formations. Fourth Army and Panzer Group 4 were to return at best speed from the south. Their task in the forthcoming offensive was to drive up the main highway which links Roslavl to Moscow. Hitler rejected Guderian's requests for time to service his worn-out panzers and to rest the tired crews. Time, Guderian was told, was of the essence and so, with no time to rest or to carry out any but the most urgent running repairs, the two German armies carried out an almost 90 degree turn and undertook the long march northwards to take their place in the battle line that would soon be advancing upon Moscow.

While plans were being laid and operations orders prepared, the battle-worn grenadiers of SS Division 'Reich' were resting. Sufficient grenadiers came in to fill the ranks and to replace the losses which had been suffered. 'Deutschland' Regiment, for example, had lost 1,519 all ranks, killed, wounded and missing since entering upon the war with Russia on 22 June. The figures for 'Der Führer' Regiment were comparable. The new men who came in had scant time to accustom themselves to the strange conditions of life on the Eastern Front. One of these was Walter Schminke who recalled his initiation into active-service life.

'The people in Div HQ sorted us out. An Oberscharführer stood on a wooden box and called out names . . . He came up to me and asked my age. "Twenty, Oberscharführer." "Right, then you take this group to the motor-cycle battalion. March from here straight on for 2 kilometres, then turn left and march for another 3 kilometres. Turn right and march for another 4 kilometres. You'll find a tree there and a guide from the motor-cycle battalion.

'There we were – my group – with orders to march without weapons, with no compass and with no senior officer in charge across the middle of Russia . . . There was no landmark by which I could plot my route, but eventually we did find a tree and the guide from Battalion. He was dressed in Russian winter clothing but I could soon make out his belt buckle and his 08 pistol . . . The battalion had cooked a meal specially for us; thick pea soup which tasted just fine . The atmosphere in the new unit was excellent. It was not exactly unmilitary but there was a complete absence of parade ground bullshit. After eating ourselves full we were able to buy canteen goods; cigarettes, schnapps, combs and writing-paper. So far, or so it seemed to me, life in the front line was good. When it got dark we went down to the Volga, at this place a river of only medium width. On its banks we were taught the words of the battalion anthem, "Unshaven and far from home." After we 36 men had sung our song we heard applause coming from the other side of the Volga. It was the Russians. Then they sang a song and we applauded. Is this really what the war was like? We went to sleep on the floor of a Russian school.' Next morning Schminke and his group of mortarmen accompanied a group which was to carry out an assault upon a Russian defensive position. Schminke suggested to Sturmbannführer Klingenberg – 'the man who captured Belgrade' – that the mortars should give covering fire and the weapons were set up by the commander's side. Twenty rounds were ordered and twenty were flung in rapid succession down the mortar tubes. 'Klingenberg jumped when the first round fired and asked if we were mad to set up the weapon so close to him and hadn't we heard of ranging in and giving correct orders. "Not necessary," I replied, rather stupidly and he looked as if he would like to shoot us. The other commanders also gave us black looks. But we were lucky. Nearly every one of our mortar bombs hit the target and knocked out the bunker. There was no need now for an attack. Klingenberg said that we had been lucky, but when I asked whether we should repeat the performance he laughed and said not, we had proved ourselves. That was our first mission. I can't say that I had any special feelings, but of course it is not a nice feeling to be a target.'

On 2 October 1941, under a cloudless, blue sky and in perfect autumn weather the new offensive, Operation 'Typhoon', began. It was clear to OKW that an operation to seize the enemy's capital city would be no easy undertaking. It was to be anticipated that every man, woman and child in the areas to the west of Moscow, as well as in the capital itself, would be employed in digging trenches and anti-tank ditches. Extensive and numerous minefields would be laid, workers' militias would be called to arms to back the Russian Army divisions already holding the line and, indeed, the whole capacity and industry of the Soviet Union would be committed to the vital task of defending the capital.

Before 'Typhoon' opened Stavka had already strengthened the existing defences of the capital and had moved a number of Russian armies to slow down and then to halt, the German assaults. That mighty battle ran until early in the New Year of 1942. By that time the assaulting German divisions which had advanced with such confidence on the sunny morning of 4 October, had been sent reeling, decimated and freezing, in the snow-storms of deep winter. OKW had planned an operation whose momentum, so it was firmly held, would send Army Group Centre crashing through the Russian forces and across the minefields, thundering over the several Moscow defence systems and finally entering the city itself before the onset of the bitterest winter weather. This operation very nearly succeeded. As the history of 'Deutschland' Regiment records: '. . . with the capture of Lenino [on 3 December] a suburb of Moscow, some 17 kilometres from the inner city, had been taken. It was one of the termini of the Moscow bus service. In the bright winter weather one could make out the Kremlin towers. My God!, how close we were to this historic objective.' But between the first day of 'Typhoon' and the retreat of the Army from the gates of Moscow lay two months of terrible suffering.

It is a story of frost-bite, of gangrene and limbs being cut off under primitive conditions in field hospitals, by surgeons operating often with no anaesthetics. Grenadiers whose boots had long since disintegrated wrapped their frozen feet in rags so that they could accompany their comrades into the attack. It was a time of wounded soldiers loaded into makeshift hospital trains who arrived dead in reception stations, frozen stiff in the unheated trucks. For those who continued to hold the battle line it was a time of lice, cold food, dysentery and the ever-present knowledge that to be wounded was almost a sentence of death. And then there were two implacable enemies: 'General Winter' and the Russian Army, whose soldiers, if not proof against the cold, were at least more accustomed to it than the Germans. The Russian Army was better clothed and better equipped to meet the terrible, freezing temperatures. But in October as 'Reich' Division moved to its new battle position, such horrors were unimaginable. So confident were the German political leaders of total victory before winter that leaflets were printed and a large order for fireworks placed which would celebrate the fall of Moscow and with it the end of the war with Russia.

Operation 'Typhoon': The Battle for Moscow

The Division began its part in Operation 'Typhoon', at 17.30 hours on 4 October, when its units moved off behind the armoured spearhead of 10th Panzer Division to capture the little towns of Krichev and Ladishino, east of Roslavl. With those two objectives quickly gained 'Reich' was ordered to swing northwards at Yuchnov and: '. . . giving no heed to the danger of an open right flank, to gain the area between Gshatsk and Vyasma'. These orders faced the Division with two tasks, both of which were difficult. Its units facing north and west would have to close the ring around the Russian forces trapped in the Vyasma pocket while those facing east and north had to frustrate the enemy's attacks to break the German encirclement. Implicit in the battle orders was the task of cutting the Smolensk Moscow highway Corps' objective was Gshatsk, whose seizure was as vital for the success of the German advance upon Moscow as its retention was for the Russian defence of the capital, for whoever held Gshatsk obstructed the free-flowing movement of the other side. The bitter battles of the first weeks of October were thus around or against that town.

Army Group Centre's first advances before 'Das Reich' moved up to make its attack had been so fast that they had encouraged the hope that the Russian Army would be finally destroyed and this time before the gates of Moscow itself. The opening assaults had forced Russian withdrawals so as to prevent 30th, 19th and 43rd Armies being trapped by a new encirclement, and German pressure on 6 October had compelled Stavka to authorize still further retreats. It seemed to those in Army Group HQ that the Russian front was beginning to break and that nothing would be able to halt the German panzer thrusts. The attacks which 'Das Reich' were to mount would first contain and further fragment the Russian armies in front of it.

To strengthen 'Deutschland' Regiment, which had been selected to open the divisional assault, it was reinforced by a platoon of SPs, 3rd Battalion of the artillery regiment plus an additional battery, a light Flak battery, an anti-tank company and Corps troops. The task of the SPs was to clear enemy troops from both sides of the thrust-line and, thereby, to protect the flanks of the grenadier regiment's attack. Mine-lifting operations were to be completed swiftly so that by 0800 hours on 7 October, the advance upon Gshatsk could begin. Second Battalion moved in at 14.20 hours supported by SPs and had soon taken the important height to the north-west of Sharaponova. An hour later the battalion had carried the advance as far as Mikeyeva, driving the Russians back northwards. Scenting victory and allowing the shaken enemy no time to reform or to set up a strong defence, the battalion pushed on and had soon captured Sloboda Potovskaya where it regrouped. During the late afternoon 1st Battalion leapfrogged through its sister battalion and struck forwards to Kamyonka. The battalion, mounted in lorries, was making good progress and was confident of reaching its given objective when snow began to fall. By comparison with the howling blizzards which were to come, this first fall was very moderate, but it was sufficient to turn into mud slicks the tracks along which the battalion's wheeled transport was advancing. Soon the lorries were hopelessly stuck. The grenadiers debussed and completed the remainder of the approach march on foot. First Battalion reached and captured Komyenka shortly before midnight. The 3rd Battalion had re-entered the battle and had cut the vital Smolensk–Moscow highway. The Russians were now trapped within a fresh encirclement.

At dawn on the following day, 9 October, 'Deutschland' Regiment attacked Gshatsk with two battalions up – 1st on the right of the highway and 3rd on the left of the road. The primary objective was to gain a railway embankment which 2nd Battalion would then protect. A recce patrol penetrated the southern suburb of Gshatsk and had soon worked its way to a position behind the enemy positions from where it ambushed a small group of troop-carrying trucks. The two assault battalions advancing up the highway made good progress despite attacks by waves of low-flying Russian fighter-bombers; assaults which did not stop until 1st Battalion's companies struck into the vast forest which bordered the road. At first grateful for this relief, the grenadiers then found that they had exchanged the fury of attack from the air for the bitterness of fighting through the undergrowth of a forest against an enemy who had constructed extensive, well-sited defensive positions. A new phenomenon encountered during this battle were Russian snipers who roped themselves to tree trunks so as to leave both hands free to hold and aim their rifles.

The relentless advance of the grenadiers could not be halted and by 13.00 hours both 1st and 3rd Battalions were in the city. Among the grisly discoveries that afternoon were the bodies of a great many civilians whom the Russians had hanged publicly before they retreated. Fighting went on around Gshatsk during the 10th, with growing evidence that the enemy was being massively reinforced. Clearly, Stavka was determined to fight hard to hold the strategic town. Fighting rose in intensity in this outpost of the Moscow defensive positions as Zhukov, the new Front Commander, reshuffled his armies. The commander of 'Das Reich' Division advised of a Red build-up, sent 'Der Führer' into an attack east of Gshatsk to disrupt Russian troop movements. The assault moved off at 08.00 hours and had captured the heights to the west of Slovoda late in the afternoon. Then on 16 October 'Der Führer' Regiment, which had taken up the running and was involved in fighting down the violent Russian reaction to its drive, reported that the first lines of the Moscow defences had been breached and that its advance guard had reached a village only 3 kilometres to the north-east of Yelnya.

An officer of divisional TAC HQ, who watched the regiment's attack go in, described the experience of being bombarded by rockets of a 'Stalin organ' (the fearsome, multi-barrelled projector which could put twenty missiles into the air at a time). 'As I had not dug a slit trench I just flung myself behind a tree and watched the terrifyingly beautiful display of exploding rocket shells. The memory of the smell of high-explosive and of black, red and violet colours as the shells detonated and took on the shape of tulip heads will always remain in my mind.'

During the night of 13 October, the sister regiment, "Der Führer", took up the fight again and continued the advance up the Moscow highway. Late in the afternoon it had forced its way against dug-in tanks and flame-throwers forming the capital's outermost defences, having in its storming advance smashed five roadblocks, fought in and across trench systems, and had knocked out concrete pillboxes. Giving the enemy no respite, the regiment's attack was continued throughout the night. Assault groups from both battalions in the line, 3rd on the left and 2nd on the right, fought hand-to-hand against the crack troops of 32nd Siberian Infantry Division. Fighting in and around the area continued for nearly two weeks with two of the climaxes of the struggle being the storming of the road junction to the south-west of Mozhaisk and the capture of that town on 18 October.

To summarize the Division's actions: from 6 October, in unbroken assault, along bad roads, usually without hot meals and in frightful weather, the élan of the SS grenadiers had brought the German battle line close to the Russian capital. The troops were now at the end of their strength and sickness had broken out; frostbite and stomach illnesses resulting from the lack of hot food had brought about a general weakening of their physique. A divisional report to SS HQ in Berlin advising of the situation stressed that ' . . . a rest of several days where possible in warm and heated billets is essential for the success of any new attack . . . '

It was expected that the OKW offensive to surround Moscow would be met with the most bitter Russian resistance. This Intelligence appreciation was fully borne out by the fighting in which 'Deutschland' Regiment was involved when it carried out an attack north of the Moscow highway. The day's objectives were Mikaelovkoya and Pushkin and as the companies moved up to their start-lines, they were smothered in a hail of rocket shells fired from massed batteries of Stalin organs. The grenadiers fought their way through the storm of explosions and against fanatical resistance until by 08.00 hours they had reached the north-western edge of the village of Otyakova, close to Mikaelovkoya. There the SS advance struck two battalions of Mongolian infantry of the 82nd Motorized Division, supported by tanks and artillery. Then began a battle of unparalleled fury as the Mongolians launched a series of suicidal counter-attacks forcing the grenadiers on to the defensive. It took over an hour and a half of hard fighting, with the SS artillery being fired over open sights, before the enemy's mass attacks were finally crushed. Paul Carrell in his book *Operation Barbarossa*, described how an officer of the General Staff, detailing the course of the battle, had tears in his eyes as he described how the SS men, lads only 18 to 20 years old, fought in hand-to-hand engagements using entrenching tools, hand-grenades and bayonets. To the grenadiers a much worse thing was the fact that inside their soaking wet jackboots, most were barefoot The weather of the past ten days had rotted the socks from their feet and there had been no fresh issue of clothing.

By the 22nd the 11th SS Regiment had suffered such terrible losses that it could not continue as a fighting unit and had to be broken up. The survivors of its battalions were used to fill out the depleted ranks of the other two regiments. The battalion commanders were kept on the divisional strength in the hope that the regiment would, one day, be reformed and returned to the Division . . . It was not to be.

The onset of the pre-winter period of deep and glutinous mud (*Rasputitza*) then brought major operations to a halt, for the mud held fast in its grip tracked as well as wheeled vehicles. But the grenadiers could still operate and were put into a series of attacks to take the Soviet capital before the bitterest winter weather halted all operations. Meanwhile the day-long downpours thickened the mud and affected the flow of supplies coming forward to the troops holding the front line. The misery of the fighting in which the regiments were involved is hard to imagine. The grenadiers, still dressed in the uniforms they had worn when the Russian war opened at the height of summer, were fighting in those same uniforms in temperatures which had fallen to a long way below zero. They lacked winter clothing, they lacked winter quarters. They were on what were little more than starvation rations because the supply trains could not get through and they were faced by Siberian élite troops, acclimatized to the extreme winter conditions. The only advantage that the SS grenadiers had, and this they had in abundance, was their knowledge that man for man they were better soldiers than their opponents. Their advance from 6 October, through rain, mud and snow had brought them from Yuknow to Istra near Lenino, only 16 kilometres from the outskirts of Moscow.

Ammunition began to run short and this coupled with the immobility forced on the panzers soon put the German Army on to the defensive. This was seen by OKW as a temporary lull for Supreme Command was still very offensively minded. In line with this attitude Corps was ordered to open an attack on 18 November. To carry out this operation 'Das Reich' Division was placed on the right wing and 10th Panzer Division on the left. The orders were that Corps ' . . . will break through the enemy positions and passing south of Bely will take Istra . . . ' A drive up the highway from Istra would form the southern pincer of the encirclement operation which would end with the capture of the Soviet capital.

At 07.15 hours on the 18th, the SS units opened their attack against Istra fighting their way forward, on this and during successive days, against heavy and repeated counter-attacks. Despite the opposition the grenadiers had forced a crossing of the River Istra by the 25th, and had set up a bridgehead out of which they exploded with such fury that the Russian units facing them broke in disorder. Small areas of Goroditsche, a town on the road to Istra and lying on a dominating ridge, were taken quickly but the battle to capture the remainder of the town endured for four whole days and only ended when 10th Panzer was put in to strengthen the grenadier assaults. The advance was then pushed forward and by 19.00 hours on the 26th, Division could report the capture of Istra, the corner-stone of the inner ring of the Moscow defence system.

The offensive to capture the Soviet capital opened at 15.00 hours on 27 November when 'Das Reich' Division moved over its start-lines covered by a short but heavy barrage. By the following day Vyssokova had been taken and the leading units of the Division had begun to close in on the capital. The night-time temperatures had now dropped to 32 degrees below zero and the grenadiers froze in the slit trenches which they had dug in the snow. The numbers of men taken out of the line with frostbite and the number of those lost through death and wounds, so reduced unit strengths that 2nd Battalion 'Der Führer' Regiment was broken up and its men distributed among the other two battalions. Similarly, the 3rd Battalion of 'Deutschland' Regiment was broken up on 1 December. The other Corps component, 10th Panzer Division, was still vainly trying to bring the advance forward although it had now only seven tanks still in action.

As early as 29 November, the GOC of Panzer Group 4 reported to Army Group Centre that: '. . . the moment will soon come when the enemy's superiority in the air and on the ground will compel the offensive to be halted . . . ' Army Group reported to OKH that the offensive would gain nothing by being continued, nor could the Army halt outside the gates of Moscow. The troops should be brought back to a defensive line in the rear. The unthinkable was being proposed – the withdrawal of a major German formation, not as a result of enemy action, but because of weather conditions. The Corps Commander's representation to Army on 1 December, was that: '. . . It is absolutely essential to pinch Corps out of the line by the actions of the neighbouring Corps . . . ' Despite these warnings from the commanders in the field Führer Headquarters forbade any construction of a defensive zone. The Führer Order of 18 December, decreed that there would be no retreat from the line presently held. The troops must stand fast.

The grenadiers, who were bearing the burden of the battle; unwashed, unshaven, freezing, lousy and desperately tried, were still determined to bring the offensive closer to Moscow and struggled to gain the little hamlets and villages in the city's outer suburbs. But by now the continuing drain of sick and wounded had reduced company strengths to frighteningly low levels. Weak in numbers the grenadiers fought on, although hardly recognizable as German soldiers for many were now dressed in winter clothing taken from dead Russians. They were encouraged in their fight by the sound and sight of the Russian anti-aircraft barrage fired against German bombers attacking the city. How close they were to their final objective . . . No. 1 Company of the motor-cycle battalion reached the terminus of the Moscow tramway system on 4 December, but then the onset of bitter weather brought a three-day pause in the fighting. The attacks by Fourth Army and Fourth Panzer Army to capture the capital had to be abandoned and as the German offensive died so did the Russian counter-offensive open. Stavka's plan, drawn up on 30 November, was for an attack by 1st Assault Army against the northern wing of Army Group Centre followed by an attack by the Briansk and South-West Fronts against the southern wing with West Front striking at Army Group's central forces. The intention was to destroy the Army Group and thus bring about the total collapse of the German Army on the Eastern Front.

For this counter-offensive the Russians put into battle no fewer than one and a half million men grouped into seventeen huge armies, and the opening move, by Kalinin Front, was made during the morning of 5 December. On the following day West and South-West Fronts opened their assaults and under their massive blows the Germans were forced back. The main Russian attacks against 'Das Reich' came in at 07.00 hours on 6 December along the sector held by 'Deutschland' Regiment. Its first assault died in the fire of the regiment's massed machine-guns. Hundreds of fallen Russian soldiers dotted the fields and their numbers were added to as attack followed attack · throughout that first day. The succeeding days consisted of periods filled with noise and the fury of battle when the enemy came on in force, regardless of loss, interspersed by periods when no sound of war broke the deep, winter silence. On 9 December, the order came for the Army to retreat, an order which was badly received by the men of the SS Division who still thought only in terms of attacking and of defeating the Russians. By midnight on 10/11 December, the bulk of the Division had crossed to the west bank of the River Istra. The slow and cautious Russian pursuit gave time for a proper defence line to be built, but these positions were not held for long. Russian penetrations of the front held by units on either flank of Corps, forced a further withdrawal to the River Rusa and into positions which were then held throughout Christmas and the New Year. Heid Ruehl, serving with 'Deutschland' Regiment wrote of the fighting in the weeks before Christmas 1941.

'Our 3rd Battalion captured the station and a factory in the northern area of Stalino. On the previous day our 2nd and 3rd Battalions, supported by the SPs, "Blücher", "Lützow" and "Derfflinger", had captured Kryokovo after bitter fighting. Losses to the battalions had been heavy and included the CO of 3rd Battalion, Hauptsturmführer Kroger, who was killed by a bullet in the head fired at close range . . . On 2 December the advance guard of "Deutschland" Regiment was directly facing Lenino and moved into the attack on both sides of the Rochdestven–Lenino road. In the woods to the west of the town both battalions struck strong Russian trench systems and were soon involved in heavy fighting, during which enemy mortar bombs exploded in the trees inflicting heavy casualties, including the regimental commander,

1942

Axis territory and general strategic movements ■

'Das Reich':
1 Gshatsk, January
2 Rzhev, February
3 'Jackboot Wood' battles, March–May
4 Germany, June
5 Le Mans, July–November
6 Toulon, November to January 1945

Schulz, and the commanding officers of both battalions. Schulz and the CO of 2nd Battalion refused to leave the field and continued to lead their men until nightfall. Fighting for Lenino went on until late in the night. To begin with there was only a foothold but then, at 23.00 hours, 2nd Battalion was ordered to attack the town from the west and capture it regardless of cost. The SPs went in with No. 6 Company but found the enemy gone . . . By gaining Lenino we had reached an outer suburb of Moscow – only 17 kilometres from the city centre and one of the termini on the Moscow bus line.'

On 16 January 1942 orders came for yet another withdrawal, this time to positions west of Gshatsk. It was, however, not all defensive fighting and attacks at local and divisional levels flung back the Russian assaults which came in at regular intervals and with increasing strength. One operation in which 'Das Reich' took a major part was the counter-attack against Russian forces that had broken through at Rzhev. This operation led to the encirclement of two Russian armies. After weeks of demoralizing withdrawals the Division was again operating offensively and one wireless message sent by 'Deutschland' Regiment to Division ended with the words, ' . . . there is a fabulous feeling among the troops . . . ' That feeling remained even though losses were high. The motor-cycle battalion lost four officers and 70 other ranks killed on 21 January, the first day of battle. In temperatures of minus 51 degrees, cold so intense that the oil lubricating the machine-guns froze and put them temporarily out of action, the 2nd Battalion of 'Deutschland' Regiment went into the attack but was stopped just short of the objective, the village of Karabanovo. Many of the grenadiers lying out on the snow froze to death. The attack was called off. Fighting continued until at last the Russian penetration to the west of Rhezev had been sealed off and the 29th and 39th Russian Armies which had made the breakthrough had been cut off. On 29 January Stavka put in furious assaults to smash through to the trapped units, assaults which were carried out by successive lines of infantry marching forward shoulder to shoulder and accompanied by massed tank formations. Otto Kumm, who at that time commanded 'Der Führer' Regiment wrote of the infantry attacks, ' . . . The enemy dead formed walls of corpses in front of the companies' positions . . . ' He estimated that there were 15,000 dead along the front of his regiment and seventy tanks which had been knocked out.

Losses to 'Das Reich' Division continued to drain its strength and with all its vehicles knocked out the SP battery was broken up and some of the men were posted to 'Der Führer' Regiment while the others were sent on panzer training courses in Vienna. The fighting rose in intensity during the first week of February when Russian armour tore a gap in the divisional lines and sought to exploit that breach with masses of infantry. The Russians advanced in masses and were shot down in masses. The climax of the battle came on 17 February, when the Russians made fresh penetrations of the divisional front and were held only with the employment of the soldiers of the Train. Stavka regrouped its tiring forces and the pause in the fighting also gave 'Das Reich' the opportunity to concentrate its units which had been separated in the fighting. Obersturmbannführer Kumm marched the remnant of his regiment to divisional headquarters and went in to make his report. Model, commander of Ninth Army, was in the headquarters hut and told Kumm that he was bringing forward replacements so as to bring the regiment up to strength. He asked, 'What is your regimental strength at this moment?' Kumm pointed to the window and replied, 'General, my entire regiment is paraded outside.' Model looked through the window. There in the snow stood thirty-five men. They were the remnant of a regiment which had gone into battle more than two thousand strong. It may well have been the memory of that sight which encouraged Model to criticize Hitler to his face. When, in 1943, the Führer asked where was the spirit of the soldier of 1941, Model retorted bitterly that the men of 1941 were dead and buried in Russia.

In the last week of February 1942 the Division concentrated to the west of Rzhev and went into reserve. Losses had now reduced it so much that it had been formed as 'Das Reich Battle Group'. There were other renamings during this period, when 'Der Führer' Regiment was reorganized as a panzer grenadier regiment. The regiment was reformed around the survivors of the winter battles and convalescents came in to flesh out the depleted ranks. New drafts of men, some 3,000 in all, joined the battalions, so that within a few weeks the panzer grenadier regiment was ready for active service.

Then in March the Battle Group moved to fresh positions, west of Rzhev, in the bend of the River Volga. From 17 March to 8 April the Russians reopened their attacks, clearly building up to a new offensive aimed at crossing the Volga. Fighting went on for villages, woods and commanding heights. One particularly bloody battle was for 'Jackboot Wood', which the Russians had chosen as a concentration area for their assault forces. Georg Schwinke, whose first impressions of life in the Waffen SS were described earlier, recalled the action in the wood during which he was wounded. This was an attack mounted on 23 March, by the motor-cycle detachment of 'Deutschland' Regiment whose own advance collided with a Russian attack which in Schwinke's words '. . . coloured brown what had been until then white, snow-covered ground. The whole terrain was brown with the overcoats of the advancing Russian soldiers. This mass of men rolled towards us, terrifying because they came forward silently and without their usual shouting . . . We lay between smouldering piles of rubble and our officer gave orders that wo were to hold our fire until the enemy was within 20 metres. We did and when we finally opened up the Russians fell in rows, piling up into a great heap of dead. Most of that first wave had come forward without weapons – cannon-fodder – to use up our ammunition. The second wave was like the first except that a few more of them had rifles. We shot them all down. Then came the third, fourth and fifth waves. By now we were nearly out of ammunition and our wireless operator sent out calls for infantry reinforcements, for artillery support, for panzers or for Stukas. Nothing came. Then we were involved in hand-to-hand fighting and we were just about able to hold them. Finally, the Russians sent in tanks and like primeval beasts they came lumbering towards us. They came on, their tracks creaking and their cannon and machine-guns firing. We had nothing left, not even one anti-tank gun. One mortar after another fell silent as did the last 2cm cannon. The machine-guns also stopped firing. They, too, had run out of ammunition. Our wireless operator continued his calls for help but we received nothing, only orders to hold to the last so as to stop the Russians from cutting the main road.

'Then, as if the squadron had been waiting for our call, Stukas began to dive. Quickly we scratched out swastikas in the snow . . . Those pilots really knew their job. Tank after tank was blown apart. Just before I pressed my face into the muddied snow I saw a bomb glide under the belly of one tank and blow it up . . . Then again we heard the sound of tank tracks and engines, but these came from behind us. They were our panzers, our infantry and our SPs.

'I was feeling terrible. My head buzzed like a bee-hive from where I had been buried when a heavy shell scored a direct hit on our dug-out. I had been slightly wounded in the head but had pulled the shrapnel fragment out of my skull. In addition, a bullet had wounded me slightly in the right leg during the day's attack. But the wound was not all that bad. I went into the counter-attack which drove the Ivans back, but because I could not run fast enough to keep up with the others I was detailed to stand guard over a sledge, but the relief which I had been promised within an hour or two did not happen until the following day. When I reached Company HQ, my officer asked why I was limping. He tried to take off my jackboot but the leg was too swollen. He cut the boot off and pus and blood poured out from a leg which was now coloured dark-blue and black . . . frostbite. Frost had got into the wound on my leg, entering a wound so slight that normally a sticking plaster would have covered it. Now I had frostbite and because there were no ambulances I had to make my own way back on foot out of that damned "Jackboot Wood".

The Red Army offensive opened at 02.00 hours on 25 March and for the next week furious but vain assaults were made against the 10 kilometre-wide stretch of front held by 'Das Reich' Division. Fighting died away during the first week of April and in the words of Corps' post-battle report: 'The first signs of spring brought to the German soldiers the knowledge that any future heavy Russian attacks would have as little success as those which had been beaten back with such heavy loss during the winter of 1941/2. The German line held . . . ' From April to 10 June there was defensive fighting in the central sector of the Eastern Front, in the area of Olenino–Nelidovo. On 30 March 'Deutschland' carried out its last operation in 'Jackboot Wood'. On 1 June the Division was relieved from the line and by the 10th of that month the units were back in Germany.

During May the divisional designation changed to SS Division 'Das Reich' and this was then changed again by Führer Order relayed by the SS Supreme Office: ' . . . At the Führer's order, with effect from 9 November 1942, the SS Division (motorized) "Das Reich" will bear the following title, SS Panzer Grenadier Division "Das Reich" . . . ' The reorganization into a panzer grenadier division brought on to divisional strength a panzer battalion of three companies equipped with Panzer III and IV, while 3rd Battalion 'Der Führer' became a fully motorized SPW battalion, as did the recce battalion. In place of motor cycles and side-cars the newly created formation was given Schwimmwagen cars and had its title confirmed as Regiment 'Langemarck'. The former motor-cycle battalion became 1st Battalion of that regiment, and a 2nd Battalion was created out of the former 4th SS Regiment.

At the beginning of July 'Der Führer' Regiment was sent to Le Mans, where it took up the duties of occupation troops under command of Seventh Army. The other regiments of the Division joined 'Der Führer' in France and the whole stayed in occupation until 21 November. As a result of the Allied invasion of French North Africa the SS Division moved into unoccupied France on 11 November and on the 27th took over the naval base at Toulon. The final reorganizations of that year were the raising of an SP battalion containing an HQ group and three batteries each of seven guns, and the breaking up of 'Langemarck' Regiment whose men were posted to the panzer regiment or to the recce battalion.

The Division stayed as part of the army of occupation until 15 January 1943 when a fresh crisis in Russia sent it eastwards again.

1943

Axis territory and general strategic movements ■

'Das Reich':
1 Kharkov, January–April
2 Kursk, July
3 River Mius, July–August
4 Fighting retreat, September to April 1944
(See sketch maps overleaf)

1943

**Eastern Front
January 1943 to April 1944**

Kursk

Oboyan
Prokharovka
Yakovlevka
Tomarovka
Belgorod
Kharkov
Merefa
Poltava
Smiyev
Kremechug
Krasnograd
Peretschepino
Pavlograd
Dniepropetrovsk

Kiev

River Oskol

River Don

Volkomovka
Kupiansk

Voroshilovgrad

River Donets

River Mius

River Dnieper

0   miles   200

N

SS Division 'Das Reich' in the Second Campaign on the Eastern Front, 1943–1944

In 1943 Germany lost the military initiative to the Eastern and Western Allies as a consequence of operations which the Allies had initiated in the closing months of 1942. The first reverse had been the defeat of the Axis forces at El Alamein in Africa and the second had been the encircling of Sixth German Army at Stalingrad. By February 1943 the remnant of Sixth Army had surrendered and that catastrophe had been followed only three months later by the capitulation of all the German and Italian troops in Africa. In order that Germany regain the military initiative on the Eastern Front a massive operation was undertaken during July by Army Groups South and Centre. Operation 'Citadel' not only failed to pinch out the Soviet salient at Kursk, but was followed up by a successful Russian counter-offensive. Then, while 'Citadel' was still being fought, invasions, first of Sicily and then of Italy by the Western Allies, caused that offensive to be broken off. The year 1943 saw a catalogue of disasters for the armies of the Third Reich.

The Russian winter offensive at Stalingrad, which opened during November 1942, struck first at the Roumanian armies on the flanks of Paulus's Sixth Army and tumbled them into ruin. The Russians then cut off Sixth Army and, leaving only a small force to reduce Paulus's host, sent other Russian Fronts striking westwards to gain the line of the Dnieper. Were the South and South-West Fronts to reach that river quickly they would have succeeded in cutting off Army Group 'A', fighting in the Caucasus, and could then concentrate upon the destruction of Army Group 'B'. While South and South-West Fronts were advancing towards the Dnieper, Briansk and Voronezh Fronts were attacking and forcing back westwards German Army Group Centre. If all Stavka's ambitious plans could be realized the Russians would have retaken much of the territory which had been lost in the German summer offensive of 1942, and would have crushed its opponents in southern Russia.

The blows of the Russian winter offensive broke the German battle line around Stalingrad by defeating first the Roumanian armies and then Hungarian Second and Italian Eighth Armies, before going on to destroy German Sixth Army. With four allied and one German army ripped from the battle line, the Russians now used their enormous superiority in manpower to breach the German line in a great many other places. These gaps had to be closed by whatever units were immediately available. There were places, as for example, the gap north of Kursk which was more than 500 kilometres wide, where there were no troops to close the rupture and only a fast withdrawal enabled the German High Command to establish a new battle line far to the west.

When Hausser's SS Corps returned to Russia its units were frequently detached to carry out 'fire brigade' actions to close gaps. It would be confusing to describe operations carried out by divisional sub-units and therefore only the actions in which the mass of the Division took part during the spring of 1943, the so-called Third and Fourth Battles for Kharkov, are described in detail.

The Battle of Kharkov

On 30 December 1942, a Führer Order directed 'Totenkopf', 'Leibstandarte' and 'Das Reich' Divisions, together forming the SS Panzer Corps, to return to Russia with all possible speed. The massive armoured force which they formed was to confront and to halt the Red Army's winter offensive. Once that first task had been accomplished Panzer Corps was to launch a counter offensive which would sweep back the Russian Fronts which were attacking Army Group South. Corps' move to the Eastern Front was begun on 9 January, and was accounted to be so urgent that the trains which carried them were given absolute priority over all other railway traffic. 'Das Reich' was the first of the three divisions to arrive and it was a visible sign of the crisis facing the Army Group, that when the Division's advance guard, 1st Battalion 'Der Führer', reached its concentration area it was given immediate orders to march in the direction of Voroshilovgrad, where a Soviet break-through threatened. The 'Der Führer' battle group contained not only 1st Battalion but also the whole of No. 14 Company, a platoon from 16 Company, two batteries of field artillery and one of Flak. The battle group came under the authority of 6th Panzer Division, and was given a length of front to hold around Alexandrovka. On 22 January, Battle Group started out on a 205-kilometre journey to the combat zone. It had been agreed that these commandeered SS detachments were to be returned to their parent Division as soon as this reached the Eastern Front, but such an agreement could not be met and it was not until 7 March, when the battle group was broken up, that the formations were finally returned.

During the last week of January, the other two divisions of SS Panzer Corps arrived in the concentration area west of Kharkov, to be told that Corps battle area was a bridgehead on the River Oskol between Kupiansk and Volokomovka. Towards that perimeter and through it were flowing the retreating fragments of Italian Eighth Army as well as the remnant of a number of German divisions, including the 320th, which will be mentioned several times in this chapter. The SS commanders were advised that the Russian South-west, South and Voronezh Fronts had torn huge gaps in the battle line held by Army Group South and that the Russians had recaptured a great deal of Soviet territory, including the important communications centre of Kursk. German Intelligence sources had learned that the objective of two

Red Army Fronts was the Dnieper and that these enemy forces were closely pursuing the shattered Italian and Roumanian armies. Heinz Macher, a company commander in the 'Das Reich's pioneer battalion met the Italians late in January 1943.

'After a drive of over 517 kilometres in bitter cold at last we were to move into warm billets . . . There we encountered problems as in some houses there were Italians, men of the Army which had been beaten at Stalingrad and who in the retreat from the Volga had been separated from their units. They had now taken up residence in what were our billets. We had to haul one Italian captain out of the bed of a Russian woman . . . ' [As an old soldier Macher knew that in such a situation of flux there would be supply problems ahead and resolved the immediate difficulty by over-indenting.] 'At that place we were supposed to receive three days' Special Panzer supplement to our rations. We soon resolved the question of how we would manage for supplies if the Company were to be cut off from the supply point. In fact, our Company's little transport Section had to send for another truck because the first lorry could not hold all the rations which were being issued on our indent. The explanation? Quite by accident, of course, we had indented for three times three days. A simple enough error.'

At this time the Russian offensive began to lose impetus as units outran their supplies. Stalin and the Stavka would not accept that a time is reached in every offensive when a halt must be called. To issue an order to halt was unthinkable to the Russian dictator. He was determined to smash Army Groups 'A' and 'B'. He had been told that the enemy line had been breached and that the German forces were in retreat. His orders were that the Red Army would continue to advance until it had accomplished the strategic tasks he had determined. Stalin's indifference to the exhaustion of his soldiers and his refusal to face facts prepared the ground for a German counter-offensive which was, within weeks, to reoccupy much of the territory that the Red Army had reconquered since the opening of the winter offensive.

But that German counter-stroke lay in the future for the Red Army's overwhelming strength still provided a momentum which carried their forces forward. The severest crisis facing the Germans was that Army Group had no strategic reserve to cover immediate emergencies, every one of its formations having been committed to battle. It could only create a Reserve by comandeering the newly arrived SS Divisions, rationalizing this violation of Hitler's plan on the grounds that the need to master the crisis demanded that the formations be committed to action immediately. The Führer's plan for the SS Panzer Corps to be used in some grandiose future massed counter-attack, had to be forfeited. Army Group's present need required that the SS units be employed on 'fire brigade' operations; plugging breaches in the line.

During the last days of January 'Der Führer' Regiment, minus 1st Battalion, moved to the Veliki Burluk sector where 2nd Battalion held defensive positions along the River Oskol. 'Deutschland' Regiment, meanwhile, was defending the woods to the south-west of Kamenka as well as the heights west of Borki, Kosinka and Olovatka. Both regiments were fighting desperately and the SITREP issued by 'Das Reich' on 1 February estimated that the Russian forces attacking 'Deutschland' 2nd and 3rd Battalions were in divisional strength. Struggling against such overwhelming odds, it is not surprising that on that first February day the units holding the Oskol bridgehead were evacuated to prevent their being cut off. For the men of 'Das Reich' Division the days which followed were a numbing procession of attack and counter-attack as the Russians, having themselves now smashed the Oskol river line, raced to reach and cross the River Donets. Their attacks drove a salient between the mass of 'Das Reich' Division and its recce battalion. To wipe out that dangerous penetration required the employment of the newly raised Panzer Regiment and 'Der Führer' battalion of SPs. But although on many days the divisions of Panzer Corps were able to achieve similar small and local successes, there was insufficient strength to hold the Russian onslaught. Stavka had now directed its main thrust at Kharkov, one of the principal communications centre in southern Russia. The importance of Kharkov was a terrible guarantee that a vast and destructive battle would be fought by the Germans to hold it and by the Russians to recapture it.

The dying Red Army winter offensive revived when it was announced that the new objective was Kharkov, for the exhausted soldiers hoped that its capture would bring the three-month-long operation to a close. With new heart the Russian formations fought on and as early as 7 February their assaults had smashed through the units on both flanks of Panzer Corps creating a pair of pincers around the city. The southern pincer, strategically the more dangerous, was thrusting through the 40-kilometre gap between the right flank of 'Leibstandarte' and the left flank of 320th Division. On Corps' northern flank the line to the north-east of Byelgorod, which was held by under-strength Army divisions, had been penetrated but not shattered. It was clear that the encirclement of Kharkov was only a matter of time and this knowledge demanded that a decision be made; whether to evacuate the city or to order the SS Panzer Corps to defend it – with the certainty that they would be destroyed in the battle.

On 9 February, under growing Russian pressure 'Das Reich' withdrew from the perimeter it held along the River Donets in an operation carried out in terrible conditions. The grenadiers conducted their painful retreat – it could not be dignified with the title of a march – in a howling blizzard, wading in thigh-deep snow and often struggling through drifts whose depth held even the tracked vehicles fast. The Russians took advantage of the weather, charging out of the blinding snowstorms upon the slow-moving SS columns. Nor, when the retreat ended on the west bank of the Donets, did the remnant of the SS regiments find the safety for which they had hoped. The Russians were already on the west bank and Corps was forced to order another withdrawal to shorten the battle line. When this was completed 'Das Reich' was positioned immediately east of Kharkov, preparing itself to meet what many feared would be its last battle.

Hausser, the Corps commander, saw as his first priority, the establishing of a closed and firm Front east of the city. In order to achieve this he must close the gap which yawned between the 'Leibstandarte' and 320th Division through which the Russians were driving to create the southern pincer. If that gap could be closed the pincer would have been amputated, but the operation needed to be swift, bold and decisive because strong Russian forces were storming against Corps' centre and left flank. The amputation would require a strong force and Hausser could only obtain that by withdrawing formations from Corps battle line. He would withdraw the line again to shorten Corps' front, detach the units he had selected and send them into battle, taking a calculated risk on gaining a quick victory. Hausser created a battle group around 'Der Führer' Regiment and the 'Langemarck' motor-cycle battalion from 'Das Reich' Division and Witt's regiment and 'Panzer Meyer's motor-cycle battalion from 'Leibstandarte'. On 10 February, the combined force advanced towards the start-line for the operation, the town of Merefa where Corps had set up TAC HQ. 'Das Reich' then suffered the loss of its divisional commander when Gruppenführer Keppler suffered a brain haemorrhage and was replaced by Sturmbannführer Stadler.

In temperatures which sank by night to below 40 degrees of frost, and shrouded by a violent snowstorm, the Battle Group opened the operation on 11 February. It was formed into three columns: 'Panzer Meyer's recce battalion on the right, 'Der Führer and 'Langemarck' in the centre and Witt on the left. Despite the weather the advance southwards made good progress against an enemy shocked to see in his rear areas and miles behind his front line, German armoured fighting vehicles looming suddenly out of the blinding blizzards. For more than fifty kilometres the SS columns thrust forward while Stukas supported their advance by wiping out the opposition. The Battle Group's thrust cut the Russian southern pincer and crushed 7th Guard Cavalry Corps. Wasting little time in consolidating this success, the drive south continued and by 16 February the Battle Group, depleted in numbers, but with its morale still high, gained touch with the 320th. The German front south of Merefa was sealed, the Russians' southern pincer had been amputated and the threat on that flank temporarily removed. Having carried out its task, the Battle Group was broken up, its components being returned to their parent units.

But while the Battle Group was making its successful drive, the other units of SS Corps had been struggling against Russian infantry and armour attacks east of Kharkov. The unrelenting enemy pressure captured Smiyev, a small but important town in the suburbs of Kharkov, but at two other key places, Rogan and Ternovoya, the line held and each penetration into the SS positions was thrown back by immediate counter-attack. Those who fought at that time recall how the Russian infantry, vast waves of men, were flung into the fight often without artillery support because their overstretched supply system could not provide sufficient shells for the guns to fire a barrage. Without regard for the losses which the units were suffering, Stavka committed them again and again and the brave assaults of those stoical Russian soldiers died in the fire of massed machine-guns. ('We were by this time equipped with the new machine-gun, the MG 42, which had a phenomenally high rate of fire, twice as fast as the old MG 34. The Russians called the MG 42, Hitler's saw, from the noise it made.') But it was not the grenadiers alone who held back the furious assaults of the enemy, for the divisional artillery and the panzer regiment fought just as bravely.

In warfare there comes a time when unlimited numbers of fresh troops, launching a succession of attacks, must prevail over defenders weakened in strength by losses and exhausted by long exposure to fighting at such an intense pitch. This was the situation which faced the defenders towards the middle of February as the fighting in and around Kharkov approached its climax. Under pressure the SS line was slowly forced to give ground and was pulled back closer to the city. Death, wounds and sickness had so reduced company strengths that in many places the line was stretched to the point where the onslaughts of the enemy were held not by platoons of men but by individual soldiers holding out in slit trenches, widely separated from one another. Now, more than ever, it was morale, training and loyalty that kept the grenadiers in their positions, fighting against the waves of Russian troops which flooded towards them in attack after attack.

Hitler's order, relayed by Lanz, the commander of the Army Detachment, to which the SS Corps was subordinated, was that Kharkov was to be held to the last, but in a situation where the city was being defended by an exhausted and under-strength garrison, military logic demanded that such an order be disobeyed. Then the Russians captured Byelgorod and the loss of that town placed an entire Russian army on Hausser's north-western flank. Meanwhile, on the north-eastern sector, Russian units thrusting through gaps in the German line, wheeled inwards towards the city. With its southern pincer destroyed, Stavka had switched the main effort to a massive blow coming down from the north which would link up with one of almost equal power coming from the east. This combined effort must surely cause the city to fall. The situation facing SS Panzer Corps was now critical and a telephone log records the conversation between the SS Corps Commander and the senior Staff Officer of Army Group. '... Friday. 12 February. Time 16.40. Telephone conversation between the Chief [Hausser] and the 1A of Army Group. Hausser: "The enemy is attacking along the entire length of the east, north-east and northern fronts. Penetrations have been made on the Luftwaffe battalion's sector ... The front will have to be pulled back ... Even if every man is committed Kharkov can be held for only two to three days. Demolitions must begin in good time." Hitler's direct order to hold the city to the last was relayed to Hausser, but he had already decided to ignore it. His decision was not an easy one. He was an SS General and the Führer had ordered Kharkov to be held. Nevertheless, he must disobey if he was to save his men. Made aware of their superior officer's intention, members of his staff sought to make him change his mind. 'The telephone rang ... The commanding General was called to the set by the regimental adjutant. At the other end was the Chief of Staff, SS Standartenführer Ostendorff. Hausser: "Yes, Ostendorff? I am with "Deutschland" Regiment and have just given the order to fight a way through [and out of the city]." Ostendorff: "Obergruppenführer! The Führer has once again expressly ordered . . . Hausser: "My decision is final." '

There is no doubt that Hausser's action saved the lives of thousands of German soldiers. More than that, by preserving the SS Panzer Corps as a fighting unit he provided Army Group with the powerful strength it needed to recapture Kharkov. In an indirect sense, Hausser's act of disobedience, accomplished Hitler's original order that the SS Panzer Corps was to provide a strong counter-attack force.

The Corps Commander's decision to evacuate Kharkov was soon common knowledge. The rank and file were aware that such an order meant that the food stores would be destroyed to prevent them falling into Russian hands and knew what measures they would take. Heinz Macher recalled.

'The war diary records that on the 14th [the day before the evacuation of Kharkov] the Company was not in action. The men could sleep but had to be at instant readiness. I was shaving when I noticed an unusual amount of activity. In front of the window men were laughing and cheering a recently arrived heavy lorry. Then another came along. That morning for breakfast Siegfried Meyer, carrying a folded napkin over his arm, had served me with a glass of champagne on a silver tray. I thought he was acting the fool but I was wrong. The Spiess came along and told me that my comrades and the Russian civilians were plundering the main ration store in Kharkov. Another of our trucks returned to the city and every vehicle we had that could carry a load was put to the task. And what my men brought back was astonishing. Stuff we had only dreamed about. Dried bananas, apricots, peaches, salmon, caviar, chocolate, skin cream, shaving soap, cigarettes, cigars, french letters, Benedictine, Cointreau, Martell, Hennessy, French champagne, etc. In addition to these goodies the Spiess, had ordered the men to bring back useful things such as salt, sugar, flour, fat, bacon and ham. Some trucks brought back half sides of pork.

'In the store-houses men looking for sugar would slit a sack and find it contained salt. In the next sack there would be flour. You can imagine the mess inside the stores. Soon my men had found the things they were looking for and in order that nothing went "missing" the Spiess organized an escort group. We lived for a long time from the things we had gathered.'

During the 15th, one of the Division's panzer battalions carried out a counter-attack against enemy troops who had penetrated into the north-western areas of the town and smashed them back with heavy loss, but at Rogan and on other sectors inroads were made. In one place forty Russian tanks forced a breakthrough. The Russians had now advanced so close to the city that the divisional supply route from Poltava was under fire and in Kharkov itself the German-held area was reduced to a narrow corridor subject to continual and heavy shellfire. The Russians had overcome the problem of a shell shortage by such primitive methods as giving each infantryman a shell to carry. Russian artillery batteries lining the entire length of that narrow corridor could now pour down a fierce fire upon the SS defenders. At 13.30 hours and then again at 17.50 hours Hausser received orders to hold the city to the last man. By late afternoon Russian troops had broken into the south-eastern suburbs and Russian civilians, joining in the battle, had begun to open fire on German columns passing through the streets of the narrow corridor. The situation was without hope of improvement and Hausser issued orders for his divisions to begin the evacuation, to head southwards and to regroup behind the River Udy. The Corps Commander's decision accorded completely with Manstein's strategy to allow the Russian advance to create a salient whose walls would be lined with German units. Then, when the enemy was at his weakest, a counter-offensive would open and crush the walls of the salient trapping the Russian units inside it.

The rearguard of 'Das Reich' Division withdrew through the narrow corridor of fire and out of Kharkov. The city had been lost, but only temporarily. Manstein concentrated the SS Panzer Corps to strengthen the battle line in the south and began to prepare its divisions for his planned counter-offensive. But first, each had to undergo a long overdue reorganization resulting in many cases in amalgamation. In the case of the divisional panzer regiment, which had suffered a 50 per cent loss in its armoured fighting vehicle establishment, its battalions were formed into a single battalion.

In the latter half of February, the situation facing Army Group South was that Russian forces were still advancing, albeit more slowly. Voronezh Front, below Kharkov, was moving westwards, South-West was thrusting in a south-westerly direction towards Dniepropetrovsk and South was moving in the same direction with the aim of establishing bridgeheads across the Dnieper. The two individual German Army Groups 'A' and 'B', were regrouped to form, once again, Army Group South (Fourth Panzer Army and two Army detachments, 'Lanz' and 'Hollidt'). Army Group held a line between Krasnograd, to the south of Kharkov, and Rostov.

As a necessary preliminary to the counter-offensive which would recapture Kharkov, Manstein needed first to destroy the Russian armies which were striking towards Dniepropetrovsk. Once that immediate thrust had been eliminated and Army Group South's battle line had been solidified and strengthened against the last blows of the Russian offensive, the counter-stroke could begin.

On 17 February, Hausser issued an Order of the Day, thanking his men for the efforts they had made:

'Since the 30th January Panzer Corps, in changing conditions of attack and defence, has stopped the storming advance of three Russian armies and caused them heavy casualties. A whole Cavalry Corps was destroyed almost to the last man.

'For the first time Panzer Grenadier Divisions "Leibstandarte" and "Das Reich", joined by "Totenkopf" have been able to fight shoulder to shoulder. All arms of Service have given of their best during these weeks and despite the confusion caused by mixing units, a confusion which complicated the tasks of the commanders, a decisive defensive victory has been won.'

The vast operation, which was Manstein's counter-stroke, was fought out between the Rivers Dnieper and Donets and lasted from 19 February to 4 March. It opened in foul weather: fog, snow and a damp cold which seeped into the bones. The strength of the grenadier companies had by this time sunk to less than 60 men, but these survivors were battle-hardened and so confident of victory and determined to share in it, that the wounded refused to leave the field. The days of retreat and withdrawal were over. Now was the time for attack. ('Today we attack and our enemy is the 6th Russian Infantry Division whose orders were to capture Krasnograd and the road which runs through it. The Stukas will support us as we strike deep into the flank of the Russian army . . . ')

The opening move in von Manstein's strategic operation was the attack by 'Das Reich', during the morning of 19 February. The intention was to destroy the enemy to the west and south-west of Krasnograd and the first objective was the capture of Peretschepino. Heinz Macher wrote of 'Deutschland' Regiment's part in that operation.

'Visibility was down to 1,000 metres, the ground fell in a gentle slope . . . The men have packed the ammunition boxes, the machine-guns and heavy weapons, such as mortars, on to sledges shaped like kayaks. We had these specially built in France . . . The last puff on a cigarette, the motor cycles start up. The gunners of the Flak Company check the ammo belts once again. The mine-laying teams are probing with bayonets because the batteries for their detectors have long since gone flat . . . The men kneel on the ground sifting through the snow and then digging out the frozen mines with bayonets. Finally a gap is cleared through the minefield. That is what our regimental commander has been waiting for. He lifts his arm. "Forward". The attack begins . . . '

At 05.00 hours on the following day, Hauptsturmführer Kaiser's 3rd Battalion of 'Der Führer' leapfrogged over 'Deutschland' and, with panzer and SP support, struck into the flank of the enemy and cut the main road. The first objective of the divisional assault had been taken and the swift Russian response was to mount a series of heavy attacks to open the highway. Each was driven back. The opening move had been completed and during the night a telegram from Hitler was received and read to all ranks waiting to go into another attack. 'I have ordered this operation by the SS Division "Das Reich" and am confident that the Division will do all in its power to bring it to a quick and successful conclusion.' Buoyed up by this personal message the units went back into action and by the 20th, at the end of two days' fighting, the Division, which had already advanced 90 kilometres against a hard fighting and relentless enemy, was then ordered to take Pavlograd, an objective 60 kilometres distant.

An SS grenadier of 'Deutschland' Regiment wrote of the events of the 22nd.

' . . . At last we climbed into our trucks. We had been regrouped to carry out the attack on Pavlograd. The roads are said to be free of the enemy. Only a few Ivans on either side of the road had to be beaten down – so our Section Leader says. We took mines on board and packed them in the trucks. If they blow up . . . Then we load hollow-charge grenades for close-quarter action against tanks . . . The Führer's order is read out at 02.45 hours . . . A decisive victory . . . We must be a marvellous mob. At about 03.00 hours we start. The engines roar into life. Well, at least we have good weather for the operation. A clear night. It'll be a nice day . . . Firing comes from the left and then from the right . . .

'At 09.10 hours we learn that a whole Russian regiment is thrusting towards the Dnieper. They are accompanied by five tanks. We debus and take up firing positions. The Ivans come closer all the time and start to bunch up . . . Suddenly there are three Stukas overhead. Our Company Commander fires signal flares and they dive to attack the Russian tanks. We knock out the one which they missed.

'During our advance we blow up two guns and are attacked by Russian cavalry waving sabres. At nightfall we dig all-round defence positions . . . Recce patrols go out. Keep your ears and eyes open. No smoking. Only cold coffee to drink. No fires to be lit. We freeze. On 24th we are in Pavlograd where we cause problems to more attacking Soviets . . . '

The pace of the advance began to increase when leading elements of 'Das Reich' and 'Totenkopf' Divisions gained touch after having been separated for a few days. Their meeting was not without incident. The battlefield area was still being criss-crossed by Russian formations and their presence led to mistakes in identification and recognition. One of these was when 'Totenkopf's panzers opened up on the 'Das Reich' units. The wireless message: 'Do not fire at us. We are the "Das Reich" advance guard', was responded to in a laconic message from the Totenkopf panzermen, 'We only fire upon worthwhile targets.' At last light on the 24th, it was clear that Fourth Panzer Army had halted the Russian forces' advances towards the Dnieper and had smashed them in and to the south of Pavlograd. The tide of battle was now swinging in favour of the Germans.

The direction of the advance changed north-eastwards and during the move German units clashed with the fresh formations which Stavka had flung into the battle. One Russian pincer had been amputated and destroyed, but Stavka still sought to reinforce the south-westerly drive towards Dniepropetrovsk and committed 1st Guards Army, Popov's Tank Group and five other armoured corps to the attack. On the German side the objective of both 'Totenkopf' and 'Das Reich' Divisions was Losovaya, a railway junction of such importance that it was defended by 1st Guards Army. There were three days of bloody fighting before the SS captured the town. Fourth Panzer Army's SITREP dated 28 February claimed that: 'In eight days of heavy fighting . . . Army has not only prevented the enemy from striking into the back of Army Group but has flung him back on a 100-kilometre wide front and for a distance of over 120 kilometres.'

The SS Panzer Corps was next directed to capture the high ground around Yefremovka, and this advance carried the divisions over terrain familiar to them from earlier battles. The new offensive opened during the night of 1/2 March in pouring rain which soon turned the roads into channels of liquid mud. Both regiments of 'Das Reich' Division were in the line and despite the mud their storming advance overrolled the enemy. Stavka, not appreciating the losses which its units had suffered, or, perhaps, unaware of the true situation and mistakenly believing that its troops were still advancing, marched 3rd Tank Army, a mighty force of three infantry divisions, three tank brigades and a Guards cavalry corps, into a gap which had opened between 'Das Reich' and 'Leibstandarte' Divisions. Immediately, Hausser closed Corps front to the west of Bereka, trapping within the pincers of 'Das Reich' and 'Leibstandarte' the divisions of Voronezh Front. The three-day battle to destroy the trapped Russian formations was fought out in snowstorms whose intensity caused the SS severe privations. The supply trucks failed to reach the units because of the road conditions and the grenadiers fought in freezing temperatures without hot food. The trapped Russian units fought fanatically to break through the encircling ring and the 'Das Reich' units fought with equal fierceness to break up the huge mass of Russian units. An incident in the fighting was recalled by Heinz Macher:

'My Company took over the lead and the fighting for the next village involved us in bitter close-quarter action. Obersturmbannführer Harmel was with me and we had soon run out of hand-grenades. The nearest vehicle was more than 50 metres away and there was no chance of our obtaining more grenades because there was no-one who could give us covering fire. The other comrades were busy on their own account. The commander and I were alone. In a bomb crater only five metres from us two Russian soldiers were defending themselves bravely, fighting for their lives. Harmel and I had to act quickly. We each picked up pieces of ice and rock and threw them at the enemy. They naturally thought we were throwing hand-grenades and ducked. We leapt up, rushed forward and in a short charge had soon overpowered and disarmed them . . . To my comment that it was not expected of a regimental commander to lead a battle patrol, Harmel's reply was, "I'll do anything to win the Close Combat badge." '

Within days the Russian troops south of the River Donets had been smashed; one hundred thousand men were killed or captured in the fighting and Manstein's plan was working. The over-stretched Russians had been attacked, cut off and either killed, captured or sent reeling back. The danger of destruction which had faced Army Group South since the opening of the offensive was now past and the recapture of Kharkov was the next objective.

Now it was the Russians west and north-west of Kharkov who were being forced to retreat.

It was the satisfying duty of SS Panzer Corps to be the troops that recaptured Kharkov and on 5 March the northward advance opened, moving in upon the city. During the afternoon of 10 March, a reinforced battle group from 'Deutschland' Regiment's 3rd Battalion and a 'Totenkopf' panzer battalion was positioned on the western side of the city. To cover the flank as Corps advanced a 'Der Führer' battle group made up of the 2nd Battalions from 'Das Reich' and 'Der Führer' faced south-eastwards. The part which 'Das Reich' Division played in the recapture opened at 08.00 hours on 11 March and met fanatical opposition. Stalin did not intend to lose the capital of east Ukraine for a second time, but the élan of the SS grenadiers was too much for the defenders and by 16.00 hours the Salyutine railway station had been taken. The Russians counter-attacked repeatedly, but each assault was driven back bloodily with heavy loss to the attackers. The situation on the Division's northern wing was not successful and the 'Deutschland' battle group, whose first attacks had begun well had, by 12.00 hours, collapsed in the concentrated fire of a Russian Pak front. The attack made no progress until Wisliceny's 3rd Battalion gained enough ground to outflank the Russians and drive them back. The leader of the 'Deutschland' battle group, Obersturmbannführer Harmel, aware of the need to maintain the pressure, contained the battle throughout the night. Meanwhile 'Der Führer' battle group had fought its way through the enemy's strongly defended positions in the southern part of the town and had gone on to cut the Udy – Merefa road. Deliberately and surely Kharkov was being recaptured by the three divisions of SS Panzer Corps.

During the afternoon, while the battle was at its height, Fourth Panzer Army, ordered 'Das Reich' to move from its positions in the west to Corps' eastern flank, in order to strike towards Smiyev and thus into the back of the Russians facing XLVIII Panzer Corps. Given the conditions under which the division was fighting, such an order could not be carried out. A new order then directed Division to battle its way through Kharkov and wheel southwards so as to trap the enemy holding out in the heavy-industry areas in the south-eastern parts of the city. But before the Division could fight its way through the city it first had to capture and cross an anti-tank ditch, establish and hold a bridgehead. This task was given to Untersturmführer Heinz Macher, OC of 'Deutschland's 16th (Pioneer) Company.

The Russians were holding houses behind the anti-tank ditch, set on rising ground and thus enjoying a good field of fire. These houses had been skilfully prepared for defence and each was a small fortress. D-Day for the mission was 13 March, at 02.40 hours. A short, sharp barrage fired by the heavy weapons of 1st Battalion, covered the opening advance of the assault group but then the SS Pioneers were struck by fierce fire coming from the very point at which they had intended to break into the Russian-held area. Macher ordered his group to advance and his men, racing forward under machine-gun and mortar fire, had soon reached the edge of the ditch and flung themselves into it. Using bayonets they hacked out steps to climb the wall on the enemy side and grouped just below the edge of the ditch. Macher gave his men a final briefing and at 02.53 hours they rushed forward cheering loudly, firing machine-pistols and flinging hand-grenades into the enemy's positions. The first houses were passed. The group divided, one section swinging left and another right, storming into the houses, driving out the Russians and turning the houses into a defensive perimeter. A third group carried the advance forward and the fourth group formed a reserve.

In a storming advance the Pioneer Company captured more houses and slowly the first perimeter was widened and deepened. Soon it was a firm base from which the Regiment could drive towards the city centre. The Russians, desperate to regain the houses they had lost, sent in not so much counter-attacks as folorn hopes. As one wave of infantry was destroyed by the SS machine-gun and mortar fire, another was already moving into the assault. By 04.20 hours the SPs had come forward to the edge of the ditch to support the Pioneers and once the walls of the ditch had been shovelled away the vehicles crossed and entered the battle firing at the enemy at close range. Less than half an hour later grenadiers of 'Der Führer's' 3rd Battalion moved into the perimeter and brought the advance into the centre of Kharkov to be followed a little later by the first panzers.

Although the Russian defenders of Kharkov were superior in number and equipment they could not withstand the SS assaults, and the troops of 1st and 2nd Guard Tank Corps and four infantry divisions holding the city were smashed. By 15 March the remaining Soviet garrison holding out in the tractor factory, six kilometres to the east of the city, had been surrounded and destroyed. It was all over. Four weeks earlier the SS had given up the city, in defiance of Hitler's order. Now they had recaptured it. But the advance did not halt there. Manstein was determined to win back the ground that had been lost and pushed the advance eastwards with 'Das Reich' still in the van of the fighting.

Three anecdotes conclude the story of the recapture of Kharkov. Anton Fehlau of the divisional artillery regiment recalled the day following its recapture:

'Our battery had to send a heavy truck to the Town Commandant who told us to drive to a German field bakery. There the vehicle was filled to the brim with freshly baked loaves. These we were to deliver to a given point in Kharkov. En route we decided on a short break, took one of the loaves and began to eat it. All the houses round about were shuttered and seemed to be empty but then an old man came out of one, approached us and made begging gestures for something to eat. Without thinking I flung him a loaf and then all the doors opened and people rushed out, falsely believing that we were distributing bread. We started the truck and drove off in a hurry but when we reached our destination in Kharkov we learned that the whole truck load had in fact been intended for the Russian civilian population.' Ewald

Ehm writing of his former Company Commander, Heinz Macher, recalled the Russian children who gathered round the field kitchen at meal times. 'They collected quickly whenever it was meal time and stood silently waiting with their huge eyes staring at the food. Nobody had the heart to drive them away and Macher decided on a course of action. He told me to go to the kitchen and tell the cook to make a thick soup out of what was still left in the field kitchen after the men had eaten. That way we fed the children. I might add that many of our comrades were already feeding the children from their own rations.' The last Kharkov anecdote is from Macher. 'After we had captured Kharkov in March the "golden pheasants" [the contemptuous term for the Nazi officials in the occupied territories] returned in April. Some had on their brown uniforms with gold embroidered swastika armbands but all of them had their motor cars and their blond girl friends. The "golden pheasants" wanted to move back into their old quarters, but we poor SS men were already in occupation. There were some incidents during which the "gentlemen" got a good beating up . . . And the ladies? They learned very quickly who the real men were.'

With the capture of Byelogorod on 19 March, the battle between the Donets and the Dnieper had been brought to a successful conclusion. During the fighting there had been changes at senior level. Keppler had suffered a brain haemorrhage and Vahl, who had succeeded him, had been wounded. Command had passed, temporarily, to Oberführer Brasack. Warm weather melted the snow and produced mud which imprisoned Army Groups South and Centre before they had been able to pinch out the salient around Kursk. That salient offered Stavka strategic possibilities, while for the Germans it held the disadvantage that its length tied down a great number of their divisions which might otherwise have been rested or employed on other sectors. Nevertheless, von Manstein could be pleased with the outcome of his strategy for this had not only driven back the Russians but had restored to the Germans the military initiative on the Eastern Front.

There then followed for the Division a period of change and reorganization. Kumm, the commander of 'Der Führer' Regiment, went off to command a new SS formation, the divisional motor cycle battalion was broken up and reformed as the reconnaissance battalion and the title of Corps changed from SS Panzer Corps to 2nd SS Panzer Corps. On 22 April the Division moved to a new concentration area.

Ahead of 'Das Reich' Division lay a summer offensive for which the regiments were already being trained, but ordinary military life continued with problems of billeting, running repairs and rations. The following three accounts recall incidents after the fighting for Kharkov and of the period between that and Operation 'Citadel', the battle for Kursk which followed it. Heid Ruehl of the divisional artillery regiment described a unit entertainment which he helped to organize.

'Our CO adopted the suggestion that we should hold an open air summer feast. Not too far away from our billeting area were a number of ladies belonging to the Signals Branch. It was not difficult to get them to come to our feast but among the preparations that needed to be made was that of constructing a dance floor. This task was given to me as a sort of "occupational therapy." I was helped in my task by the Russian mayor, the Starost, to whom I went for advice and help. He started off with a string of excuses; no wood, no saw mill – therefore – no boards. Very logical. But he was up against a very stubborn German NCO and once he had agreed I was astonished at the way in which the Russians improvised . . . Within two days a tree-felling commando had brought in some tree trunks and the Russians began to erect a platform in the village square and to cover this with well-cut planks – all done within a couple of hours. We were all very impressed with this performance and filled with admiration at the capability of the Russians. As a reward – money was not asked for – we promised the Starost that he would use the wood for his own people after our unit had moved out. That promise may well have been the impetus for the speed with which they worked. In an open space in our bivouac area we had soon created a sort of Bavarian festival site and the dance floor was almost ready . . . '

Heinz Macher was one of the members of a four-man advance party which was sent to find billets for 'Deutschland' Regiment in Merefa, a small town to the south of Kharkov.

'We came to a house which seemed to be undamaged. Thank Heaven!: for a couple of days at least we would be able to sleep under a roof and perhaps even in proper beds. We had spent the past weeks criss-crossing an area between Kharkov–Dniepropetrovsk and Poltava – weeks in which we had seldom got out of our lorries and during which we had not had the clothes off our backs.

'Matka [the lady of the house], was shaken when we demanded to be let into her house. She may have been concerned, and perhaps rightly, for the three young girls who lived with her. The first of these was Helena, her daughter. She was about the middle twenties and was an architect in Kharkov. When fighting for the city broke out she had brought her friend Genia with her and had also given shelter to her cousin from Merefa whose own house had been smashed to pieces in the fighting.

'I have no wish to describe here any sort of love affair. The girls were all attractive but had resisted other advances as Helena, who translated for us, told us later. We cracked jokes and there were things we laughed at. Such things would have been remarkable enough in a wartime situation but during the evening of the second or third day as we sat talking somehow the subject turned to music. One of my comrades asked whether I could play the piano and I confessed that a teacher had once tried to knock some idea of rhythm and harmony into my head. Questions and answers produced the information that Helena's cousin owned a piano and that the instrument was buried under the rubble of her house. In a spontaneous decision we decided to rescue the piano and to bring it to Helena's house. Apart from slight damage caused by falling rubble and a couple of strings that had been broken the instrument was in excellent condition. Transport was no problem and once we had brought it to the girls' house they cleaned it thoroughly.

'I could once play from sheet music but it was years since I had touched a piano and I soon stopped maltreating the ears of my poor comrades with my miserable attempts. Genia then sat down at the piano and having struck a few arpeggios began to play a Strauss waltz, went on to some Russian folk songs in which the other girls joined and then finished up with Beethoven. She had never told us that she could play and so our astonishment was all the greater at her ability. From that time on there was no problem in passing away the hours and days before the rest of the group arrived. Nor, from that time on did we have problems with finding quarters for our group. Doors opened as if by magic and with Helena as our interpreter all our problems vanished. In this quarter of the town one saw only women. Any men who were still about were very very old. All the others were serving in the Forces. One day Helena told us that her father and brother had been taken away, some six or seven years earlier, together with a number of other men from the street, and that nothing more had been heard of them.

'Today I recall with pleasure that in those days I acted according to my conscience and not according to orders. I am also pleased that our battery commander was able to prevent the house being occupied by other troops when we pulled out.'

Horst Herpolosheimer, formerly of No. 11 Company 'Der Führer' Regiment, recalled one of the Russian prisoners taken during the winter battles around Kharkov.

'In February 1943, our Spiess checked through all the prisoners whom we took, looking for one who could repair boots. He needed a cobbler very badly to repair a pile of worn-out felt boots, jack boots, belts and other leather equipment, because there was absolutely no way in which we would receive any new equipment for a great many months to come.

'My platoon was in position on the railway embankment at Bereka. The morning of 16 February had been a very quiet one. There had not been much in the way of shellfire or enemy action of any sort when suddenly thirty Red Army men came in to surrender. They were absolutely terrified. One of my comrades acted as interpreter and through him I asked whether there was a cobbler among the group. A middle-aged man, trembling from head to foot, admitted that he could repair boots. I calmed him down, gave him cigarettes and later that evening took him to our "B" Echelon. Not long afterwards I was wounded twice and spent a long time in hospital. What with convalescent leave and a number of other things it was not until a year later that I met that Russian again and, this time, in southern France.

'Quite by chance I went into his little shop in "B" Echelon. He saw me, fell on his knees and kissed my hand in gratitude. I told him to get up and asked an interpreter what he was saying. The interpreter told me that my Russian said he had never been so well treated in all his life. He worked well, received the same rations as a German soldier, was paid for his work and could buy a bottle of wine every day. Whenever we met he continued to thank me. In all my war service I never saw such a contented and happy man as my Russian cobbler.'

Operation 'Citadel':
The Battle of Kursk, July 1943

The spring of 1943, did not present the senior commanders at OKH with the problem of where to launch their summer offensive. The location was obvious – the great salient around Kursk. Nor was there any dispute about the need for a summer offensive. One had to be mounted in order to retain the military initative on the Eastern Front. There was another imperative. Hitler needed to deal the Red Army a blow which would weaken its offensive potential for a very long time to come. This would leave him free to concentrate upon the probable invasion by the Western Allies of either southern Europe or France. If the German Army, through the offensive at Kursk, were able to inflict a defeat on the Red Army by pinching out the vast salient, the battle line in the East would have been straightened and shortened by some 500 kilometres and this would release formations to form a reserve to be employed against invasions in the west. There was yet another factor in favour of the offensive. The expected German victory would destroy the Russian armies holding the salient and those Russian soldiers who were not killed would be prisoners. Germany needed labour for her factories and farms. Hitler anticipated that the manpower needs of the Reich would be met from the prisoners taken during the Kursk operation.

The German plan, code-named 'Citadel' was for a pincer movement. Model's Ninth Army, made up of three panzer corps, striking down from the northern wall of the salient would meet the upward thrust of Hoth's Fourth Panzer Army erupting from the southern wall. Hoth's Fourth had on its establishment three panzer corps and the one that is of interest to us is the SS Corps, made up of the 'Leibstandarte Adolf Hitler', 'Totenkopf' and 'Das Reich' Divisions.

The Soviet High Command, which had been warned by its agents in OKW of 'Citadel', prepared the battlefield carefully. Line after line of trenches covered the length and breadth of the salient. Vast and deep minefields were laid, designed to channel the panzers into killing grounds dominated by huge blocks of anti-tank guns. Stavka was well aware of how important the operation was to the Germans and took these measures to ensure that it would fail. Further – they intended, once 'Citadel' had been smashed, to swing without pause from a defensive to an attacking posture. The first move of the counter-stroke would be made against Second Panzer Army positioned to the north of Model's Ninth Army. A successful blow against Second Panzer

Army would threaten Model's flank and rear and force him to detach units to meet the challenge. Thus his southward drive would be weakened.

Both sides were aware of the decisive nature of the Kursk operation. Hitler is reported to have said that at the very thought of it his stomach turned over. He knew that it was the German Army's last chance in the east. The Soviets, for their part, had every confidence in their battle plan, but it was misplaced optimism because it was based upon a false premise. The slim volume, *Bitva na Kurska*, a series of lectures given by the Red Army's High Command and describing the battle from the Soviet point of view, admits that Stavka had been wrong in predicting that the German main thrust would be made by Model in the north. The massive blows which were made by Hoth's Fourth Panzer Army in the south and, particularly, those of the SS Panzer Corps, compelled the Soviet High Command to withdraw some of the armies of Central Front and rush them southwards to where the forces of Voronezh Front were under terrible pressure and where a German breakthrough and victory seemed certain.

'Citadel' lasted from 5 to 18 July, when Hitler broke off the offensive rationalizing his decision on the grounds that Sicily had been invaded and the SS Panzer Corps was needed in the Italian peninsula. During the two weeks of fighting there were several climaxes, the most interesting of which was the tank battle at Prokharovka, the greatest clash of armour in the history of warfare; the so-called 'Death Ride of Fourth Panzer Army'.

The Intelligence Summary produced by Fourth Panzer Army on 28 June, calculated that the Russian forces occupying the first line of trenches on its sector would number four infantry divisions with a further two holding the second line of defences. ' . . . In addition it is likely that an armoured corps will either be in or immediately behind the second line with a further armoured corps south of Oboyan . . . After breaking through the second line of defences attacks must be anticipated against the eastern flank of our attack by several armoured corps as well as attacks on the western flank by three or four infantry divisions . . . '

Orders from Fourth Panzer Army to its subordinate formations included the directions that ' . . . On D-Day Panzer Army will break through the enemy first line positions on the heights Belgorod–Korovino . . . Enemy resistance in the second line will be broken, the enemy armoured forces smashed and then, passing eastwards of Oboyan, Army will strike towards Kursk and exploit to the east of that place . . . The operation will be protected on its eastern flank by . . . Army Detachment Kempf [an armoured formation], whose left flank formation, 6th Panzer Division, will attack via Belgorod, and Stabynino towards Prokharovka . . . SS Panzer Corps . . . will break through the enemy's defensive zone in the Beresov–Sadelnoye sector . . . One Division will attack towards Shsuravliny and open the road from Belgorod to Yakovlevo . . . Corps will then attack the second enemy position between Lutschki and Yakovlevo

... and is to hold itself ready to cross the Pssel sector and to advance in a north-easterly direction with its right wing on Prokhorovka ...'

Those orders thus placed upon SS Panzer Corps the burden of Fourth Panzer Army's assault and indicated that the key to the battle would be the high ground around Prokharovka. Progress from that point would depend upon how well the other formations of Panzer Army did, but the planners at Fourth Panzer Army HQ did anticipate that the SS attack would punch a salient in the south of Voronezh Front's battle line; a salient which would become one arm of a pincer. The advance by Kempf's Army Detachment would produce a second pincer and between this pair of jaws a mass of the enemy in the south would be encircled and destroyed. The SS Panzer Corps and Kempf's Army Detachment, united into a mighty armoured fist, would then strike upwards towards Kursk and also exploit eastwards. Panzer Army anticipated that a similar encirclement would occur on Corps' western flank. Thus a large number of Russian units of Voronezh Front would have been smashed and when Fourth Panzer Army met up with Model's pincer the way would be open for the final thrusts which would pinch out the salient and destroy the other Russian armies holding it. Operation 'Citadel' would have been brought to a successful conclusion.

Among the armoury of weapons which the German army fielded for the new campaign were Panther tanks – of doubtful value since they had a habit of bursting into flames – and a Heath Robinson contraption which slung an anti-tank cannon beneath a Ju 87 dive-bomber. This weapon proved to be so effective against Russian armoured units that whole squadrons of the Luftwaffe were fitted with it and used it up to the last stages of the war. Self-propelled guns played an important part in the battle and were considered by the Russians to be so dangerous that the Red Air Force fighter-bomber pilots were told to consider SP guns as primary targets. Heid Ruehl recalled how in the summer of 1943, his unit of the divisional artillery regiment was converted to an SP formation, ' ... In order to give support to the panzer units , we were given "Wasps" [10.5cm howitzers] and "Bumble Bees" [15cm guns], both mounted on panzer chassis ... We carried out familiarization training, but these new weapons brought problems we had not had to face before – finding fuel and spare parts.'

During the night of 29 June 1943 the divisions of SS Panzer Corps marched into their concentration areas, along roads turned into a morass of mud by two days and nights of rain of almost monsoon intensity. For the opening attack of the offensive Panzer Corps deployed on its 20-kilometre wide front: 'Totenkopf' on the left, 'Leibstandarte' in the centre and 'Das Reich' on the right flank. On 3 July 'Das Reich' moved into its form-up positions to the south of the Belgorod–Tomarovka railway line. In the first hours of 5 July several Orders of the Day were read out to the troops stressing the decisive nature of the operation to which they were being committed.

Hitler's proclamation stated that 'Citadel' would be decisively important to the outcome of the war. The Order of the Day issued by Gruppenführer Krueger concluded with the exhortation, 'The Führer depends upon our élan. Our country and our loved ones depend upon our success. Our fallen comrades accompany us in this battle. With them – on to victory.' Knowledge of the importance of 'Citadel' strengthened the resolve of all ranks of 'Das Reich' to gain the victory which their Führer and their nation demanded.

Corps intended to break through on a narrow sector with the point of maximum effort being made by the units on the inner flanks of 'Leibstandarte' and 'Das Reich' Divisions. 'Totenkopf' would be held ready to exploit any breakthrough. On 'Das Reich's sector 'Deutschland' Regiment would undertake the first assault with 3rd Battalion leading. Although H-Hour for the opening of the offensive was set at 06.00 hours on 5 July, assault detachments of 3rd Battalion, accompanied by pioneer groups with flame-throwers, went out some hours earlier to infiltrate the Russian outpost line. Those patrols crawled across no man's land, avoiding detection by sentries, and reached their attack positions. There they waited, silent and unmoving, throughout the short hours of darkness until the time for action came. Then the twelve flame-thrower sections struck first into the backs of the Russian outposts, changed direction and went on to attack the main line positions. So swift and effective were these assaults that as early as 02.45 hours, that battalion's storm troops could report that they had taken one village and were advancing. The 2nd Battalion, which went in once the enemy outpost lines had been taken, was less fortunate. Within minutes of the battalions leaving their trenches they and the accompanying mine-lifting pioneer detachments, were forced to ground by heavy artillery and machine-gun fire. Only slowly could the 2nd Battalion grenadiers fight their way forward through the annihilating shell, mortar and machine-gun fire. This first operation opened under an evil omen of things to come. At 01.30 hours, while the regiments were still in their concentration areas, a heavy Russian barrage had crashed down, causing the first casualties. Although the bombardment lasted for only a short time, its sudden fury and the losses it brought were a bad beginning.

The main body of Wislicency's 3rd Battalion, which had moved off at 03.00 hours, had soon become involved in bitter hand-to-hand fighting in which entrenching tools were more effective than a rifle and bayonet. One man recalled that his overwhelming impressions of that first day were associated with smells. The scent of wet grass filtering through the more intense stinks of wet clothes, cordite and mahorka (the coarse Russian tobacco whose smoke hung in the air inside Russian dug outs). The objectives which 'Deutschland's 3rd Battalion had been set were the capture of a line of trenches in front of an anti-tank ditch, to cross the ditch and to go on to capture Beresov, a village on its far side, ending the day with the capture of an important ridge. The infantry had been promised the support of both panzer and SP guns, but fought their way across the trench line and towards the ditch without that support. The fault was not that of the panzer and SP commandants but in the condition of the ground which had been turned into a swamp, trapping and holding fast the heavy armoured fighting vehicles. By the time the first SPs had freed themselves and had come forward the grenadiers had already taken the anti-tank ditch and were defending it against counter-attack. But support was needed urgently.

Just after 06.00 hours 3rd Battalion, which had reached the west bank of the River Vorska, was smothered by a concentrated barrage of shells and its advance was halted. Not until the Stukas went in did the advance resume. By 08.15 hours the battalion's leading elements had by-passed Beresov and had reached a point to the north of it. Then the direction of the advance changed as the grenadiers, covered by dive-bombing strikes and spearheaded by flame-throwing groups, swung southwards and entered the village. Hans Huber was in a flame-throwing detachment and recalled that battle.

'The enemy artillery fire forced us to take cover. One might almost add, thank God because the equipment was damnably heavy . . . Soon we knew from the Very lights being fired that our No.2 Platoon had gained a foothold in the village. Section commander Kiesel grew impatient. He ordered me to get the flame-thrower ready and we worked our way forward into the trenches ahead of us. I fired a burst of flame as we approached every zig-zag in the trench and at every enemy strong point. It was a strange feeling to serve this destructive weapon and it was terrifying to see the flames eat their way forward and envelop the Russian defenders. Soon I was coloured black from head to foot from the fuel oil and my face was burnt from the flames which bounced back off the trench walls or which were blown back at us by the strong wind. I could hardly see. The enemy could not fight against flame-throwers and so we made good progress taking many prisoners.'

A. Gaerntner wrote of a comrade named Mueller, in his Company in 'Deutschland' Regiment, whose imperfect gift of tongues had often been put to good use when dealing with the Ukrainian civilians and who used it to take prisoners

'When we attacked on 5 July, there was in one pillbox a Russian garrison which would not surrender. Along came Emil and in a curious mixture of German/Polish/Russian (which he later translated for us) shouted out, "Little lads [his standard form of address] come on out of there. You stay there you get cold arse. At home the little wifie and kiddies are waing for you. Your comrades already have their hands up . . . " Not another shot was fired and with no further casualties the group of Russians in the bunker surrendered.'

Wisliceny's 3rd Battalion should then have captured a ridge; Point 233, some six kilometres to the north of Beresov, but, exhausted by the strain of battle and reduced through losses, its attempt failed. Reinforcement was essential to maintain the tempo of the advance and during the early afternoon Weidinger's 1st Battalion of 'Deutschland' Regiment passed through Wisliceny's 3rd and by 16.00 hours had captured the hill. Although the regiment's objectives for the first day had all been taken, Division decided to exploit the gains which had been made and ordered that the advance towards the enemy's second line defences be pressed forward relentlessly. The enemy must be given no time to rest or regroup.

Ahead of Weidinger's grenadiers the ground north of Beresov was covered by a vast web of minefields. These created such difficulties that Corps cancelled the attack by 'Das Reich's panzers which should have accompanied the grenadiers. But the panzers of the 'Leibstandarte' had had better luck and by 19.30 hours were only 500 metres short of the southern edge of Jakovleva, a village well within the second line of defences. Poor road conditions delayed 'Das Reich's infantry companies as they moved towards their start-lines forcing Corps to postpone the attack until the following morning.

The onset of night on 5 July, the first day of 'Citadel', did not end the fighting. Patrols and minor operations to take out enemy posts went on throughout the hours of darkness. Huddled in their slit trenches the remnant of the assaulting battalions ate their hard tack and tried to rest after the strain of battle. It had been a hard slog and a costly day. The battalions had attacked a determined enemy, had crushed his counter-attacks, had been bombarded by more than six hundred guns and had been bombed and strafed by swarms of Russian aircraft. And it had rained and rained all day long.

On the other side of no man's land Stavka decided that the only way to halt SS Panzer Corps and Army Detachment Kempf was, irrespective of the situation on other sectors of the salient, to commit a major formation from its strategic reserve – 5th Guards Tank Army. Its task would be, by constant aggressive action, to blunt the two German pincers on the salient's southern side.

For the second day of battle 'Der Führer' Regiment passed through the positions held by 'Deutschland' Regiment, its grenadiers struggling forward through knee-deep mud to open an assault against a tactically important piece of high ground – Point 243. The hail of artillery and machine-gun fire which struck the 1st and 2nd Battalions 'Der Führer' caused them to falter, but when in the late morning the divisional artillery and heavy weapons were concentrated and brought into action, their fire 'lifted' the grenadiers on to the objective. This success was important for it opened the road towards Lutschki allowing the armour to come forward and smash through the breach which the grenadiers had made. Now the advance towards Prokharovka could begin.

The massive blows inflicted by SS Panzer Corps, produced a fresh crisis which Stavka met by further reinforcing the formations holding the ground to the east of the breach which had been made. Units were rushed to the threatened area and with Stavka's attention now fixed on the southern front, 'Citadel' began to move towards one of its climaxes. The Russian commanders brought into battle armoured trains and regiments of tanks against the three SS divisions now fighting for the high ground north of Prokharovka and for the railway line at Belenichino. The first attacks by 3rd Battalion 'Der Führer' to take its objectives collapsed in the face of repeated air attacks as well as a fierce defensive barrage fired by guns and multi-barrelled mortars. But with the support of 2nd Panzer Battalion and covered by a divisional 'shoot' of guns and Nebelwerfers the attack picked up momentum again. The other two 'Der Führer' battalions, meanwhile, were fighting in the teeth of long and heavy artillery barrages and fierce air attack to widen the gap in the enemy line once again.

Heid Ruehl recalled that the Red Air Force singled out SPs for attack and that he had two narrow escapes.

'While a small wound was being dressed at the Regimental Aid Post, Russian aircraft attacked our battery and cost us one hundred and eight casualties, including the Company Commander . . . I had a slight collision with a Tiger which damaged my own vehicle. I went back to 'B' Echelon to collect a replacement machine and arrived there just at the start of another air raid. Once again I was slightly wounded – this time in the back. Some sort of liquid with a high alcoholic content was poured on, a sticking plaster applied and I returned to the battery to find more of my comrades had been killed in the time that I had been away.'

By 8 July the intensity of the fighting had reached new heights as Stavka put in more and more armoured formations to halt the SS advance. The Soviet High Command, acutely aware that if the effort by Hitler's élite soldiers could be broken 'Citadel' must fail, crammed the area across which the three divisions were advancing, with formations drawn from both Central and Voronezh Fronts. The battle's fury moved towards its climacteric.

The staff officers of Fourth Panzer Army could see that approaching climax from the changing arrows and lines drawn on the operations maps, but the infantry fighting his way forward on foot across the wide and open hill country south of Kursk, would have seen little other than the ground which he was crossing. Grenadiers in their SPWs saw even less, while the view afforded to panzermen in a closed down vehicle was limited to a small patch of ground immediately in front of the machine. Those who carry upon their shoulders the crushing and personal burden of battle see little, know less and are only aware of victories when these occur close at hand as, for example, Sturmbannführer Kaempfe's battle report on the action of his No.10 Company.

'During night attack by No.10 Company against the railway embankment at Belenichino, the Company was confronted by strongly held enemy positions. Fire, opened at close range, struck the Company and forced it to ground. Untersturmführer Krueger rose to his feet and led his platoon, with all weapons firing, into the first line of enemy trenches. When the Company Commander, Obersturmführer Heinz Werner, was wounded, he took over command. Tirelessly, and at times in hand-to-hand combat, the Company battled its way forward for six hours until the day's objective was gained. Despite being wounded twice during the day he [Krueger] not only stayed with the Company, but was always to be found where the fighting was heaviest. An enemy T-34 whose enfilade fire threatened to halt the

Company's advance was attacked at close quarters by Untersturmführer Krueger.

'A rifle bullet struck his pocket and ignited an incendiary grenade he was carrying. Untersturmführer Krueger tore off his trousers and underpants and continued to fight on dressed only in a jacket, shirt and with his lower limbs completely naked. He fought at the head of the Company until the objective was gained.' Krueger did not have long to live – he fell, on 14 July, in the closing stages of the Kursk battle. Sturmbannführer Stadler described a special task force which 'Der Führer' set up. Serving with that group were six Russian Hiwis, whose job it was to listen in to Soviet radio traffic. The information which the Hiwis gained was of importance and especially so on one particular afternoon.

'We listened into the Russian transmissions. Both Corps and Army on the enemy side were blaming each other and threatening all sorts of dire things, because the Reserves which had been promised had not arrived. The reason for this was that they had been put in on other sectors. On the enemy side there seemed to be a definite panic. I drove to 1st Battalion of "Der Führer" and we exploited the situation. No.3 Company under Hauptsturmführer Lex, carried out an attack at last light and passed through a gap in the enemy lines. Suddenly he saw a well-constructed TAC HQ occupied by a Russian infantry brigade and captured the completely surprised brigadier, as well as his staff and the HQ Defence Company.'

At senior command level on the German side optimism was high concerning the outcome of 'Citadel'. On the Russian side the initial mistake in deploying the mass of forces against Model was being corrected and strong formations from the northern wall of the salient had now entered the fight on the southern battlefield, usually at the end of long, forced marches.

The thrust by the SS Panzer Corps had, as planned, struck into the flank of the Russian units around Prokharovka and had created a dangerous pincer arm which threatened with encirclement the Russian formations facing Kempf. Stavka's reaction was immediate and violent. Waves of tanks were put into battle against the panzer spearheads and one particular counter-thrust against Teterevino was only held when 3rd Battalion 'Der Führer' was rushed from where it was embattled in order to strengthen the line on the threatened sector. Every unit of 'Das Reich' Division was by now in action, fighting for the high ground and for the villages on those ridges; villages whose existence was previously unknown to the world in general, but whose names are now part of the military history of the Second World War – Gresnoya, Teterevino, Yashay, Polyana, Netshayevka, Oboyan and above all, Prokharovka.

Bitter fighting raged for the greatest part of the morning of 7 July, across ground saturated with the rain that had fallen throughout the night. The fighting which had died away in the latter part of the 7th, flared during the 8th as heavier and more frequent Russian tank attacks were put in against Hausser's Corps. It was during this day's fighting that the Luftwaffe introduced the technique of destroying Russian armour by aircraft cannon fire and developed this to such good effect that pressure on the SS sector was eased. But such relief could only be brief. Stavka, fearful of a German breakthrough around Prokharovka, created *ad hoc* infantry and armour groups and sent these masses into desperate assaults to wear down the German forces while behind these almost suicidal charges Reserves were being collected for the counter-stroke. The Red Army's losses in men and *matériel* were fearful. The bodies of Russian infantrymen and burned-out hulks of tanks covered the whole battle area. For the men of 'Das Reich' Division the days were marked with attacks of a weight and ferocity not previously encountered and with a frequency which eventually forced the SS Corps on to the defensive.

One such attack spearheaded by sixty tanks and followed by several battalions of infantry, went in east of Gostischchev with the aim of cutting the main road from Belgorod to Oboyan. Unknown, perhaps, to Stavka, that particular drive posed a threat to the SS Corps supply route. The threat had to be stopped. The 'flying anti-tank weapons', the cannon-firing aircraft, smashed fifty tanks and behind the dive-bombers came low flying fighter-bombers whose anti-personnel bombs broke up the Russian infantry masses, causing them fearful loss.

Throughout the 8th reports came in to Corps HQ that large numbers of Russian tanks were driving down from the north and north-east. The fiercest fighting against these armadas was on the Teterevino–Lutschki sector held by 'Das Reich'. An indication of the Soviet determination to smash the SS Corps can be seen in the fact that as early as 13.30 hours 'Deutschland' Regiment had fought off its third tank attack of the day. The Panzer Corps War Diary reported that during 8 July 290 Russian tanks had been destroyed, many of these in close-quarter combat. The divisional panzer regiment played a major part in the successes of that day when it struck into the flank and rear of one group of more than a hundred Russian armoured fighting vehicles heading westward from Prokharovka to Teterevino.

Corps regrouped during the 9th, and concentrated its divisions, deter-mined to renew the attack and thus wrest the initiative from the enemy. That was to prove a difficult task because Stavka, using units from 1st Tank Army, was now trying to encircle Corps which was itself trying to encircle Russian tank forces on its eastern flank. The opening moves of this Russian pincer operation came when armour from 2nd and 5th Guards Tanks Corps, 3rd Mechanized Corps and 6th Guards Tank Corps struck from three different directions. Despite heavy loss they had pressed home their attacks, but although 'Das Reich' was badly hit by the savage armoured blows its units stood firm. Disregarding the threat that was being posed, Fourth Panzer Army directed that for the 9th, the SS Corps was to advance, destroy the enemy north-east of Beregovoy and reach the eastern bank of the River Salotinka. The task of 'Das Reich', holding post on the right, or eastern, flank, was to be a defensive one while 'Leibstandarte' and 'Totenkopf' sought to carry the battle northwards towards Prokharovka and the River Pssel. Throughout 9, 10 and 11 July, 'Das Reich' Division stood fast while its sister divisions fought their way through heavy rain and clinging mud towards the Pssel, the last natural obstacle south of Kursk. To stand on the defensive is not to imply that 'Das Reich' had no fighting to do. It had, and 'Deutschland' was especially heavily involved. The regiment was echeloned behind the 'Leibstandarte' to protect that division's right flank during the advance. The emphasis in the fighting switched between 'Leibstandarte' and 'Totenkopf' as Hausser probed to find a weak spot in the Russian line which could be exploited to speed the advance. The battle plan of Fourth Panzer Army had intended XLVIII Panzer Corps to strike northwards across the River Pssel and then wheeling eastwards together with SS Panzer Corps, to gain the landbridge from Prokharovka before the Russian armour could cross it and expand out of it. This essential part of the German plan was jeopardized by Army Detachment Kempf which had still not fought its way forward to the appointed area by 9 July.

The predictions by Fourth Panzer Army's planners that attacks were to be expected against the eastern flank of the assault had been realized and these had come in a rolling succession. Although outnumbered the SS divisions were a match for their opponents. The intensity of the fighting can be gauged by the fact that 6th Guards Tank Army and 1st Tank Army, both formations committed to Stavka's pincer operation, were driven, ruined, from the field together with a miscellany of smaller formations of 5th Guards Army which had been rushed to the battle. But behind the remnant of these two Russian armies a third, General Rotmistrov's 5th Guards Tank Army, was nearing the southern flank after a long and arduous journey, and was heading towards Prokharovka. The SS Corps was directed to smash the enemy south of that place and to establish a base for the next stage of the advance. Hausser's Corps deployed about 600 panzers while Rotmistrov had in excess of 850. Both sides were employing the greater part of their armour and these two vast fleets of fighting vehicles were charging towards Prokharovka. On the morning of 12 July, a rainy, cloudy day, the climacteric of Operation 'Citadel' finally arrived when these clashed.

It is not possible to describe the movement of units during that July day. The fighting was in essence similar to a clash of armoured knights on a medieval field – a confusion of small actions without central direction, a battle of annihilation in which victory would go to the side which could continue to put in fresh reserves of men and machines. While on the ground panzer fought tank, above them the Luftwaffe and the Soviet Air Force wrestled for control of the skies. Both sides knew that supremacy in the air was the key to victory on the ground, not that that could be determined so soon. Rotmistrov in his account of the day's events describes how he sat on a hillside overlooking Prokharovka and watched the battle roll beneath his feet. He had ordered his units to close with the Germans in order to annul the advantage which the panzermen had in their long-range, 88mm guns. The Russian tanks, not so heavily gunned as the Germans, would have to destroy the enemy vehicles at close range.

All day the noise and thunder of battle raged among the hills around Prokharovka. Columns of smoke from burning vehicles rose above a battlefield on which no quarter was asked or given. Advantages of armour thickness or gun calibre vanished in savage duels of tank versus tank. No one observing the battle could determine who was attacking and who was defending and it was only the fading light of that hot July day that brought the exhausting battle to its close. Perhaps neither side knew at the time just how decisive that particular day's fighting had been. Certainly Panzer Corps did not for it issued fresh attack orders as if the greatest tank battle in the history of the world, for such it had been, were just another incident in the offensive. Corps directed 'Totenkopf' and 'Leibstandarte' to destroy the enemy on the east and west banks of the River Pssel as well as those Russian forces advancing in the area to the south-east and south-west of Petrovka.

'Deutschland' Regiment continued to protect the flank of the advancing 'Leibstandarte' while the rest of 'Das Reich', still on the defensive, flung back a succession of infantry and tank attacks. One interesting incident was the employment against the Russians of T-34s, which 'Das Reich' had seized from a factory in Kharkov. During the day's battle a column of fifty Russian vehicles was seen driving along one of the balkas or valleys, which are a feature of the terrain in that part of Russia. The direction of the column's advance showed that it was moving to attack 'Der Führer'. On the high ground above the Russian column stood the division's group of captured T-34s which opened a destructive fire upon the Russian tanks. The panzermen's tactic was one which they had learned early in the war with Russia; kill the enemy's command tank first. It was the only machine fitted with both a radio receiver and transmitter. The other vehicles had only receivers and could not communicate by wireless with one another. There was yet another weakness in Red Army tactics. Russian tanks carried on their rear deck a metal drum containing reserve fuel supplies. A hit on the drum ignited the fuel and caused the tank to 'brew up'.

With the onset of darkness the noise of battle died away and rain which fell in torrents prevented 2nd Guards Tank Corps from attacking 'Der Führer's unprotected right flank; unprotected because Kempf's panzers had still not gained touch with the SS. During 13 July, Hausser switched his main thrust from 'Totenkopf' on the left wing to 'Das Reich' on the right, intending that the latter should attack via Pravorot towards Prokharovka, creating and exploiting a gap in the enemy line. Although aware that all his Divisions needed rest and reinforcement the Corps Commander directed that if 'Das Reich' lacked the necessary strength, 'Leibstandarte' was to be employed to reinforce the attack. Hausser was determined to break through. During the day the arrival of III Panzer Corps strengthened Hoth's army, but in the north Model, who had regrouped his forces to begin a fresh attack, was forced to abort this. The Russian counter-thrust had struck into the back of Ninth Army forcing Model, as Stavka had planned, to withdraw some of his assaulting divisions to meet the threat to his flank and rear. On that day, too, Anglo-American troops landed in Sicily.

At 04.00 hours on the 14th, 'Das Reich' opened Corps' new drive with an artillery and Nebelwerfer barrage followed by an infantry assault spear-headed by the grenadiers of the 1st and 3rd Battalions of 'Der Führer'. Stolidly they accepted casualties from the extensive minefields across which they marched to gain the high ground south-west of Pravorot. The first houses in Belenichino, a village at the foot of the high ground, were taken by midday, but then the fighting was from house to house and hand-to-hand. Twelve of the Russian tanks which intervened in the battle were destroyed by grenadiers using hollow-charge grenades, while overhead Stukas dive-bombed the Russians, destroying their resistance inside and outside the village. With Belenichino at last in German hands the grenadier battalions regrouped under the protection of the panzer regiment whose counter-attacks flung back the Russian armour in confusion. Panzer regiment then led the Division's attack for what remained of the day and continued this throughout the hours of darkness. But the attack which began with good promise during the night of the 15th, lost momentum as heavy rain washed away the road surfaces. Corps' other order, to gain touch with III Corps, was accomplished when the Panzer Regiment met the leading elements of 7th Panzer Division. That junction surrounded the enemy forces in the Gostisch-chevo – Leski area and destroyed them. Despite this successful operation it was clear that 'Citadel' could not succeed, for on both the northern and southern flanks the German advances had not gained the ground expected of them and there was still more than 130 kilometres between the pincers of Model's and Hoth's armies – 130 kilometres of trenches, minefields and Russian armour.

The Battle to Hold
the Dnieper

It was stated above that victory would go to the side that could reinforce and replace its wasted units. It was the Soviets who achieved this. The Germans could not replace formations that had been destroyed in the fighting and indeed, were already preparing to remove some from the battle line in order to meet the political crisis brought about by the invasion of Sicily. In response to Manstein's promise of victory in the south of the salient Hitler allowed 'Citadel' to continue on that sector, but decided to detach the SS Panzer Corps from the battle. Manstein's hope of victory was a vain one and soon the last major offensive of the German Army on the Eastern Front came to an end.

The extraction of SS Panzer Corps did not follow immediately, nor when all the moves had been completed did the whole Corps travel to Italy. Part of the Red Army's counter-offensive smashing forward on both flanks of the Kursk salient, struck the German units holding the River Mius. The only unit available to meet the Russian drive towards the River Dnieper, with all the catastrophic results to Army Group South that such a success would entail, was Hausser's SS Panzer Corps. The battles along the River Mius, the last water barrier before the Dnieper, lasted from 30 July to 28 August.

Heinz Macher of the Pioneer Company of 'Deutschland' Regiment took part in and was wounded during that first operation to recapture the Mius positions.

'. . . We were told off to attack Stepanovka on the Mius. Two platoons of No. 16 Company were placed at the disposal of 2nd Battalion . . . in open order we climbed a gentle slope on whose other side lay the objective; Stepanovka. Just below the crest of the reverse slope was 2nd Battalion's Medical Post. As I passed it I called out to Dr Axmann that he should get his bandages ready because I would be back in a quarter of an hour. He shouted back, "You're mad." A few minutes later a small piece of shrapnel from a 17.2 shell hit me in the left forearm and our platoon stretcher-bearer put on a field dressing. For a scratch like that one did not abandon one's mates. Five minutes later I fell to the ground. Another fragment from a 17.2 shell had hit me. This one had severed the nerve in my upper left arm. End of the Act. Dr Axmann looked quite surprised when I was brought into the Aid Post on a motor-cycle combination . . .'

Heid Ruehl was another who recalled very vividly the fighting along the Mius.

'For one attack I was in No. 2 OP Panzer as Forward Observation Officer and was surrounded by Tigers which were widely spread out. We soon came under the well-directed fire of some 17.2cm guns which halted the attack. Some Tigers were hit and knocked out. The attack was broken off until a new thrust line had been reconnoitred.

'I was then ordered to take my vehicle into a hollow behind the infantry front line and to use it as a signals relay point to direct a curtain barrage as well as to support the infantry . . . Our infantry was fewer than a Section in number and the enemy was in a row of pines about 50 metres distant with the likelihood that they had a listening-post even closer than that . . . When I brought down a barrage so close to our own line the commanding officer was astonished. The infantry group lay as flat as flounders as the shells whistled low over them . . . Our attack went like an exercise although we lost wireless contact with the battery just after the barrage started . . . I was ordered to return; somehow my panzer had suffered a hit which must have come from some small hills at the edge of the hollow in which we had been concealed. I was surprised to see, on the edge of that hollow, lined up like beads on a necklace, thirteen T-34s, all burning . . . An NCO told me that the first shot fired by the leading T-34 had penetrated our hull, but then some SPs and panzers had come forward and had destroyed all the enemy machines before they could fire another shot . . . On the following day we were supporting an infantry attack against the Mius bridgehead and I halted near some knocked-out Russian tanks. Oberscharführer Toepfer, an infantry platoon commander, stopped with me and we both lit cigarettes. He died in my arms, but no shot had been fired. The doctor found that the cause of death was a hand-grenade splinter which had struck and penetrated his temple. He had been wounded on the previous day but had refused to go back. He was determined to stay with the attack until it was finished.'

On 4 August, before 'Das Reich' could entrain for Italy, the following signal was received from Army Group South:

'To the Kempf Army Detachment: (1) A Führer Befehl has placed Division "Das Reich" under the command of Army Group South and it is to concentrate in the Kharkov area. All preparations which Division has made for a possible move are hereby halted. (2) Division 'Das Reich' is to be taken by Sixth Army transport, beginning during the evening of 4 August, to the north-west of Kharkov, so that it can advance [to battle] in a northerly direction, formed into at least two columns . . . ' The Panzer Corps eventually grouped around Stalino and Heinz Macher recalled an Army directive, used as a prophylactic measure, which reported the unlikely story that all the women in that town were infected with syphilis.

Army Group intended to thrust into the side of the Russian armies as they drove forward, through a 55-kilometre-wide gap in the German line, to capture Kharkov and this counter-attack needed for its success a strong panzer force. One was to hand – the SS Panzer Corps. Before 'Leibstandarte' left for Italy it handed over to 'Das Reich' its armoured fighting vehicles so that the division, even if its panzer establishment was not up to full establishment, would certainly be strong enough to fight a successful engagement.

The departure of 'Leibstandarte' meant the end of II SS Panzer Corps and a third corps was created with 'Das Reich', 3rd Panzer Division and 'Totenkopf'. While the other formations of III SS Panzer Corps were assembling, 'Der Führer' Regiment had begun the first moves in the counter-offensive. As the regiment carried out its approach march to the Mius on 30 July, it clashed with Russian formations which had broken out of the bridgehead they had created on the west bank of that river. One early clash came when a Russian tank column opened fire on an anti-tank detachment. The SS gunners quickly unlimbered and went into action, killing eight vehicles in a few minutes. The remainder of the column turned tail and withdrew to the safety of the perimeter.

Despite Army Group orders to Sixth Army to 'lift' 'Das Reich' as a whole, it had only been possible to bring forward individual units which were then transported up the line as fast as they arrived in the concentration area. 'Der Führer' went into action with an *ad hoc* group and the other 'Das Reich' units were inserted into the division's 40-kilometre-wide battle zone as they arrived. Intensive reconnaissance patrolling was the first necessity; to establish where the enemy was and in what strength. One patrol sent out by the Panzer recce battalion gained touch with Fourth Panzer Army, thereby sealing the German front. When 'Deutschland' and other regimental units arrived to thicken the line the patrolling became more aggressive with battle patrols moving into no man's land to dominate the enemy. By 2 August the SS battalions had driven in the Russian perimeter along the Mius and had flung the enemy back across the river. The situation on that sector was secure and the old German defensive positions had been retaken and re-occupied, but on other sectors, notably at Bogoduchov, the situation was fraught with danger. The spearheads of Russian 1st Tank Army had over-rolled the German units facing them, had captured the town and were driving westwards.

It was at that time that the German counter-stroke was made and 'Das Reich' struck at First Tank Army. How fierce was the fighting during those days is shown by the 7th Company of 'Der Führer' Regiment which battled against the attacking Russian armour and infantry and who died to the last man. However determined the 'Das Reich' counter-attacks; however skilfully led and admirably supported their panzer assaults, they could not halt, nor long delay, the masses of men which Stavka had committed to take the principal objective, Kharkov. The Red Army offensive opened on 18 August and led to the fourth battle of Kharkov. The 53rd Army struck down from the north forming one Soviet pincer, the second pincer, 57th Red Army, swung in from the south and Rotmistrov's 5th Guards Tank Army stood ready to make the killing blow. A situation was developing which paralleled that which had faced the Germans at Kursk in July – but here it was reversed. Now, in August, it was Army Group South which had had time to set up a pattern of deep defences against which Rotmistrov's armour made, in the early stages of the battle, very little headway. Indeed, the losses which his tank Divisions suffered at the hands of 'Das Reich' panzermen, destroyed his army, for a short time, as an effective fighting force. On 19 August, the second day of battle, 184 Russian tanks were attacked and destroyed. Even the prodigious output of the Soviet arms factories could not cover such shocking losses.

A crisis on another sector took 'The Führer's Fire Brigade' out of the line at Kharkov to master the new disaster and on 22 August, during the time that 'Das Reich' was away, Manstein, his forces threatened with encirclement, pulled them out of Kharkov, again in defiance of Hitler's direct order. The Field Marshal retorted to those who questioned his decision, that he would sooner lose a city than the six divisions which were defending it.

With Kharkov evacuated, 'Das Reich' fought a defensive battle against waves of infantry and tanks, often with outstanding success. One such victory was gained on 22 August when, in the early hours of the morning, No.2 (Panther) Company came under heavy artillery bombardment. When the barrage ended about eighty T-34s were seen climbing the hill on which the Company was halted. At 2,000 metres' range the Panthers opened up on the Russian tanks. When the three-hour tank battle ended 23 Russian tanks, as well as lorries and anti-tank guns, had been knocked out. On that one day, the day on which the Panthers first went into battle, the battalion destroyed 53 enemy vehicles.

A divisional Order of the Day issued on 22 August records the successes which had been gained. ' . . . In the period from 6 to 20 August we have destroyed or captured, 6 aircraft, 271 tanks, 6 assault guns, 2 scout cars, 30 guns, 4 Stalin Organs, 4 Flak guns, 230 anti-tank guns, 47 mortars, 162 anti-tank rifles, 313 machine-guns, 324 machine-pistols and a great number of lorries, horse-drawn carts and a vast amount of equipment. We have taken 24 officers and 1,141 NCOs and men prisoner. More than 5,000 dead have been counted. Other enemy losses behind his lines and the number of his wounded cannot be known . . . ' On 23 August the Panther battalion had another successful day but such victories could not hold back the Russian pressure indefinitely and under the weight of mass attacks by 5th Guards Tank Army the divisional line was so often penetrated that preparations were begun, on 28 August, to pull it back. That retrograde movement began on 2 September, was completed by the 15th, and was followed only a few days later by preliminary orders for Army Group South to withdraw to the west bank of the Dnieper. This was certain to be a difficult and wasteful operation because forty Russian infantry divisions and twelve armoured corps were racing towards the river, pursuing closely and harrying the retiring German' formations.

During the fighting of 12 September, a miserable day of heavy and prolonged rain, a group of more than eighty T-34s struck at the positions held by the recce battalion. Behind the deeply echeloned block of armour Otto Weidinger could make out masses of Russian infantry trudging stolidly forward to wipe out any pockets of resistance which the tanks had not destroyed. His orders were passed from slit-trench to slit-trench; let the armour roll over our trenches and kill the infantry. Although this tactic was by now a familiar one, there was always the fear that a Russian tank commander might spin his vehicle round and round over a slit-trench, pushing down lower and lower with the heavy tracks, until the grenadier in it was crushed into bloody pulp; a lonely and terrible death.

The Russian armour advanced through the pouring rain and across the grenadiers lying huddled at the bottom of their slit-trenches. Then the vibration of the tank treads was behind the infantry line. Now, it was time to stand up and open fire upon the ranks of brown-uniformed men marching across the open ground. Astonished by machine-gun fire coming at them from men they had thought dead, the Russian infantry wavered and then broke. To add to their destruction Weidinger called down an artillery 'shoot' on his own positions. This scattered the enemy completely. The T-34s, meanwhile, carrying on with their advance, had run into a carefully laid trap. Fourteen Panthers lay in wait, in hull-down positions, and in the short fire-fight which followed 78 enemy tanks were destroyed.

The difficulties of withdrawing to the Dnieper were compounded by the fact that when 'Das Reich' reached the area near Kremechug, which it was to defend, it found that Russians formations had already crossed the river and established bridgeheads on the west bank and were busily engaged in reinforcing them. Another complication which affected not just 'Das Reich' Division but the whole of German Eighth Army, was that across the Vorskla, a river barrier east of the Dnieper, there was only a single bridge, near Kremechug. The rear guard of both grenadier regiments and the reconnaissance battalion carried out a fighting retreat towards the bridge and the recommendation for the award of the Knight's Cross to Obersturmführer Roehder of the SP battalion indicate the intensity of the fighting.

'On 20 September 1943, No. 3 Battery received orders from Division to hold the area around the strategically important bridge across the Vorskla at Poltava until it was blown . . . At about 14.00 hours it was learned that the bridge was about to be destroyed and the SP detachments were ordered to move back in quick succession to the bridge. At about 17.00 hours the rearguard commander, Obersturmbannführer Stadler . . . gave orders for the SP platoon to cross the bridge . . . One of the SPs was hit by a Russian anti-tank gun whereupon Roehder took a motor-cycle combination and drove back over the bridge to the damaged vehicle. During the journey he came under fire and, dismounting from the machine, he and the driver moved back firing their pistols and driving off the pursuing Russian infantry who were intent upon cutting off the German units which had not yet crossed the bridge . . .

'Roehder decided to defend it together with two of his men while the motor-cyclist was ordered to contact the SP battery and to bring it back. A 3.7cm Flak standing on the west bank of the river was towed on to the bridge by Roehder and was positioned about 30m on the bridge . . . The Russians who had worked their way through the gardens and houses of the village took the small group under fire at a distance of about 70m. At that time the Commander of a Pioneer Company called to Roehder, "Hold the bridge while I bring back four demolition teams" . . . The SP battery came back and Roehder formed this in a half-circle on the eastern bank of the river. The fire of the SP guns held down the Russians. Some fifteen minutes later Hauptsturmführer Fleischer and the four demolition teams arrived . . . Covered by the fire of the SP guns the final preparations were made to blow the bridge and when these had been completed Roehder took the SPs back across the bridge. As the last vehicle crossed, the bridge across the River Verkla was blown. When they saw the SPs preparing to cross the Russians pressed forward and their leading troops were blown up with the bridge . . . '

The course of future operations, particularly the defence of the Dnieper was now in doubt as the Russians had already established small bridgeheads around Grebeni, on the west bank of the river and were in the process of widening and reinforcing these, using paratroops and armoured corps. On 28

September the Division opened an attack to recapture seven hills in the Dnieper bend which the Russians had captured and which had become strongpoints in his vast bridgehead. The first assaults by 'Der Führer' made no ground and the assault died in the fire of Russian machine-guns and artillery. The 3rd Battalion was sent forward in support and that, together with 15th (motor cycle) Battalion's assault, reduced the Grebeni bridgehead a little. Orders from XI Corps and Eighth Army for Division to smash the Russian perimeter were rejected by the commanding officer of 'Der Führer' who pointed out in vain that the strength of his regiment had sunk to only 500 men. As ordered, on 30 September, 'Der Führer' marched into the Grebeni sector to reduce the enemy perimeter. Horst Herpolsheimer describes the part played by 3rd Battalion after the attack by the 2nd had failed. For this new assault No. 11 Company would be supported by two flame-throwing panzers.

'Our SPWs came out of the copse in which they had been concealed and drove forward with all weapons firing, closely following the flame panzers which were squirting great streams of fire at the enemy. Our No. 2 Company then attacked the wood to their front, drove the enemy out of it, pursued him and, finally, took up position in the north-western sector of the bridgehead. There the dismounted grenadiers of Nos. 9 and 10 Companies joined them. Because it was believed that the enemy had no heavy anti-tank weapons on our sector we in No. 11 Company were ordered to smash through his positions, capture Grebeni and gain touch with an army unit on the far side of the enemy bridgehead. For this operation our Company was additionally reinforced by an anti-tank gun and two SPWs from No. 12 Company, mounting anti-tank weapons. Our attack was to be supported by artillery.

'At this time casualties had reduced Untersturmführer Neudeck's No. 11 Company to little more than platoon strength, but we had five personnel carriers commanded by Hauptscharführer Staiger as well as a headquarters troop which I led. With wide intervals between vehicles we charged the enemy . . . racing towards and then across his positions. In front of us there was a vast field of sunflowers cut by a path leading to a village. As we drove up that path we came under heavy fire from both sides of it as well as from the village. Every type of weapon was being used against us, including large-calibre anti-tank guns which the Russians had ferried across the river. It would have been madness to turn back in such open country and in the middle of an enemy bridgehead. There was no other choice than to drive on despite the anti-tank guns. The first SPW was hit and stopped. The following one, which tried to drive past it, skidded and tipped over. By this time our vehicle had reached the spot and Neudeck wanted to drive past and carry on, but I convinced him that this was senseless. He ordered the remaining vehicles to halt and for the grenadiers in them to dismount. We took up all-round defence in the ditches and soon had the unwounded and the lightly wounded men as well as the machine-guns positioned on both sides of the track. Behind us an SPW tried to turn round and go back but was hit and burst into flames. The enemy on the right flank was firing at very close range and those on the left began to close in.

'From the forty men who had made up the battle group there were now only 25 left in action. Then a mortar barrage caused us more casualties. An NCO, FOO who was with us took over on a machine-gun. Our MGs and MPs kept up a continuous rain of fire and we changed our positions frequently to deceive the enemy as to how few we were in number. In that way we kept the Russians at bay. None of us expected to come out alive from this situation but we were determined not to surrender and to fight to the last. When one of our MGs ran out of ammunition I had a quick look round in the vehicle which had tipped over and found a few blood-smeared belts. In the heat of the action we had forgotten about our wireless but then the Company Commander told the operator, who was acting as a sniper, to raise battalion on the set. This he could not do but he did manage to contact No. 10 Company whose OC promised to pass to battalion the news of our position.

'By this time the Russians were working their way down the path. It began to get dark. We had lost all sense of time. By last light the enemy soldiers had closed to within hand-grenade range and their shouts of "Hurrah! Hurrah!" meant that they would soon charge. We prepared for the end. When the charge came in we fought desperately and our concentrated fire stopped them. At intervals we fired flares to see if they were creeping up on us. Just when all hope was gone we heard the sound of motor engines. Coloured Very lights rose in the sky and suddenly there was the cry, "Its our flame-throwing panzers." Some 50 metres right and left of the track the two vehicles drove slowly forward spewing out the death-dealing fire. They came up to us and we consolidated our position. The CO had also come forward to organize the recovery of our SPWs. They had all been hit several times and one of them was a burnt-out wreck. This had to be left behind. The badly wounded and dead men were put in one vehicle and we moved off still unable to believe that our little group had held out for so long against a superior enemy. On the following day we received orders to renew the attack but before we moved off were ordered to another sector of the line where we not only carried out the attack but captured the village and gained touch with our army comrades.'

Not until 5 October did the fighting for the Grebeni bridgehead die away and in his Order of the Day the divisional commander paid tribute to the panzer grenadiers, ' . . . who, of all the arms of service, were the ones who led the way into the enemy's positions . . . '

Throughout the following weeks the German front line was pulled farther and farther westwards with the divisions manning it defending, attacking or counter-attacking as the situation demanded. Army Group South was forced to give up Kiev on 5 November, and through gaps in the ruptured German front the Russians struck into western Ukraine. 'Das Reich', meanwhile, was holding a line to the south-west of Kiev, defending it against minor attacks.

This relatively easy time ended when the Division was ordered to capture Fastov and with that operation 'Das Reich' entered, once again, into a period of defence and attack. These see-sawing operations endured until 25 November, when Division was ordered to an area east of Zhitomir where it was to spearhead a counter-offensive in the Korosten–Berdichev–Radomyshl area. That operation opened well but was halted when it struck the strong reinforcements which Stavka had rushed forward to counter it. The Russian attacks forced 'Das Reich' on to the defensive again and as a result of the incessant enemy assaults, by 10 December the battalions had almost bled to death. The SS soldiers had fought from Kharkov in the spring, through the summer offensive at Kursk and into the fighting retreat of autumn and early winter. They had been in action, almost without pause or let up, committed to unceasing, murderous battle for nearly ten months.

By this time it had been accepted that 'Das Reich' was no longer capable of carrying out the tasks given to a full-strength division and orders were issued to create a battle group from the units still fit for action. This group would stay on the Eastern Front while the remaining divisional elements returned to Germany. On 17 December 1943 the Panzer Battle Group was constructed out of Panzer Grenadier Regiment 'Das Reich': a composite formation of 1st Battalion 'Deutschland' and 2nd Battalion 'Der Führer' Regiments. Two companies of armour constituted the Panzer Battalion 'Das Reich' and also on strength were the recce battalion, artillery, Nebelwerfers, pioneers, a heavy infantry gun company and two SP companies. The battle group was really a miniature division in composition, although it had a strength of only 5,000 men. For administrative purposes, Panzer Battle Group 'Das Reich' was placed under XLII Corps, which was holding a sector to the south-east of Radomyshl–Guta Sabelozkaya. The villages around that area were left deliberately unoccupied. The Germans had long since learned that deep woods offered not only better concealment against the Russian Air Force, but also some measure of protection against the bitter winter weather.

That a Soviet winter offensive would soon be launched was clear to all ranks, but they were determined to show that although small in number their fighting will had not diminished. The lull over the battlefield in those dark December days was broken when, at 06.00 hours on Christmas Eve, the Russian artillery opened an hour-long barrage behind whose fire and explosions came the infantry. Within hours two Russian salients had been driven into the German front. Stavka sent forward armoured regiments to fill these penetrations and great numbers of Russian AFVs advanced to battle. They were destroyed in such great numbers that at the end of the first day sixty had been knocked out.

But against the overwhelming enemy strength which was being pitted against it, Corps had no choice but to issue an order for its units to pull back to a line east of Zhitomir. This decision came too late. Russian troops had already cut the road down which the formation would have to withdraw. Realizing that his battle group did not have the power to fight its way through the block,

Obersturmführer Sommer, the unit commander, swung it off the road and across country heading for the Tetrev. Arriving on the banks of the river, Sommer had to make a hard decision. No bridges spanned it and the ice was too thin to bear the weight of the group's armoured fighting. vehicles. It seemed, at first, that if the group was to escape all the heavy equipment would have to be abandoned. The pioneer officer suggested a bridge over the 60-metre-wide river pointing out that timber was no problem – the group was pulling back through a heavily wooded area. The grenadiers were told that the line must be held until the bridge had been built and the battle group had crossed the Tetrev.

While the infantry fought hard against waves of Russian infantry and tanks, the pioneers and others from the non-fighting detachments toiled, sawing, hammering and building. The bridge was finished; the first lorries crossed, then the armoured reconnaissance vehicles and behind them, singly and slowly, the heavy armour. All night the vehicle column rumbled over the hastily constructed bridge and before dawn the grenadier outposts were called in, leapfrogging in a fire and movement operation back to the safe bank. At 03.00 hours the HQ detachments began to cross under Russian artillery fire and shot at by infantry. Machine-gun and mortar fire held back the attackers who were flung into the fight to seize the bridge before it could be destroyed. The order to blow it up was given but when the detonating handle was turned, nothing happened. The cable had been severed by the track of an SP. A fuze was lit and when it reached the detonating charges at last the bridge blew up leaving the enemy on the far bank. For a short time at least, Russian pressure on the Battle Group would be relaxed. Hans Werner Woltersdorf's *Picnic between Biarritz and Zhitomir*, recalls the savagery of the fighting during the Russian winter offensive of 1943/4, which he experienced as a junior officer in a 'green' replacement battalion.

'Christmas Eve 1943, was spent in the Bulishety Forest between Kiev and Zhitomir. We had each received a Christmas package and post from home – and although this was usually weeks old it was very welcome. We had tried to make things like a traditional Christmas, with a tree and candles . . . This had been a quiet area for weeks but there seemed to be something brewing out there. Reports from our listening-posts confirmed that something was up . . . The enemy artillery fire grew in strength and the sound of tank tracks was borne on the wind . . . I reported to Battalion who passed on my reports to Regiment, where they were not taken seriously. The OC of the right-hand unit to mine also complained that his reports were not believed that the Russians had worked their way forward to within 50 metres of his positions.

'By 4 in the afternoon it was pitch dark. I brought up a 5cm Pak SP and we fired HE at the Russians lying camouflaged in the snow. They began to move, hand-grenades began to fly about and then the whole mass of the enemy began to retreat . . . Then a rolling thunder like an earthquake ending in a screaming, howling tornado of explosions. We knew that when the barrage lifted the infantry would make their charge but the barrage did not stop. It crept backwards and forwards across our strip of ground destroying everything . . . When at last it did stop we rushed to man our firing positions but these were in a changed landscape. The forest had been destroyed and now there were only the stumps of trees rising out of the fog and smoke. We looked to where our main line had been. In the dawn's light we could make out a T-34 only 50 metres from our Pak, and there was a second Russian tank in a slight rise, with its track torn off. There was no other sound or movement . . . The Russians were now behind us enjoying the contents of our Christmas packages, the biscuits, the chocolate and the six cigarettes that each contained.'

Woltersdorf led his small group through the shattered woods capturing, disarming and then releasing Russians they encountered and carrying their own wounded until they regained the German lines.

'In Studenizza, which was a collecting point, I found space in a room packed with soldiers and fell immediately asleep. It must have been about midnight when fighting broke out close at hand. Through the windows we could see fur-hatted Russians. Some of our men fixed bayonets and rushed into the street. The whole town was like a firework display. We began to pull back towards Zhitomir. Nobody could tell me where regimental Tac HQ was located. Then I saw a sign "Train Pi Btn DR and 1st DF". On New Year's Eve I saw again the 5cm Pak which we had mounted on to a half-track as a sort of SP gun. I had not expected to see that weapon again and it was like a Christmas present. I stroked it like a horse . . . A few minutes before the Old Year died, just as we had filled our mugs with vodka to drink in the New Year, the fireworks began again. Karlemann, my No. 1 on the SP Pak, pointed to a T-34 standing on the bend of the road leading into the village. I took over his seat and looked through the sights. "Fire!". A hit in the turret but had the shot penetrated? "Reload!" "Don't fire!," someone whispered to me. "Karlemann has gone forward to finish the T-34." He had filled a shell case with petrol, had walked forward to the tank, poured the petrol over it and lit it. It began to burn brightly.

'Another T-34, carrying infantry, came into the village but a shot drove it off and the SS detachments moved to where a bridge was being built . . . At dawn the Russians started firing their MPs and shouting out their terrible hurray cry. They came in supported by a mass of tanks. Then a new order was given to take our SP gun north-east of the bridge where at least twelve enemy tanks had broken through. My gunners held their fire until the T-34s were at about 1,000 metres' range. Fire two shots, change position; two more rounds and change position again. We had to bluff the Russians into believing that they were facing a well-camouflaged Pak front. There were sounds of fighting coming from the bridge and we raced back there but found the situation well in hand. There was a pause in the fighting and we took the opportunity to look into the first tank we had knocked out. The interior was sickening. A headless torso, bleeding flesh and guts spattered the walls. The men from the Train told us that the driver was still breathing when they got him out of the machine. Now he lay there dead with his chest covered in decorations for bravery. The back of his head had been smashed exposing his bloodied brains. There was froth on his lips, typical of this type of wound where the brain is dead but the lungs are still working.

'The pioneers have worked well and the bridge is ready. The first lorries cross and head westwards. We have a brew-up and something to eat. We park our version of an SP outside the house in which we are brewing tea and until the heater boils relive the fighting of the day. Everybody is thinking of, but nobody mentions, the flesh spattering the walls of the tank and the headless torso . . . By the time we rejoined the regiment's positions it had already left for France leaving behind two of the Division's battalions as Battle Group "Das Reich" for special combat missions. The battle group had no adjutant, so I was assigned the post and served Lex, the commanding officer . . . '

The retreat continued through deep snow drifts and in the face of howling blizzards. The Russian winter offensive had been revitalized and struck again at the weakened Battle Group whose fighting retreat had by now resolved itself into a wearisome pattern. During the day the units fought off their Russian pursuers; by night they marched, but no longer the impressive distances of summer. One night march of 16 kilometres was considered an outstanding achievement having been made through a snowy forest. Rations were scarce. The Battle Group could not live off the land and hot meals for the grenadiers lying out in the snow were a rarity.

The inability of higher staffs to comprehend the privations suffered by the grenadiers was illustrated on 13 January when a counter-attack with limited objectives went in at Krasnopol. Such importance was placed on the success of this operation that Panzer Group 'Peiper' of the 'Leibstandarte' accompanied the 'Das Reich' Battle Group's attack. When, despite the most strenuous efforts, this was called off, staff officers came forward to insist upon it being renewed. Made aware that Peiper's command was reduced to just three vehicles and that these were confronting a Russian Pak front, the staff officers accepted the local commander's decision. There was a pause in the fighting and the grenadiers put that time to good use to improve the positions they had dug on the heights north of the line Mal–Bratalov–Grinovshky. The reduction of enemy pressure lasted until mid-February with ski-patrols sent out to harass the enemy and to dominate no man's land. The losses which the Battle Group had suffered – 1,121 all ranks from a total of 5,000 men – coupled with the fact that not a single replacement had been received, forced Army Group to evaluate the combat ability of the Battle Group's infantry component. The conclusion drawn was that one battalion was only 60 per cent and the other only 55 per cent mobile. It was time they were withdrawn and rested.

A resumption of the Red Army's offensive led to the fear that the Battle Group might be outflanked and cut off and it was withdrawn to a new sector where it met the assaults aimed at cutting off First Army. The SS group recaptured Isyaslavl and the Russian drive was halted. Fighting around Isyaslavl lasted until 14 March and so great were the losses to the depleted grenadier companies that the distances between the individual slit-trenches had increased to 400 and 800 metres. The Battle Group, terribly weakened, still had more battles to fight. On 3 March a Soviet spring offensive opened, mounted by four armies. The whole of Army Group South was threatened with destruction as the Russians blows separated one German formation after another from the neighbour on its flank. Battle Group then found itself part of a 'wandering pocket', a group of German formations which, surrounded and cut off, moved steadily westwards until at Buszacz it gained touch with Fourth Panzer Army.

On Easter Sunday, 8 April 1944, – the Battle Group, which had now reached Kartanovche in Galicia, went into reserve and a week later carried out an 80-kilometre foot march to board the train home.

To set the seal on its 13-month record of service, the Battle Group parade-marched (goose-stepped) into the station forecourt. Weapons were handed in, the train left on 20 April and by the 27th the survivors, 800 in total from the 5,000, reached Toulouse. They had returned to the Division, at last.

1944

Axis territory and general strategic movements ■

'Das Reich':
1 Toulouse, April–June
2 Normandy, June–August
3 Ardennes, December to January 1945
(See sketch maps overleaf)

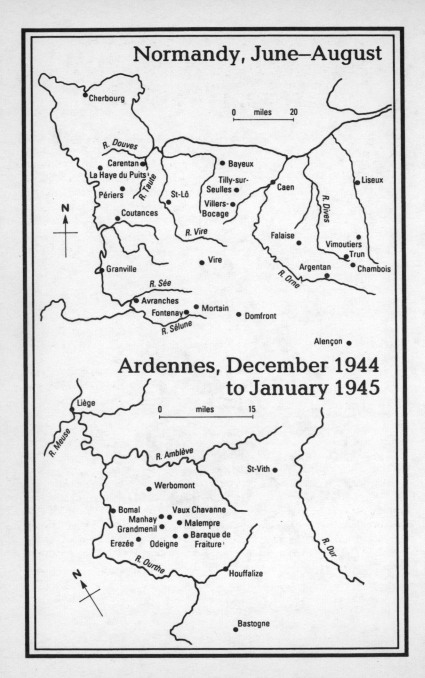

Normandy, June—August

0 miles 20

Cherbourg

R. Douves

Carentan
La Haye du Puits
Périers

R. Taute

St-Lô

Bayeux

Tilly-sur-
Seulles
Villers-
Bocage

Caen

R. Dives

Liseux

Coutances

N

R. Vire

Falaise

Vimoutiers
Trun
Chambois

Vire

Argentan

R. Orne

Granville

R. Sée

Avranches
Fontenay
Mortain
Domfront

R. Sélune

Alençon

Ardennes, December 1944 to January 1945

Liège

0 miles 15

R. Meuse

R. Amblève

St-Vith

Werbomont

Bomal
Manhay
Grandmenil
Erezée

Vaux Chavanne
Malempre
Odeigne
Baraque de
Fraiture

R. Our

R. Ourthe

Houffalize

N

Bastogne

2nd SS Panzer Division 'Das Reich' in North-West Europe, 1944–1945

With the break up of Battle Group Weidinger in April 1944, and the return of its constituent units to their parent bodies, 'Das Reich' Division, once more complete, passed into the strategic reserve of Supreme Commander West. As such it formed part of LVIII Corps, garrisoning the Toulouse area. Its given task was the defence of the coast in the event of an invasion of southern France.

During its time in the Toulouse area nearly 9,000 replacements came in and were posted to regiments where these inexperienced but keen volunteers were taught the practical aspects of active service life. The recruits came under the command of officers and NCOs who, although battle experienced, were themselves not much older than the men they commanded. The divisional commander, for example, was only 36 years old. The heavy losses which the Division had suffered included, of course, many veteran junior commanders for shells and bullets make no discrimination between young soldiers and seasoned campaigners. But sufficient veterans remained to imprint upon the new men the stamp which marked a soldier of 'Das Reich' Division.

The strong regimental spirit which animated the men of 'Das Reich', as it does for the men of all élite units, is evidenced by a great many accounts about men of the Division struggling against obstinate bureaucracy in order to return 'home' to the old mob. An example of this was supplied by Oberscharführer Ehm, who during a period of convalescence confided to his superior officer, Heinz Macher, his determination to make his way back to his old company, the 14th of 'Deutschland' Regiment. Macher, an officer of the same unit, determined to accompany the NCO and applied to the local Commandant for movement orders which would allow them both to return to unit. Macher insisted that he was fit but the commandant replied that the hospital papers told a different story and ordered him to strip to the waist. All was revealed. His shoulder and back were in plaster which was blood-soaked and his wounds had turned septic.' Such determination by even badly wounded men to return to active service so as to carry on the fight alongside their comrades is expressed over and over again.

Normandy

During the time that the Division was in the Toulouse area the level of partisan operations had increased, an indication that events in France were reaching crisis point. From May onwards there was a rise in the number of attacks on soldiers and indeed, during the period from March to D-Day, no fewer than a hundred men of the Division were murdered or had been kidnapped and nearly as many had been wounded. With the news that the Allies had invaded Normandy, 'Das Reich' went on to first stage alert. In order to meet the need for greater mobility when the second stage alert was ordered on 7 June, civilian vehicles were requisitioned. The Division's first contingents, the wheeled units, set out for the invasion area leaving the tracked vehicles to be loaded up and taken by train. John Keegan in his book, *Six Armies in Normandy*, claims that the actions of the French resistance delayed significantly the move of 'Das Reich' Division to the invasion area. ' . . . Some wheeled vehicles got on to the road that day [6 June]. The tanks . . . were assembled at Montauban to load on to railway flat cars but had to wait four days for trains. The marshalling yard was then bombed . . . and when the first trains reached the Loire on June 11, they found only a single-track span in use at Port Boulet . . . Not until 23 June did the last of the division's rail elements reach the battlefield . . . seventeen days on a journey which in normal time would have taken five . . . ' This claim that the Division was prevented from playing its part in the early days of the invasion is denied by 'Das Reich' officers who point to the fact that the Division was put into Army Group Reserve when it reached Normandy; indicating that it had not been urgently needed in the battle zone.

It was during the Division's march to Normandy that punitive action was taken against the village of Oradour sur Glane. It is not my intention to discuss the actions of the French Resistance in this matter nor the counter actions of 'Das Reich' Division. The Allies saw the men and women of the Maquis as resistance fighters determined to liberate France. Front-line soldiers see such people in a different light – as *franc tireurs* who commit murder and who deserve no mercy. I intend to say no more on this matter other than that a murderous attack was carried out near Oradour sur Glane and that this resulted in savage reprisals being taken by some units of the Division against the civil population of that village.

Much has been written in books and many films and television programmes have been produced depicting German soldiers, especially those in the SS, acting in a brutal, repressive way towards the French civil population. In view of the accounts which I have received from men of 'Das Reich' Division and in which they recall excellent day-to-day relations with the civilians, the media view may be seen to be subjective and its accuracy may be called into question. One account records an example of restraint shown by the SS towards members of the Maquis discovered in the possession of firearms. Under international law partisans taken under such conditions can be summarily dealth with as *franc tireurs*. That was not the action of Anton Fehlau and his comrades from 'Das Reich' artillery regiment.

'During the campaign in France in 1944, I served on a 15cm gun in No.9 Battery. We had broken off a counter-battery action when it was realized that ammunition was running low and we had, in fact, fired our last rounds to stop an enemy tank attack. Orders came for us to move to a new position and the guns together with the prime movers got away without too much interference from the enemy artillery.

'I was one of those left behind with the battery commander and a handful of men, several wounded comrades, equipment and instruments, all of us waiting for a lorry to carry us away. Towards midday the truck driver reached us. He was on foot. His vehicle had been attacked by low-flying fighter-bombers and he himself had been lightly wounded. He said that no other truck would make the trip to reach us until last light. As we expected to be attacked at any minute we, naturally, looked for a way out of our difficulty, less for ourselves than for the wounded and for the equipment.

'There was a farm close by and three of us were sent to requisition some farm carts. Although enemy shells were falling close by the farmer helped us to harness the horses and we drove away, leaving behind us a very sad farmer whose best horses had not only been taken away during harvesting but had also been commandeered just before the Allies arrived. Our promise to return the horses must have been little consolation and we ourselves did not really expect that we would be able to keep our word. Once back with our little group we loaded the wounded and covered the equipment under foliage. We three drivers took off our steel helmets and uniform jackets to disguise ourselves and we reached the unit's new positions without being attacked by Allied fighter-bombers. The horses and carts were handed over to "B" Echelon and we returned to our batteries to man the guns.

'We stayed in that sector for a couple of days, but frequent changes of position took us further and farther away from the farm where we had commandeered the horses and carts. One day the Spiess asked if we would like to return them. "The situation is not without danger," he told us. "Which is why the Battery Commander does not want to order you to do it. The front line is being pulled back tomorrow so this afternoon, or at the latest the coming night, will be the last opportunity to return everything." We three were willing to carry out the task and after reporting to battery HQ, went back to "B" Echelon. We harnessed the horses had something to eat and drink and then set out. The Spiess gave us up-to-date information about enemy movements and had also drawn us a sketch map. "There is no firm front line in the sector where you are heading, so it is not certain whether there are any enemy troops there." Then he pointed on the map to a crossroads which was under constant artillery fire. Finally, he said that partisans were holding many of the farms in the area.

'We left quite late in the afternoon and after a couple of hours' driving reached an isolated farm in a wood where we intended to feed and water the horses. By now it was beginning to get dark and we heard from the farm the sound of several men speaking French. We tied up the horses and moved carefully towards the house. We knew the men must be partisans and that it would not be possible to pass the farm without making a noise. We had no wish to get shot in the back and we also needed food and drink. Quietly we opened the door and saw, seated around a table, a group of young men smoking and drinking. Our sudden appearance gave them no time to hide their weapons. To show our peaceful intentions we did not carry our MPs in a firing position, although we each had a couple of egg hand-grenades ready for use in an emergency.

'Our signaller was from Alsace and in perfect French greeted the group and pointed out the blunder they had made. "How could you sit around and not put out a sentry?" he asked them. "You are civilians and are armed. Tomorrow the war will have passed this place. Do you really want to die on the last day?" One of the group replied that no German soldiers had been seen in the area for several days past and he and his comrades were convinced that the Germans had all pulled out. Another reason for their slackness was that they had all drunk too much wine. I should mention here that we were just as frightened as the French lads. Then an old man came in, obviously the owner. I went outside with him, watered the horses and gathered some feed for another meal. My comrades joined me and then we left that dangerous area. Shell explosions which grew louder and louder showed that we were on the right road. Then the shells began to land very close to us. This had to be the crossroads. The barrage was almost continuous and the animals were trembling with fear. We could not go forward, nor could we go back through the partisan-held area and we did not want to turn the beasts loose. As "old Gunners" we knew that batteries must rest occasionally and that is what happened. The gunfire died away and we led the horses by their reins across the shell-torn ground. Although shell splinters whizzed around us, within ten minutes we had passed through the danger zone. Bathed in sweat and with trembling knees we took a short rest. We crept along for a couple of hours but then the horses realized that they were nearing home and increased their pace. The animals brought us to their stables, a place which we would never have found in the total darkness. Awakened by the noise we were making the farmer and his wife came down and were very pleased to get their animals back. They thanked us so warmly that any doubts that we might have had whether it was worth taking the risk to return there horses was quickly answered. Yes it had been. The farmer and his wife fed us and we enjoyed a few hours' sleep in the barn. The farmer kept watch over us and woke us at the proper time. When we left his wife loaded us with food and he came with us part of the way taking us through short cuts. We reached the battery about midday only to find it changing position once again. We leapt onto the trucks, glad to be back "home" once again.'

On 14 June the first elements of the Division reached the concentration area to the south of Domfront and while moving into the area were attacked by Allied fighter-bombers. This was a new and frightening encounter. The veterans of the Russian campaign had had experience of being attacked by Russian low-level aircraft, but nothing in the east had prepared them for the rocket-firing aircraft which cruised around the sky in 'cab ranks', waiting to be called into action against anything that moved behind the German lines. Some accounts recall that even individual soldiers were shot at by Allied airmen. The experiences of those first few raids caused it to become second nature for crews to camouflage their guns or vehicles and to park them under trees. That first demonstration of Allied air power had happened as the units were moving into the concentration area and had resulted in sixteen lorries being set alight and burned out. It was also on 14 June that Sturmbannführer Weidinger took over command of 'Der Führer' Regiment upon the appointment of Standartenführer Stadler to lead 9th SS Panzer Division.

Although the self-propelled artillery, the 1st Battalion of the divisional artillery regiment, the Flak battalion and part of the panzer regiment all reached the divisional area during the night of 19/20 June, concentration was not yet complete. Some grenadier battalions were still in the Toulouse area. Until such time as the Division was completely assembled a few units were sent on temporary postings to other formations. Thus the order from Seventh Army which came in during the evening of 26 June, directed that an artillery battalion and a panzer battalion be sent to support II Fallschirmjaeger Corps to the north of Torigny-sur-Virein in the St-Lô area and that a battle-group, made up of the 1st Battalions of 'Der Führer' and 'Deutschland' Regiments was to be temporarily assigned to 2nd (Army) Panzer Division for a proposed counter-offensive along the Villers-Bocage–Caen road. In the opinion of Bayerlein, GOC of Panzer Lehr Division, under whose aegis the battle group had now passed, the units holding the area had been so badly mauled, there could be no question of an offensive operations. He proposed, as a greater priority, that the SS battle group be employed in stabilizing the front east and north of Noyers by closing the gap between its flanking neighbours – Panzer Lehr and 12th SS Divisions. Once the front was closed the counter-attack in the Villers-Bocage area could be considered. His plan was agreed and the group moved off with 1st Battalion 'Deutschland' on the left, 1st Battalion 'Der Führer' on the right and with a Panther company in support. The advance to reach the positions which had been allocated had to pass through a heavy artillery bombardment which brought the first casualties. 'D' Battalion suffered more heavily as the result of a clash with British infantry advancing out of Tessel.

The situation in Normandy at that time was that the Allies were seeking to extend the British sector of the bridgehead through an attack across the River Orne. The intention of Operation 'Epsom' was that a strike to the south of Caen would isolate the city, forcing its determined German defenders to pull back. With that achieved a base would then have been created for the eventual breakout of the beachhead perimeter on the British sector which would tie in with a similar operation being prepared in the American area. The British formation committed to 'Epsom' was VIII Corps, fielding 15th Scottish and 49th West Riding Divisions. In support of these two infantry units was 11th Armoured Division as well as a number of independent brigades. The British corps opened 'Epsom' and as a counter-blow II SS Panzer Corps was to strike into the flank of VIII Corps as it thrust between Caen and Villers-Bocage. The 'Das Reich' battle group was placed tactically, under command of 9th SS Division 'Hohenstaufen' and the German thrust began to roll at 14.30 hours on 29 June. Its weight, combined with the close-quarter combat skill of the SS soldiers, brought initial success and halted the British advance. But as the columns of SS men and their vehicles fought their difficult way through the close, verdant Norman countryside they came up against increased resistance from British infantry and armour which slowed the advance. Last light did not end the day's fighting and both sides stress the intensity of struggles which were fought out in the rainy, dark night; battles which were often hand-to-hand.

German and British sources describe the difficulties of fighting in the bocage country of Normandy and British VIII Corps report on the operation states: ' . . . Because of the cut-up nature of the ground the advantage lay with the defenders and the enemy used that advantage to the full. Fighting was usually carried out at very close range . . . The enemy held his positions and let our men roll past him . . . only to emerge when suitable targets presented themselves. It is worthy of note that in every case groups of the enemy fought until they were all killed or until the position was taken . . . If we achieved a breakthrough on a narrow front our flanks were in the air. He [the enemy] lost no opportunity of attacking our flanks . . . ' Again both British and German sources stress that the battle resolved itself into small unit actions which were controlled by junior officers of even by NCOs. The thick, tall hedges which were a feature of the Normandy bocage restricted vision to such an extent that Sturmbannführer Weidinger was forced to issue the order that, 'a good field of fire takes precedence over cover'.

The difficulty of controlling the fire of artillery regiments in such close country was one which the Germans were not able to resolve as efficiently as their opponents. The British enjoyed a benefit denied to the Germans – air superiority. This allowed them to use artillery spotter planes; flying OPs, to bring down upon the opposing units the concentrated fire of 900 artillery guns and the fire of warships, including cruisers and a monitor. To the indiscriminate fury of ground and sea artillery fire was added the more direct terror of attack by rocket-firing aircraft. It was in the face of a prodigal use by the British of shells and rockets and against their massed tank squadrons that the assault by II SS Panzer Corps had gone in. The Sitrep produced by German Seventh Army on the evening of 29 June includes the words: 'The tank battle in the Caen area which the enemy opened around Tilly-sur-Seulles and for which he is using several fresh divisions, reached a climax when the spearheads of II SS Panzer Corps entered the fighting at 14.00 hours. By the timely intervention of II SS Panzer Corps, the enemy's attempts to expand his salient [across the River Odon] were frustrated and the penetrations he had made were cleaned up despite his material superiority on the ground and in the air . . . ' The real situation which faced the hard-fighting grenadiers was less optimistic than Seventh Army's report suggests. They were fighting to

Above: Oberführer Heinz Harmel, CO of Panzer Grenadier Regiment 'Deutschland', who went on to command 10th SS Division.

Above right: Sturmbannführer Heinz Hauser who commanded 1st Battalion 'Der Führer' Regiment in the fighting for Vienna, 1945.

Right: Hauptsturmführer Klingenberg, who was awarded the Knight's Cross for his dramatic action in forcing the surrender of Belgrade with only ten men.

Above: This picture, taken in December 1943, shows, left to right: Schlink, Gruppenführer Krüger (GOC 'Das Reich' Division); Obersturmbannführer Sarg; Obersturmbannführer Sylvester Stadler, commanding 'Der Führer' Regiment.

Below: Scharführer Adolf Peichl, a platoon commander in No. 12 Company, 'Das Führer' Regiment, showing his awards. These include the Knight's Cross, the German Cross in Silver, the Close Combat badge, arm stripes to show the single-handed destruction

of enemy tanks, the infantry assault badge
and the wound badge.

Opposite page, bottom right:
Obersturmführer Rentrop, commanding the
divisional Flak battalion, which attacked and
captured the important railway bridge over
the River Desna, September 1941.

Above: Oberscharführer Emil Seibold of
No. 8 Company of the panzer regiment, who
was the Division's highest-scoring ace. He
was awarded the Knight's Cross on 6 May
1945, after 'killing' his 65th victim.

Above right: Oberführer Felix Steiner, the
innovative genius, who commanded
'Deutschland' Regiment, and who rose to
command an Army by the end of the war.

Right: Obersturmführer Franz Vogt was one
of the first winners of the Knight's Cross in
'Das Reich' Division. He gained his award as
a member of the reconnaissance battalion in
1940.

Left: The last contingent of recruits to 'Deutschland' Regiment before the outbreak of the Second World War. They are seen here taking the oath in East Prussia, August 1939.

Centre left: Men of 'Deutschland' Regiment posing in the first Polish shellholes on the road to Mlava, September 1939.

Bottom left: The motorcyclists of Battle Group Steiner have brushed with the enemy and the advance is temporarily halted. At the side of the road light panzers wait for the order to advance, Poland 1939.

Above: The casemates and pillboxes of No. 1 Fort at Modlin, after their capture, September 1939.

Below: The pioneer company ferries units of the Division across the River Beresina, Eastern Front July 1941.

Left: Grenadiers move into the close-pursuit stage of the attack. They are carried in lorries so as not to lose touch with the retreating Russian forces, summer 1941.

Below: Grenadiers in a captured Russian village, waiting for orders to continue with their attack. Eastern Front, 1941.

Right: Grenadiers moving through deep forests during the advance to Mozhaisk. Eastern Front, October 1941.

Right: A photograph taken during the defensive battle at Yelnya during the autumn of 1941. Despite the strain of the fighting the two men in this slit-trench seem remarkably cheerful.

Right: Gruppenführer Hausser, the divisional commander, and his IA (centre) being briefed on the situation by Hauptsturmführer Klingenberg. Eastern Front, 1941.

Left: A scene from the fighting around Kharkov, 19 February 1943. The swift advances of the summer and autumn have been replaced by hard slogging as these men of 'Deutschland' Regiment, moving up the line to a new attack, tow sledges loaded with weapons and supplies.

Centre left: A heavy machine-gun group of No. 12 Company, 'Deutschland' Regiment on the march to Vel Burluk, 5 February 1943.

Bottom left: Grenadiers waiting along the side of a road, before opening an attack in the fighting to the east of Kharkov, winter 1942/3.

Top right: An SP gun protecting the thrust-line to Losovaya, 25 February 1943.

Bottom right: Grenadiers riding on the outside of a vehicle of the panzer regiment as 'Das Reich' attacks Kharkov in von Manstein's counter-stroke, spring 1943.

Left: The *rasputitsa* (the thick mud of Russia) which held fast even tracked vehicles. In this photograph an infantry gun and its towing vehicle are bogged down. Note the divisional sign on the back of the prime mover.

Opposite page, bottom: A commanders' conference, 1943. Right to left: Heinz Lammerding, IA of the Panzer Corps; Hausser,

the Corps Commander; Harmel, commanding 'Deutschland' Regiment; Kreutz, commanding the divisional artillery regiment.

Above: A two-man slit-trench in the front line, Eastern Front 1943.

Below: A 'Wespe' of the SP battalion preparing to go into action east of Zhitomir, 1943/4.

Opposite page, top: A 5cm Pak, mounted on a one-ton half-track. This improvised SP gun, built in the divisional workshops, is seen here preparing to move out to intercept a group of twelve T-34s. Godycha, February 1944.

Opposite page, bottom left: The unit war photographer, Grigoleit, who accompanied a recce patrol to the east of Isyaslaval, February 1944.

Opposite page, bottom right: Himmler during an inspection of the Division after the fighting at Kharkov.

Above: A heavy infantry gun moving forward on bad roads, south of Stuhlweissenburg (Hungary), 1945.

Below: The last panzer in the area of the Florisdorf bridge. Vienna, 13 April 1945.

Above: Field Marshal von Manstein who defied Hitler and evacuated Kharkov, thus producing the conditions leading to the retaking of the city, 1943.

Above right: Obersturmbannführer Werner Ostendorff, commanding the 'Reich' battle group, 1942.

Below: A heavy gun of 47th Regiment, which supported Battle Group Steiner, here seen firing on No. 1 Fort, Modlin. Poland, 1939.

Right: Men of the motorcycle battalion in Russia, 1941.

Right: A machine-gun outpost during the winter fighting of 1942/3.

Right: A 10.5cm gun from 2nd Battalion of the divisional artillery regiment firing from a reverse slope position.

Above: The improvised SP which was commanded by Woltersdorf in the winter battles of 1943/4.

Below left: A heavily camouflaged Panzer IV on the Normandy front, 1944.

Below right: A Tiger of the Heavy Panzer battalion. Ardennes, December 1944–January 1945.

survive in the storm of British gunfire, against tank assaults and infantry thrusts. There comes a time in battle when even the most courageous soldiers cannot maintain an advance against such opposition. Thus it was that the efforts of II SS Panzer Corps first faltered and were then halted by the hurricanes of fire which swept across the battlefield. And when the SS assault died away VIII Corps seized the opportunity and counter-attacked to such good effect that a squadron of Shermans penetrated as far as Battle Group TAC HQ., and were only stopped when No. 14 Company's anti-aircraft machine-guns backed up by the flame-throwers of No. 16 Company, knocked out four of them.

During the night of 29/30 June the Battle Group's shattered remnant regrouped and prepared to meet the challenges of the coming day. The survivors were now terribly few in number. There had been a 40 per cent loss of effectives in 1st Battalion of 'Der Führer' as a result of the bitter fighting of the past days; a percentage figure which was to rise to 60 per cent by the time that the offensive was finally called off. The statement by VIII Corps that 'groups of the enemy fought to the last' recognized the soldierly qualities of the men of the battle group and the loss of 846 men in the operation was a blood letting which was soon to make it incapable of continuing as a fighting unit.

But that time was not yet and during the night of 30 June SS Panzer Corps issued orders that a pre-dawn attack against the British salients was to begin at 03.00 hours on 1 July. Details of the Corps plan did not reach the commander of 'Der Führer' Regiment in time for him to deploy his battalions, neither could he, because of the radio silence which had been imposed, use the radio to contact 'Hohenstaufen' Division whose panzer regiment was to collaborate in the attack. By the time that Weidinger's battle group was ready it was already 06.00 hours. His grenadiers would have to make their attack in daylight. Worse news was to come. Sturmbannführer Weidinger then learned that his battalions would be without the support of the Hohenstaufen panzers. The ground was considered to be unsuitable for armour. Despite all these changes the companies crossed their start-lines and at first made good progress. Then, without consultation 'Hohenstaufen' Divisional HQ cancelled the attack and ordered the assaulting units to return to their form-up area.

To break off an attack and move back in daylight under enemy fire is not an easy task, nor can it be conducted without loss. The British battalions, sensing perhaps the confusion which existed on the German side, launched fresh attacks which, although they caused more casualties to the grenadier companies, were beaten back. However, there could be no longer any question of II SS Panzer Corps continuing its own offensive. Hitler was forced to accept the situation and ordered: ' . . . the present positions are to be held. A firm defence or local counter-attacks will halt any further enemy breakthrough . . . ' Although the Germans had had to break off their offensive, the SS grenadiers had won a victory, albeit a Pyrrhic one. In retrospect it can be seen how crucial had been the role of 'Der Führer' Battle

Group in the third Battle of Caen, in stopping a breakthrough to the River Orne and the seizure of the high ground to the south of Caen by British VIII Corps. Two under-strength SS battalions, whose soldiers fought often hand-to-hand against the British infantry, using entrenching tools, hand-grenades and machine-pistols, had helped to hold Normandy in obedience to Hitler's order.

The Führer's directive ordering a firm defence or local counter-attacks against British assaults no longer applied to the shattered 'Der Führer' Battle Group. At 15.00 hours on 2 July it was relieved from the line and on the following day reverted to 'Das Reich' control. Those units of the Division which had reached Normandy were now grouped in the Mesnil–Vigot area and were still in Seventh Army Reserve. Although technically the units were out of the line there was no respite for the grenadiers. Time after time, throughout the weeks which followed, the under-strength battalions and other divisional units were formed into small battle groups and put into 'fire brigade' actions. The reputation for élan in attack and staunchness in defence which 'Das Reich' had gained on the Eastern Front, worked against it. On the Western Front, just as had been the case in the east, squads were inserted into the line to stiffen the defence of some wavering unit or to support the faltering attack of some other formation. In vain did Hausser, as divisional commander, and his successors stress that such actions brought with them a higher than usual casualty rate and that among the losses were junior commanders, the natural leaders, upon whom the Division depended.

Such protests went unheeded and in Normandy the Division was not once able to fight as a single, cohesive unit. Although nearly a month had passed since the order was issed for the Division to march from southern France, not all its units had arrived in the Normandy concentration area. Still in the Toulouse region were 2nd Battalion 'Deutschland', 2nd Battalion 'Der Führer', a company of the reconnaissance battalion, 3rd Battalion of the divisional artillery regiment, a company of the pioneer battalion and all the divisional troops. None of these units reached the combat zone before 17 July.

In the confused conditions which prevailed in Normandy on the German side the question of supplies and its concomitant, meals for the fighting troops, was a vital one because ration trucks were often shot up by the Allied figher-bombers. In the following anecdote the unit Spiess is shown using his initiative to feed his men.

'During June 1944, a great many of our marches towards the invasion area had to be carried out at night. At the end of one particularly strenuous night march, No. 11 Company was spread out along a typical Norman road. Our vehicles were widely spaced and camouflaged with foliage; a vital precaution because Allied fighter-bombers were very active.

'Our rations were depressingly monotonous and the only change came through the masses of butter and cream which we bought from the farmers. They were only too pleased to sell their produce to us because they could not get to market as Allied aircraft attacked everything which moved along the roads.

'As I said, our rations were monotonous and we had not eaten meat for some time. It was something we missed and our Spiess was aware of this. We relied on him to get meat because a good Spiess should be able to "organize" anything. Our NCO hit on a plan and lay in wait near a burned-out omnibus, the victim of former air attacks and often mistaken for a target by Allied pilots. The Spiess waited, pistol in hand, for the next attack and when the Allied aircraft came in with cannon and machine-guns firing, he went into the nearby field and shot a cow. He went across to the farmer and bought the dead beast from him. The farmer, of course, blamed the American air force for the death of his animal and was only too glad to sell the carcase. I can only say that we were very pleased to eat meat again. As I said, a good Spiess can organize anything.'

The Division was now serving as part of LXXXIV Corps, but still was not able to fight as a single unit. Once again there was that 'splintering' from which 'Das Reich' had suffered so much in the past. The divisional units now held the Périers sector near St-Lô and soon after they moved into their concentration areas, on 4 July, orders came for battle groups to be created. The first of these, made up of panzers and artillery and led by Sturmbann-führer Weidinger, was placed under the command of 353rd Division and given as a first task the strengthening of that division's defence. To carry out the other task of holding La-Haye-du-Puits against the American assaults Weidinger's battle group took up positions on either side of the small town. The second battle group, which was ordered to support 17th SS Division's counter-attack north-west of St-Lô, consisted of 'Das Reich' divisional headquarters with the HQ and 2nd Battalion of the panzer regiment, the HQ and 4th Battalion of the artillery regiment, the Nebelwerfer battalion and the Flak battalion. These units took up position on either side of Sainteny. A third divisional group, under the command of Obersturmbannführer Wisliceny and made up of HQ 'Deutschland Regiment and two of its battalions, together with the pioneer battalion, was also en route to the 17th SS. A smaller 'Der Führer' group formed a counter-attack reserve behind II Fallschirmjaeger Corps.

During the time that these battle groups of 'Das Reich' were in action with other formations, the Division's panzers began a spectacular run of 'kills' and the man most closely associated with those victories was Unterschar-führer Ernst Barkmann. Although he had fought successfully on the Eastern Front, his many victories in Normandy led him to become known as one of the most successful panzer commandants in the whole Division.

His first success in the west came on 8 July. On the previous day, American infantry of the 9th and 30th Divisions, had crossed the Rivers Vire –

Taute and were pushing on towards Le Dézert. The tanks of 3rd Armoured Division passed through the breach which the infantry had created determined to exploit and widen it. To meet that critical challenge Seventh Army ordered an immediate counter-attack and detailed the panzer regiment of 'Das Reich' Division to carry it out.

The counter-attack opened and at a point north-east of Sainteny, No. 4 Panzer Company, acting as point detachment for 1st Battalion, met and exchanged shots with an American unit. In that exchange Barkmann destroyed his first Sherman. American artillery responded promptly to the German challenge and brought down a bombardment which halted the SS counter-attack. The situation was reversed on the 9th and for several days thereafter when probes made by the units of 3rd Armoured Division were met with German tank gun fire which drove them back.

Only days later, at dawn on the 13th, Barkmann spotted a group of six Shermans crashing through a bocage hedge to enter a field some 400 metres from him. The first shot fired from the 75mm gun struck the leading Sherman low down in the hull and 'brewed it up'. The dramatic suddenness of that 'kill' confused the other US tankmen and the group halted. One commandant began to swing his main armament towards Barkmann's Panther but his action came too late. A shell from the panzer's gun struck and tore off the Sherman's track. The Panther's next shell destroyed the now immobilized tank. A third Sherman was smashed before it and the others could pull back into cover.

While Barkmann had been in action against the enemy tanks to his front, American infantry and anti-tank detachments had infiltrated past his position and were about to attack him from the rear. Warned of the threat by a grenadier Barkmann began to smash it using high-explosive shells and machine-gun fire. But before one American gun was put out of action its shells had hit Barkmann's Panther and set it on fire. The crew put out the blaze and brought their damaged vehicle back to the Workshops Company for battlefield repairs.

Orders received during the morning of the 14th took Barkmann back into action. Four panzers of No. 4 Company had been cut off and his new mission was to take some reserve machines and rescue his trapped comrades. This operation successfully concluded, he and a small panzer group were then sent out to rescue some wounded men of the Division who were cut off in a house in no man's land and who had been taken prisoner. Once again Barkmann led the detachment in and had soon returned with the wounded grenadiers.

Although to include the next action at this point is to take Barkmann's greatest exploit out of chronological sequence, it is recorded here in order to show how his reputation was gained. The operation took place on 27 July, and resulted in an otherwise obscure road junction in Normandy becoming known in military history as 'Barkmann's Corner'. The Panzer Lehr Division, which held post on the left of 'Das Reich', had been all but destroyed in the US bombing raids which opened the American offensive. To cover the gap where once Panzer Lehr had held post, 'Das Reich' panzer regiment had to be taken from its place in the line and put in to cover the open flank.

Positioned at Le Lorey, at the junction of a minor road on the main highway running from St-Lô to Coutances, Barkmann watched a group of Shermans coming from the direction of St-Lô and decided to engage them. Moving stealthily between the bocage hedges to avoid attack from the fighter-bombers overhead, he drove slowly forward and took up position at the crossroads under a huge oak tree. The 75mm gun on the Panther faced eastwards towards the approaching American tanks. They were within 200 metres' range before Barkmann opened fire and 'brewed up' the leading pair of Shermans. Their blazing hulls blocked the road. The petrol tankers and soft-skin lorries which had been following the tanks halted, clearly uncertain of what to do next. Barkmann opened fire and destroyed them. Clouds of smoke from the burning oil bowsers reduced visibility but through the gloom Barkmann saw another pair of Shermans, which had crunched their way past the obstructions in the road, and were now quite close. The shells of the first Sherman missed the target but Barkmann's return fire did not and hit the lead tank. It blew up. The gunner of the second American tank scored two hits on the Panther before shells from the 75mm struck it. It, too, began to burn. The Americans, determined to destroy this single panzer which was obstructing the advance, called in fighter-bombers to take it out. One bomb fell so close that the Panther nearly turned over and another bomb damaged the running wheels. During this air assault other Shermans came into the battle. They smothered the lone Panther with fire but fighting furiously Barkmann 'killed' two more. One of the shells which struck the Panther tore off a track and knocked out the ventilating system. By this time short of ammunition Barkmann decided that the time had come to pull back and ordered the driver to reverse the badly damaged tank back to TAC HQ. There he learned that he had destroyed nine of the fourteen Shermans which had attacked him. This was not the end of the victories which he scored in Normandy; on the following day he 'brewed up' another pair of Shermans. A reputation had been gained which was to endure to the end of the war.

To return again to the situation as it was in the first weeks of July. The German forces which had already endured nearly a month of fighting were now facing Bradley's First Army which fielded, in the Périers – St-Lô sector, no fewer than fourteen divisions. Against that host the German could put up only six divisions and a single panzer division.

Throughout the following days and nights Battle Groups Weidinger and Wislicency, undertook local attacks and carried out counter-attacks to seal off US penetrations. By 14 July the diminishing strength of all units in LXXXIV Corps, as well as the unrelenting US pressure around St-Lô, forced a withdrawal. The town itself was of great importance to the Americans for it was to be the springboard from which their imminent offensive, Operation

'Cobra' would be launched. Although there was only one panzer division to oppose the American armoured preponderance, the nature of the terrain aided the defence and did not allow the US armoured divisions to be used in the role for which its men had been trained. The US tankmen had expected to fight an open and mobile type of warfare but the Normandy 'bocage' of small fields, high hedges and few roads, was ideal defensive country and it was being defended by men who knew how to exploit its potential. By the first week of July, the town of St-Lô had been reduced to a ruin which lay deserted between both armies, neither of which was strong enough to hold it. This situation changed when General Omar Bradley made another bid to break out of the confinement of the Cotentin peninsula. His first attempt, in early July, had been halted on the line of the River Douves. With his second, to open on the 25th, he intended to capture St-Lô, which would launch Operation 'Cobra', a smashing of the German positions between the Rivers Vire and Lozon. Bradley intended that General Collins' VII Corps, forming the spearhead of the advance, would pivot on St-Lô and drive southwards towards the base of the Cotentin peninsula. Through the breach which VII Corps had created, George Patton's Third Army would come storming across terrain which, south of the 'bocage' country around the bridgehead, was open and, therefore, considered to be 'good going' for armour.

For the soldiers of 'Das Reich' Division the days and weeks up to 25 July were passed in patrol activity or with handfuls of determined grenadiers defending their positions against American attacks and in launching immediate counter-attacks to regain lost ground. Among the losses which the Division suffered during the course of 24 July, was the divisional commander, Brigadeführer Lammerding, who was wounded while on a tour of inspection of the panzer regiment. Obersturmbannführer Tychsen, commanding the panzer regiment, assumed command until a new General could be appointed.

Panzer Lehr Division, on the left flank of 'Das Reich', recorded in its history, a phenomenon which occurred during the morning of 25 July. The men in the Division's outpost line reported that the American soldiers on the far side of the charred and battle-scarred ground around St-Lô, were leaving their trenches and withdrawing from the battlefield. The explanation for this evacuation was not long in coming. Squadron after squadron of Fortresses were flying in to bomb ahead of their own infantry line, with the intention of blasting a fiery passage through the German positions; of creating a gap along which the US armour would pass. General Bayerlein, commanding Panzer Lehr Division, upon whose positions the greatest weight of that enormous bomb load was to fall, wrote of how ' . . . carpets of bombs wiped out artillery positions, overturned and buried panzers, flattened infantry positions and destroyed all roads . . . ' Paradoxically, that crushing weight of bombs and the damage they caused, did not speed up but, instead, retarded the US advance. Bradley had not learned the lessons of Cassino and Caen, that aerial bombing creates as many difficulties as it resolves. Bombing might destroy the enemy on the ground, but it creates a lunar-type landscape which halts any advance until the obstructions it has created are removed, the craters filled in and roads restored again.

The relative calm which prevailed in the pre-dawn hours of 25 July, on those sectors of the German front held by 'Das Reich' battle groups, was broken when the heavy bombers of the Allied air forces opened the first of three major strikes on the units holding the narrow strips of territory to the west of St-Lô. The weight of these air bombardments and the barrage of artillery shells which then fell indicated that a major ground offensive had opened. Behind the air strike the infantry of VII Corps advanced, their attacks designed to open the way for the follow-up armour. A curtain of artillery shells marched ahead of the assaulting troops and that part of the barrage which fell at first light on the right flank of 'Das Reich' Division marked the start of a day in which thirteen separate infantry and tank assaults were launched against it. Each was met, held and then repulsed. Many of the American armoured attacks were smashed by SS recruits using hollow-charge grenades and other close-quarter weapons. These young soldiers had learned from the veterans of the Russian front that tanks without infantry support were at a fatal disadvantage against determined men armed with Panzerfausts and Panzerschrecks. And that fatal disadvantage was exploited to the full in the claustrophobic Norman countryside. Success did not, however, always attend upon the German efforts and one counter-attack which 'Der Führer' Regiment launched with panzer support, collapsed and died in a hail of well-directed artillery fire.

While 'Das Reich' was holding its own against overwhelming odds, LXXXIV Corps issued a stream of conflicting orders concerning withdrawal to new defence lines. Order and counter-order produced disorder and as confusion piled upon confusion a number of 'Das Reich' units that had begun to withdraw were caught on the move, attacked and overrun by US tank units. Bradley's First Army was now striking down the Cotentin peninsula towards Avranches, and although his Army's attacks in the Coutances sector where LXXXIV Corps was holding the ground were not particularly heavy, they were severe enough to threaten Corps with encirclement. That threat was not yet apparent to the rank and file of 'Das Reich', for a soldier in action sees only what is to his immediate front. Of more immediate concern to those men were the consequences arising from the confusion arising from Corps' conflicting orders. The feelings of the grenadiers can well be imagined. They had been bombed and shelled out of one series of positions to the west of St-Lô and, en route to a new battle line, which they were nearing after a long, exhausting night march, had been ordered to move again. Corps' new order was that they were to take up a line to the north of the St-Gilles–Coutances road and extending from Savigny to the north-eastern edge of Coutances itself. The late arrival of that second order – it did not reach the units until 03.00 hours – meant that the march to the new positions was made in daylight and under continual air attack. Suffering from the effect of that bombing the fragmented units then found that as a result of the conflict of orders, whole stretches of the defence line which they should have taken up were already held by the enemy. The grenadiers had to launch attacks to drive out the Americans before they could dig themselves in and set up a strong defence.

The weight and frequency of the enemy assaults soon produced a crisis within the Division. Losses to the grenadier companies had been so severe that there were now too few men to hold the line and to gain more men there was a comb-out of 'B' Echelon personnel in divisional headquarters where the cooks, clerks and other non-combatant personnel provided sufficient men to form a small battle group. This hastily improvised unit was ordered to attack, seize and hold a road junction east of Tully. Heavy tank-gun fire stopped it from reaching the designated area and the men dug in on the western side of the road junction. During the evening of the 28th Corps flashed a signal that the vehicle in which Tychsen, the divisional commander, was riding had been hit by a shell and that the GOC was feared killed. The recent losses among senior commanders showed how closely they shared the dangers which their men were experiencing.

By this time, around Coutances, American thrusts and probes had almost cut off LXXXIV Corps and the time had come when its units would have to fight a way through the encirclement. As yet the US ring was not fully closed nor would it be strong enough to withstand a concentrated attack. But forces to smash through could not be mustered from the rifle companies nor would another comb-out of divisional units produce the numbers needed. The SS acted pragmatically. A group would be created through the amalgamation of 'Das Reich' and 'Götz von Berlichingen' – the 17th SS – and both units would share a common Command structure. Once the attack had succeeded the SS units were to set up a defensive line on each side of Percy. The break-out attempt did not succeed. The SS units were attacked from the air and intercepted by US tank formations lying across their retreat lines. Under this combined battering the amalgamated force was smashed and LXXXIV Corps almost ceased to exist as a fighting force.

During its retreat from the Coutances pocket 'Das Reich' suffered severe losses. 1st Battalion of the artillery regiment was wiped out; the lowest percentage loss (30 per cent) was that of 2nd Battalion of the panzer regiment. Pounded by artillery and rocketed by aerial assault the scattered fragments of 'Das Reich' Division struggled through the Norman countryside towards Percy where security cordons collected them. Rested, refreshed and re-armed, they were formed into new battle groups and allocated defensive positions. These fragments of remnants were then ordered to hold to the last.

Meanwhile, on 30 July in another sector of the Cotentin peninsula, a barrage of 20,000 shells fired by the artillery of US First Army smashed a fresh gap through which the Americans struck. The impetus of this thrust forced the German left wing away from the sea at Avranches, and through the gap which had been created Patton's divisions fanned out south-westwards and headed towards Brittany. In an attempt to form a cohesive line German Seventh Army authorized LXXXIV Corps to withdraw south-eastwards. It was a fatal mistake. The direction ordered should have been south-westwards in order to close the gap in the line. Upon receipt of the order Corps pulled back its left wing, a movement which widened the gap. The German error was immediately exploited by Montgomery who ordered Bradley's tankmen to swing away from Brittany and back into Normandy in an armoured advance that threatened to roll up the southern flank of the German forces in Normandy. To meet that threat at the base of the Cotentin peninsula, OKW and the commanders on the ground drew up plans. That of von Kluge, Supreme Commander West, was roughly similar to that drawn up by the Führer and a compromise battle plan was agreed. Hitler had proposed an unrealistically ambitious operation which would not only recapture Avranches but which would go on to drive up the peninsula and smash the American original lodgement area on the Normandy beaches. Von Kluge's proposal was for a spoiling attack with limited objectives designed to fling the US forces off-balance and gain time for the German Army to conduct a planned withdrawal through France and Belgium.

Planning and preparation for this offensive took so long that it was not until 5 August that Seventh Army was ready to launch Operation 'Liège'. For the thrust towards Avranches a total of 120 armoured fighting vehicles would traverse the ground between the Sée and Sélune, using those rivers to protect both flanks of the advance. 'Das Reich' Division came, temporarily, under the command of XLVII Corps which was to conduct the operation. Corps' plan was that the first wave of the attack would comprise detachments from 1st SS Panzer Division ('Leibstandarte'), 2nd SS Panzer Division ('Das Reich'), 116th Panzer Division and a battle group from 17th SS Panzer Grenadier Division ('Götz von Berlichingen'). The second wave of the assault would be made up of the remainder of 1st SS and the 9th and 10th SS Panzer Divisions.

'Das Reich' created three battle groups. The task of 'Der Führer' Regiment on the right was to bypass Mortain to the north, take the heights to the north-west of the town and gain touch with the 'Leibstandarte', its right-flank neighbour. To strengthen its own right wing 'Der Führer' Regiment was to be supported by the divisional SP battalion. The centre battle group was that of 17th SS Panzer Grenadier Division 'Götz von Berlichingen'. Its task was to capture and hold the tactically important Point 317. The left-flank battle group comprised 'Deutschland' Regiment and the divisional recce battalion. Some elements of the latter formation were to make a wide sweep southwards to reach a line running from Fontenay to Milly while other detachments were to retake Mortain. The Division's main effort was to be made by the left-wing units and these would be supported by the panzer regiment.

'Der Führer' Regiment plan was for its 3rd Battalion to lead the battle group, supported by four SPs and followed by the regiment's 2nd Battalion and No. 16 Company. The plan failed even before it could open up. The Regiment crossed its start-lines promptly, but barely had its first elements moved off than they encountered the 'Leibstandarte's armoured columns which had been delayed and were late in reaching the start-line. The 1st SS Division had absolute priority in right of way and having to wait delayed 'Der Führer'. The consequence was that the Regiment lost so many valuable hours that it was already first light before it could open out into battle formation. Corps and Army Intelligence appreciations had predicted only light American resistance, but that forecast proved to be incorrect; units of US 30th Infantry Division holding the village of L'Abbaye Blanche, directed a storm of artillery and mortar fire which forced the grenadiers to leave their SPs and to go into the attack on foot. That delay cost even more time and while the firefight was in progress Allied aircraft entered the battle and destroyed two of the SPs supporting the Regiment's assault. Pinned down under a barrage of aircraft rockets 'Der Führer' could not advance until early in the afternoon when the fighter-bombers at last flew away. The American infantry had made no aggressive movement while the air attacks were coming in, but had used the time to strengthen the defences. This was done to such good effect that when No. 9 Company opened a fresh attack it lost nine vehicles, six of them SPs.

The assault by 17th SS Division, the battle group in the centre of the line, had also been unsuccessful and its units had not taken their objective, Point 317. On the left wing 'Deutschland' Regiment had ordered its grenadiers to foot march into the forming-up area so that the sound of SP vehicle engines would not alert the Americans. The Regiment's attack, which went in at 02.30 hours, was also silent, with no preliminary or covering barrage. The assault flowed well to begin with; the 2nd and 3rd Battalions pushed rapidly westwards and 3rd Battalion had captured Mortain by 10.00 hours. Then the recce battalion took up the running and its advance gained touch with the Division's left-flank neighbours.

Despite these initial successes it was soon clear that the offensive was losing momentum in the face of stiffening US opposition, and despite Hitler's order to continue Operation 'Liège' using fresh troops it was clear that the offensive had no chance of achieving its aims. Soon any movement forward had stopped and the attacking forces, who had attacked buoyed up by Hausser's Order of the Day that ... 'the success of this operation will determine the outcome of the War in the West ...' passed over to the defensive.

While the German formations of Operation 'Liège', had been fighting their way forward new threats were building up. On their left the armoured divisions of Patton's Army had begun a huge wheeling movement that would soon take them racing for the River Seine. Behind the right flank of the German group at Mortain a Canadian–British–Polish army had begun to drive from the coastal lodgement area towards Falaise. It needed no staff-trained brain to realize that both German Seventh Army and Fifth Panzer Army were in danger of being trapped in a huge encirclement. Hitler had once declared that each metre of ground in Normandy was worth five kilometres of ground in any other part of France. So far as he was concerned there would be no withdrawal from the Mortain area and the men of Fifth Panzer Army and Seventh Army paid in blood for his insistence on holding ground in Normandy.

The Falaise Counter-Attack

Within days it was clear to the High Command that Operation 'Liège' had no hope of success. Indeed, unless prompt action were taken to pull back the assault divisions, they would be caught in the encirclement which was building up around Falaise. During the night of 8/9 August 'Das Reich' Division was ordered to halt its ttacks and go over to the defensive. Sensing that the SS offensive had been broken, the Americans struck hard in well-mounted operations and throughout the following days the regiments of 'Das Reich' Division were involved in ferocious battle. They counter-attacked when they lost ground to the US infantry and destroyed enemy armoured thrusts with Panzerfausts and Teller mines. There was bitter, often hand-to-hand fighting and the War Diary of 'Deutschland' Regiment's pioneer company contains an interesting entry for 10 August. '... a number of Americans pretended to be dead but we could pick them out quite easily because they all lay face downward with their head to one side and with their eyes closed ...' The grenadiers and panzermen, the ones most deeply committed to the unequal struggle, were aware that the offensive could no longer bring the military advantages that the Führer had demanded of it and at 18.00 hours on 10 August, Corps ordered 'Das Reich' to pull back east of Mortain. The dying Operation 'Liège' was brought to a close on the following day.

Throughout the second week of August the Division conducted a fighting retreat under fighter-bomber attacks which struck at anything using the roads. Allied command of the air had not only, and almost through its own power, stopped an offensive by massed panzer units, but went on to strike at the German armour as it withdrew towards Falaise. Air power was the key to victory and the Allies held that key. On 15 August there was an ominous sign of the deterioration of the German military situation in Normandy and of the speed with which the US forces were exploiting the situation. 'Deutschland' Regiment had been ordered to hold the town of le Bourg St-Léonard to the east of Argentan, but found it already occupied by American units. The SS battalions had first to fight their way into and capture the town before they could obey the order to hold it. In the confused and difficult fighting which marked the progress of that and successive days, 1st Battalion of 'Deutschland' was struck and dispersed by well-handled and aggressively led armoured units. 'Das Reich' was experiencing the symptoms of *Blitzkrieg*. One US thrust on 16 August drove through 'Deutschland' Regiment's front and Shermans reached the TAC HQ of 2nd Battalion before they were halted and destroyed.

On that day the Division was taken out of the line and ordered to reach the area of Vimoutiers, a town outside the noose which the Allies were placing around the German armies in Normandy. Supreme Command West, aware of the threat, planned that a strong force would either hold open an escape route or, if Allied pressure closed this, would attack to reopen it. The reason for the sudden move to Vimoutiers was now clear. II SS Panzer Corps was to be that strong force. As a consequence of being taken out of the pocket in good time 'Das Reich' was not one of the fifteen divisions which suffered and perished in the encirclement. Division was to see and experience much in the days to come, but at least it was spared the worst horrors described by General Eisenhower when he wrote that, ' . . . it was literally possible to walk for hundreds of yards at a time stepping on nothing but decaying flesh . . . '

The two divisions of II SS Panzer Corps drove through the pocket and by the 18th 'Das Reich' had reached its designated area. Although the divisional units were involved in brushes with Canadian troops in Trun the mass of 'Das Reich' escaped with little trouble. That the move had been made in good time was borne out by the War Diary of Fifth Panzer Army which records that by the evening of 18 August, ' . . . at the eastern exit of the bottleneck . . . no movement of any kind is possible due to the continual air attacks by fighter and fighter-bombers. These machines attack even individual soldiers. Nor is it possible to sort out the intermingled units . . . Communications have broken down . . . ' By the next day the encirclement by Allied units was complete but not in strength. A determined strike by an aggressive German formation would be certain to rupture it.

It will be appreciated that there is certain to be confusion when the intermingled units of one army, trying to fight their way out of a trap, clash with the troops of an enemy army endeavoring to hold them in. Let us, first of all, look at the situation as it was on the Allied side in those crucial days when the Americans, Canadians and Poles were striving to contain the trapped German formations and to prevent their escape between Trun and Chambois.

Field Marshal Montgomery directed the Polish Armoured Division to advance southwards on 18 August and close the pocket by capturing Chambois and the road through the village. The 2nd Polish Armoured Regiment, without waiting to refuel or take on fresh supplies of ammunition, set out in the gathering darkness. Its commander was aware that this thrust to link up with the Americans south of Chambois must take his units across roads which led out of the pocket towards Vimoutiers. He would also have known that his move would cut the roads along which German foot, wheeled or tracked units were streaming. Thus the Polish regiments would not only and inevitably become involved in furious firefights against enemies seeking to escape destruction but would be struck by 'Das Reich' as it made its thrust to break open the encirclement.

By mistake the squadron leading 2 Polish Armoured Brigade was misdirected towards les Champeaux and not to Chambois, a mistake which was not at first realized because in the dark of the night and in the heavily wooded terrain there were no distinguishing features. To confuse the situation further there were in that area two trignometrical points, both identified as Point 262. One of these was to the north and the other to the south of the Vimoutiers road. A mispronounced name, the intense darkness, coupled with unfamiliarity with the terrain and compounded by confusing, identical trignometrical points, all played their part in directing the Polish brigade, not southwards to Chambois but eastwards across the thrust line of 'Das Reich' Division.

During the morning of Saturday 19 August as Allied units in the Trun–Chambois area began to move cautiously towards one another, Field Marshal Model, the successor to von Kluge as Supreme Commander West, learned that the Canadians had taken Trun. His response was to order attacks to be launched by units inside the pocket and by the 2nd and 9th SS Divisions outside it. It is upon the fighting which raged in the small area of ground between those two places, and on the roads and in the hills to the east of them, that we must concentrate. The Polish 1 and 2 Armoured Brigades, together with the motorized light infantry battalions, were positioned on Mont-Ormel, a steep-sided ridge which the Poles nicknamed the 'Mace'. The head of the Mace lay north of the Chambois–Vimoutiers road and the shaft of the Mace crossed that road to the south. Viewed tactically, the 1,500 men and 80 Shermans constituting the Polish forces were in an almost impregnable position and one which, furthermore, dominated the German escape roads. It must be remembered, however, that the Polish armoured regiments had not been re-ammunitioned or supplied and that they were, as a result, ill-equipped to fight a long and wasteful battle. The Poles were isolated, in a sea of German formations who were determined to fight their way out of the trap. That sentence needs qualification. Not all the German units were seeking to escape from the ring. As we have seen, II SS Panzer Corps was committed to an attack that would smash gaps in the encirclement.

Orders to the Panzer Corps on 10 August were that its attack was to open at 05.00 hours on the following day. Corps decided that the main burden of the assault would be carried by 'Das Reich' which was placed on the left flank. Division proposed a three pronged assault. The emphasis would be with 'Der Führer' and the remaining panzers, on the right wing. The unit in the centre of the divisional line would be the recce battalion with 'Deutsch-land' on its left flank. As a protection to its open left wing, below 'Deutschland', Division created 'Blocking Force Reimann', a battle group made up of Flak and pioneer detachments. Divisional orders stressed that attacks would continue to be made until contact had been established with the units trapped in the Falaise pocket.

The task given to 3rd Battalion 'Der Führer' was to thrust quickly into the ring via Champosoult and Mont-Ormel. To achieve this the battalion would be carried in SPs and would have a Panther and two Panzer IVs in support. The battalion crossed its start-line at 05.45 hours and drove along a narrow road littered with smashed vehicles and teams of dead horses, victims of the

Allied fighter-bombers. It was, perhaps, the fact that the Allied aircraft were active over other sectors of the shrinking pocket that kept the battle group from 3rd Battalion free from attack during its advance. On the road towards its objective the battalion met individual German soldiers who had escaped from the trap; then these single soldiers became small groups and finally large numbers, most of whom, the SS noted with contempt, were not carrying their weapons. A post-battle report prepared by 3rd Battalion contains a very sober account of the opening of the day's fighting. '... After passing through Champosoult the leading unit, No. 11 Company, came under fire from both front and flank from an enemy on the heights at Vigan [sic] and at a road crossing below Point 262, app. 1 km from a junction on the road up which we are advancing ... '

Throughout the long hot afternoon of 20 August the grenadiers launched a series of attacks. In some places the sides of the 'Mace' were so steep that the SS men were bent double as they pulled at bushes and shrubbery to bring themselves towards the summit. At other places there were small open spaces in which, as some veterans recalled, there were little hollows which gave no shelter for they were swept by shells from the tank guns and by bullets from the Shermans' machine-guns. Against that murderous fire the grenadier advances faltered, but then quite suddenly, in a blind rage of desperation and frustration, the survivors regrouped and once again stormed forward into a last assault that was almost berserk in its primitive fury. That final charge died, as had all those preceding it, in a rain of shells and bullets.

In the following post-battle reports the words are sober and unemotional. It is left to the reader to imagine for himself the fury, the noise and the stench of the battle which raged around the Mace, along the roads and in the houses and villages around Trun and Chambois. The report of 3rd Battalion quoted above, continues:

'... The Company debusses and returns fire. It is then ordered to advance on both sides of the road to Vigan [sic] ... The enemy armoured vehicles [occupying the high ground] are unaware of this as they are facing either north or west in order to cover the escape routes from the pocket. It is clear that we must have reached the outer perimeter of the pocket and that when we gain the crossroads, about 1 km ahead, we shall be in touch with our troops trapped inside it. The attack was resumed at 08.00 hours. No. 10 Company on the right side of the road strikes in a south-westerly direction, crosses the Camambert road and attacks St-Léger-cour-Beaumon [sic], so as to dominate the northern and western area. No. 11 Company on the left of the road strikes south-eastwards towards Boijois [sic]. No. 9 Company supports No. 11 Company.

'Heavy enemy artillery and small-arms fire threaten to break up the attack. The battalion CO, Haupsturmführer Werner, decides to outflank the enemy on the right and goes over to where No. 10 Company is positioned and leads it onto the high ground around St-Léger. At that place we see 10 Shermans with their guns firing westwards, i.e., towards the pocket. They are standing in the open and broadside on to us at about 1 km distance. I issue orders to Obersturmführer Manz, No. 10 Company Commander, for his men to dig in against an anticipated enemy attack from the west or north, but that his men are not to show themselves.

'Our own panzers are still in Champosoult near 3rd Battalion HQ. I jog-trot back about 2 kms to TAC, outside which stands a Panther which has just been repaired. I order the platoon commander to bring his vehicle forward where it is urgently needed. This he refuses to do as he is awaiting orders from Panzer Regiment. I insist that he comply with my order but he still refuses and at last I draw my pistol and tell him that I am the one issuing the orders here. He agrees. I clamber on to the back of the turret and guide him to the point I had earlier left from which we can observe heavy shellfire falling upon Nos. 9 and 11 Companies. The Obersturmführer and I go forward on foot and I show him the Shermans still standing on Point 262 and firing into the pocket. The young commander issues orders and within a minute three enemy tanks have been knocked out. He continues firing until he has knocked out five Shermans and inflicted damage upon several others. I move to No. 9 Company.

'The two Panzer IVs have attacked the enemy armour at Vigan [sic] which takes the pressure off the two attacking Companies and I then move towards Point 262. I meet up with one of the platoons of No. 9 Company, some 200m west of the crossroads which is under heavy fire. The bulk of No. 9 Company has already crossed the road and are fighting in the woods on its far side, supported by a Panther and two Panzer IVs. These have taken up a position on the road to the right of the crossing. No. 11 Company is attacking the woods at Boijois [sic]. I crawl along the ditches until I reach the crossing which is under constant artillery fire. I see that our Panzers are engaging the enemy armour and call across the road to where there are a few men of No. 9 Company in a cutting. Together we creep forward until we contact the first of the men inside the pocket. They had just reached this place and had been preparing to move forward and out of the encirclement. I direct No. 9 Company to keep this gap open. The destruction of the five Shermans has led to other tanks being pulled back from Point 262, thus creating a new gap in the pocket. Through this streams a succession of units despite the heavy barrage which continues to fall in the area.

'Those who have escaped are either rested at regimental TAC HQ a farm some 2 kms west of Champosoult, or else sent on eastwards. So far the number has reached 4,000 men. Now vehicles begin to arrive from Chambois, passing through our front line and driving at full speed for our TAC HQ. The contents of cider barrels give the men a first refreshing drink. Many still have their personal weapons with them.

'At about 12.00 hours orders come for the battalion to continue the advance to Coudehard and Chambois, so as to extend the existing gap. The enemy who has now recovered from 3rd Battalion's attacks launches a series of counter-attacks which run parallel to our own line of attack but, he occasionally changes direction so as to strike into the flank of No. 10 Company. While No. 10 Company is heavily engaged, No. 9 is having a quieter time, always excepting the artillery and mortar fire, but No. 11 Company is also under intense pressure. It is clear that Division's orders to continue the advance cannot be carried out because the battalion is having enough difficulty in maintaining its present position against enemy counter-attacks. No. 10 Company is ordered to change front to face northwards and protect the road to the north. No. 9 Company in the woods around Boijois [sic] is to hold the gap open. No. 11 Company is to hold the area to the south of Menior [sic]. By 14.00 hours all Companies report that they are under growing pressure.

'The CO reports to Regiment which forwards it on to Division. "Pocket opened to the west of Champosoult. Touch gained with units escaping from the pocket and heading eastwards. The regiment requests Military Police units to control traffic to RHQ." Division is urged by Corps to continue with the attack upon Chambois but in view of the enemy's pressure this is not possible. Even if the battalion's attack were to gain ground it would be easy for the enemy to seal the gap behind 3rd Battalion because it is isolated and unsupported.

'The 3rd Battalion is ordered to send a fighting patrol into the pocket to bring out the Commander of Seventh Army, Colonel General Hausser, but that order is cancelled because Hausser, Meindl and three other divisional commanders, staff officers, regimental commanders and about 300 other officers together with some 5,000 men, have now escaped. Wisch of the LSSAH sends all his ambulances to evacuate the wounded coming out of the encirclement.

'In the afternoon Sturmbannführer Weidinger goes forward to 3rd Battalion's position at the road crossing to the south-west of Champosoult where he expects to meet the battalion. In a hollow he finds arms and equipment, obviously belonging to a group which had been captured as it tried to break out. He can find no sign of our own troops and assumes that 3rd Battalion has pulled back from the crossroads. The regimental commander is now in no man's land. Machine-pistol fire forces him to take cover and not until last light is he able to return to TAC HQ.'

On its sector 'Deutschland' Regiment crossed its start-lines at 05.30 hours on 20 August, with the aim of capturing St-Pierre-la-Rivière. No. 2 Battalion moved off in echelon formation along the road with its right wing touching 2nd 'Der Führer'. The 1st Battalion 'Deutschland' was in touch with recce battalion. The heavily wooded country through which the grenadiers had to force their way slowed the pace of the advance to only 500 metres in a couple of hours. During the advance the battalions were fired at by Shermans from 1st Polish Armoured Division, but these were attacked and destroyed at close range. The methodical advance by the 'Deutschland' battalions although slow, eventually brought them to a place where they, too, broke into the pocket. The time was 15.30 hours. The post-battle report of 'Deutschland'

Regiment recorded that among the troops who came through their gap were Fallschirmjaeger marching in step and singing, with their officers leading the shattered companies as well as the divisional headquarters group of 12th SS Panzer Division 'Hitler Jugend'.

It will be recalled that the reconnaissance battalion held the centre of the divisional attacking front, and the following is a brief summary of the laconically worded report written by the commanding officer of that unit. From his words it is difficult to realize that what he described was fighting of an intensity which had not, until that time, been met with in north-west Europe, as well as situations and a loss of life unimagined by anyone who was not in the pocket or who did not, after the fighting was over, see the results of the Allied air and ground assaults.

'... At this critical time "DR" received an order to prevent the enemy from capturing Trun and to prevent the enemy from striking into the flank of the encircled German forces ... The Recce battalion flung itself into an attack against enemy armour north-east of Trun, the battalion making its way with difficulty through the press of vehicle columns and marching units fleeing out of the encirclement. Following a short O Group, the 2nd Battalion of "DF" advanced and seized the north-easterly road hard to the north of Trun. The Recce battalion, together with the SP battalion struck into the flank of strong enemy tank formations to the north-west of Trun. Six British tanks were destroyed within a few minutes, but the enemy, ignoring his losses, maintained the assault with undiminished fury and lost a further three tanks. By interrogating an enemy DR who had lost his way we learned that the 1st Polish Armoured Division was on our sector. No other unit which we had met since the invasion fought so well as these Polish formations. Enemy assaults ended during the hours of darkness. During the following morning [21st] the enemy made a number of armoured probes, indications that a major attack would not be long in coming. No orders were received from either Division or Corps. We were already outflanked by enemy armour but did beat off all his infantry assaults. It was the opinion of the commanding officer of the Recce battalion that his group had now carried out its given task and he decided to try and gain touch with Division.

'The battalion had smashed a breach at Chambois and had halted enemy assaults in that area. Obergruppenführer Hausser and an escorting officer escaped and reached Recce battalion HQ where Dr Rüff bandaged the General. Hausser was completely out of touch with the current military situation outside the pocket and did not know of the Allied invasion of southern France. He refused to be evacuated and set out for Corps HQ in order to knit the front together.

'Deutschland' Regiment and the other formations had opened the pocket and through the gaps which had been created there poured a flood of men from a miscellany of units. As we have seen from other post-battle reports the 'Das Reich' units held open the gaps throughout the 20th and then for much of 21 August. In the early afternoon of that day the numbers of men escaping declined sharply and by 16.00 hours had almost totally ceased. The Division could be pleased with its efforts, for through its breaches 20,000 soldiers out of a total of 50,000 had escaped. Included in that total was General Wisch, the commander of 'Leibstandarte' Division, as well as Generals Funk and Mahlmann. One Army lieutenant who had broken through with his Panther detachment, placed this under SS command and performed excellently.

With its task ended Division began a slow retreat eastwards, covered by an outpost line made up of the recce battalion, the SP battalion and Blocking Group Reimann. The post-battle report of the recce battalion concludes with this paragraph: 'Following a zig-zag course the battalion . . . moved towards Rouen. Near Elboeuf it, together with "DF" regiment, was once again involved in heavy fighting. The excellent traffic control across the Rouen bridge had been organized by Wisliceny, the CO of "Deutschland" Regiment . . . The Recce battalion, together with several SPs, was active on outpost duties at St-Etienne, to the south of Rouen, until orders came for it to cross the bridge that night.'

The Division's participation in the battle for Normandy and in the Falaise pocket, was at an end.

The autumn of 1944, saw the German armies in the west, withdrawing under Allied pressure, back through France and Belgium, until at last the shattered formations were knitted into a firm front where they prepared themselves to hold the western frontier of the Fatherland against their Anglo-American enemies.

The part played by 'Das Reich' in that fighting retreat began when the divisional units crossed the Seine near Elboeuf, at the end of August, withdrawing on a line that was either northwards or eastwards. There was only the occasional respite from the closely pursuing enemy; such as the short defensive battle along the River Maas from 5 to 7 September. It was clear that the line along the Maas could not be held for long. The weakness lay not in the SS divisional area where the assaults of the enemy were held, albeit with difficulty because the companies were so reduced in numbers. Then, at last, reinforcements came. The recce battalions took on charge two companies of naval volunteers; men who had sailed the special craft; one-man torpedoes or two-man submarines. Another unit which came in to flesh out the depleted recce battalion was an anti-aircraft machine-gun battalion manned by the Reichsarbeitsdienst.

The weakness in the defence of the River Maas was on those sectors held by less determined units. There the Allies had soon forced a crossing of the river compelling 'Das Reich' to conform in a withdrawal to the Schnee–Eifel region of the Westwall (the Siegfried Line). This slow retreat was carried out through difficult country and always under pressure from American tank and infantry groups. To add to the problems Belgian partisan attacks grew in number and size, harrying the SS detachments as they struggled through the dense woods and along the poor roads of the Schnee–Eifel. By 9 September Division was pulling back across that area of the Ardennes over which it was to advance during the Battle of the Bulge. At 15.45 hours on 11 September 'Das Reich' crossed the German frontier. There its units began to occupy bunkers and positions in the Westwall and, lacking instructions from a superior authority, the CO of 'Der Führer' ordered his battalions to take up positions between Brandscheid and Leidenborn. The regiment was thus covering three times a normal length of front; 16 instead of 5 kilometres.

To increase divisional numbers a battalion-sized battle group from 'Hitler Jugend', the 12th SS Division, was taken on strength and put into the battle line between 'Deutschland' on the right flank and Recce on the left. There were other and less welcome detachments. Otto Weidinger describes how 'A battalion of Russians came on to "DF" establishment and was posted to 2nd Battalion, although it was obviously unusable. The men abandoned some bunkers taking, according to reports, both their weapons and their NCOs with them. It is inexplicable that a battalion of such men should have been used on the German side.' Other replacements included Luftwaffe squadrons that had been converted to infantry status for lack of aircraft and who considered their new posting as a sort of punishment. They were quickly lost in the destructive fighting in the Siegfried Line.

Although American historians and military writers make a great deal of the Siegfried Line campaign, the system of block houses and bunkers which comprised its defences was not the frightful wall of death as popularly supposed. Many pillboxes had been used for years as storehouses by the local farmers who were reluctant to return them to their military owners and a great many bunkers could not be used because the firing slits which had been designed for the weapons of 1939, were too small for those in service in 1944. To add to these deficiencies there were not enough men to garrison every one of the strongpoints. In view of these, and other shortcomings, Otto Weidinger wondered why the Americans, who had been closely pressing the retreating German forces, made no attempt to 'bounce' the Siegfried Line by a direct and massive assault. Certainly, when 'Das Reich', took up its positions in the West Wall, the weaknesses would have made a strong defence impossible. Whether Hitler knew of the run-down condition of the West Wall is not known, but in an Order of the Day issued on 15 September, he declared that the wall was of such decisive importance to the battle for Germany that every strongpoint was to be held to the last round and the last man.

An example of how closely the grenadiers obeyed that order is Otto Weidinger's account of the last action fought by men of his No. 10 Company. 'Der Führer' was holding the Krefeld area and the main American effort came in against 3rd Battalion. The US infantry had suffered heavy losses in their attacks against the pillboxes of the Siegfried Line and sought a tactic to take them out. They knew that the small grenadier garrisons had no anti-tank guns and that weapons, such as the Panzerfaust, could not be used inside the confined space of the concrete boxes.

Exploiting these deficiencies the Americans brought up Sherman bulldozer tanks which scooped up the earth outside the bunkers blocking the firing slits. The waiting US infantry outside the pillbox entrance then shot down the grenadiers as they tried to escape. A bunker, held by men of No. 10 Company, came under attack and the NCO in charge telephoned for help. Weidinger listened, distraught, as the NCO described what was happening. The regimental commander was powerless. The whole regimental front was under intense attack and he had neither reserves nor armoured support except for one single panzer. Over the telephone Weidinger heard how the American advance was covered by flame-throwing detachments and that the pillbox was shaking as the US infantry detonated high-explosive charges on its outside walls. The surviving grenadiers tried to fight their way out using MPs and hand-grenades, but were forced back to make a last stand in the bunker's living-quarters. Over the telephone came the NCO's final words: 'The room is filled with fire from the flame-throwers. The heat is frightful. There are flames and smoke everywhere. I cannot hold out any longer . . .' Then the line went dead. To the last bullet and to the last man had been no empty oath for the grenadiers of No. 10 Company.

During the second week of October orders came for the Divisional units to be relieved from the line. The depleted 3rd Battalion 'Der Führer' was first to leave and was followed by 2nd Battalion on the 20th. In time the whole Division was taken out and rested, replacements were received and the lessons of the past months of conflict evaluated. Slowly, 'Das Reich' began to build up its strength and to retrain for the new battles it would have to fight.

The Ardennes

At 23.30 hours on 11 November, 'Das Reich' Division, which had been resting and refitting in Sauerland, was ordered to move westwards. It was to take part in 'Watch on the Rhine' a new German offensive, better known as the Battle of the Bulge. Hitler's plan was for three armies to strike out of the Ardennes and by D-Day plus 7 to have captured Antwerp, thereby separating the British armies to the north of that port from the Americans to its south. The Allied forces were then to be destroyed in succession. Hitler forecast that during the operation fog and low clouds would nullify Allied air supremacy and allow the panzers to roar across Belgium without fear of air attack, refuelling as they advanced from captured supply dumps. The main thrust of 'Watch on the Rhine' would be made by Sixth SS Panzer Army on whose establishment was II SS Panzer Corps, consisting of 'Das Reich' and 'Hohenstaufen' Divisions. After several postponements D-Day for the operation was finally set for 16 December and H-Hour at 05.30 hours.

Although the movement order to 'Das Reich' to cross the Rhine was issued on 11 November, it was not until the 24th that the last contingents of the Division reached the western bank. There it encountered the familiar situation of having units taken away to serve with other formations. On this occasion the detached units were formed into battle groups to defend Corps' flank against possible enemy attack. 'Das Reich' moved by stages to its concentration area where, on 18 December, two days after the new offensive had opened, orders came for II SS Panzer Corps to follow the spearhead unit, I SS Panzer Corps, with the aim of either strengthening the thrust of the sister Corps or guarding its flank. A further weakening of the divisional effort came when an armoured car company of the recce battalion was detached and placed at the disposal of II SS Panzer Corps HQ with orders to carry out reconnaissance in the breach which it was anticipated the German offensive would by that time have made in the American lines.

Lack of space prevents me from analysing the reasons for the failure of the German offensive except to say that any enterprise, predicated upon bad weather and upon capturing enemy fuel supplies to maintain its advance, stands on brittle glass. 'Watch on the Rhine' depended for its success upon both those factors. Because of shortages within Germany the amounts of fuel which were actually issued to the fighting units were quite inadequate. General Staff calculations were that 12 fillings of petrol per vehicle was the minimum amount needed to cover the duration of the battle. That number was calculated on the figure of one filling equalling 100 kilometres of driving on dry and level roads. Instead of twelve fillings only three were in fact issued. In addition there was insufficient ammunition for the artillery or tank guns; there was a shortage of winter clothing and boots, and the manpower strength of 'Das Reich' was 10 per cent below establishment. Although the attack towards Antwerp was planned as a seven-day operation, supplies were issued for just five days.

To give an illustration of the deficiencies affecting 'Das Reich', the 1st Battalion of 'Deutschland' Regiment had no motor transport and the grenadiers were mounted on bicycles, most of which had to be repaired before they could be issued. That such an élite Division as 'Das Reich', could be committed to battle 10 per cent below establishment and without its basic needs in mechanical vehicles is evidence of the state to which the German armed forces had been reduced by the end of 1944. It comes as no surprise, therefore, to learn that 'Watch on the Rhine', an operation dependant upon bad weather and undertaken by weakened, poorly equipped units, with uncertain fuel supplies, failed to gain the objectives given it. But then no senior German military commander had ever considered Hitler's ambitious plan as having any hope of success.

Within two days of the operation opening, the narrow, insufficient and inadequate roads of the Ardennes were jammed with lorries that had run out of fuel and had been abandoned. The roads were jammed for miles and, as a result, the flow of reinforcements and supplies to the units in action was reduced to a trickle.

Throughout 19 December the units of the Division rested and awaited orders to move forward although, given the traffic jams, this would not be an easy directive to obey. Then, in the early evening of 20 December, a signal from Corps directed that the mass of the Division, having relieved 560th Volks Grenadier Division at the Baraque de Fraiture crossroads, was to fling back the Americans defending that tactically important area and then to advance as far as Manhay, with the aim of establishing a bridgehead at Bomal. With those objectives gained the Division was then to strike for Erezee from where it would have an uninterrupted drive to the Maas. Given the fuel shortages such an ambitious plan had no hope of success. Because there was no fuel the Division's wheeled and tracked units were held, immobile, for the whole of 21 December. Had there been fuel the élan of the SS Division and the confused state of the American defence in the area might well have taken the attack forward to the Maas. But already, within a few days of the offensive opening, the belief that 'Watch on the Rhine' could be fuelled from US dumps was proving to be false and as a consequence the German advance ground to a succession of halts as units waited for the arrival of petrol-bowsers which had, in most cases, filled up at dumps in Cologne. This fuel and time-wasting extravagance played its part in causing the offensive to fail.

That delay of a whole day gave the US forces time to regroup and bring forward new troops to oppose the German drive. The American formations holding the sector which 'Das Reich' Division had been ordered to capture had used those hours of inactivity to put the villages, hamlets and even individual houses into a state of high defence. Tank regiments of the 3rd and 7th Armored Divisions as well as the élite paratroopers of 82nd Airborne were rushed forward to contest the German assault, and against such formations the anticipated swift defence deteriorated into a hard slog to capture a series of strongly defended, fortified villages. The battlefield on which 2nd SS Panzer Division was to fight extended across an area from the Baraque crossroads to Vaux Chavanne and from Grandmenil to Malempre. In that small area and for much of the offensive 'Das Reich' was to advance, fight, bleed and then withdraw when the German forces committed to 'Watch on the Rhine' were forced back under the relentless pressure of the American ground and air forces.

The first fuel trucks arrived on 22 December and with its vehicles at last tanked up, Division prepared to advance. Although the first stage of the attack, the assault by 'Der Führer' Regiment upon the Baraque de Fraiture crossroads, opened at 15.00 hours on 23 December, it is a smaller assault which went in later that day that is first described. This operation was a preliminary to the night attack which 'Deutschland' Regiment was to make against the village of Odeigne. That regiment and 1st Panzer Battalion had failed once to take the village and to ensure that a second assault would succeed the regimental commander combined the pioneer company, two AFVs mounting 2cm Flak and two platoons of the divisional Storm Company into an assault group. By 16.15 hours the pioneers and storm platoons were in position, some 900 metres to the south of Odeigne. There had been scant time to carry out reconnaissance but the ground was believed to be covered with bushes and clumps of trees and to dip steeply down to a frozen stream before climbing again towards the village. At 16.30 hours the Flak vehicles opened fire, with the intention of confusing the enemy as to the direction of the attack. Exploiting that diversion the pioneers and storm troops charged into the village and by 21.30 hours Hans von Twistern, the commander of the pioneer company, reported that the village had been taken and that a hot meal had been served to his men. One feature common to the pioneer and grenadier casualties was frostbite brought on as a result of the attacking troops having to wade through the stream below the village.

While 'Deutschland' was fighting to the west of the crossroads 'Der Führer' regiment was preparing to seize that important road junction from the US infantry and armoured detachments which were holding it. The 'Der Führer' commanding officer planned an attack to be made from two directions and for it to be preceded by a short but intense barrage upon the crossroads and the Manhay road. The 2nd Grenadier Battalion, supported by Panzer IVs from No. 7 Panzer Company and reinforced by the Infantry Gun Company and part of No. 14 (Flak) Company was to attack frontally up the road to the objective. Once the attention of the US defenders was fixed on that thrust, 3rd Battalion, carried in SPs, and supported by an SP Company, would strike from the west.

The attack opened at 15.00, but made only slow progress against the Americans who fought bitterly to hold the crossroads and it was not until well into the night that the objective was finally gained. Those SS companies which went on from the crossroads to fight in the wooded area around Malempre were involved in bitter, close-quarter struggles against US soldiers whose orders had been to hold the area at all costs.

Among the successes of that day can be included those of the panzer and the SP battalions in destroying 17 Shermans and 34 half-tracks for a loss of four Panzer IVs. It was the grenadier battalions that had suffered shockingly high casualties. The intensity of the day's fighting as well as the scale of losses incurred were to be the pattern for the following five days and nights of battle, but despite the exhausted state of the 'Der Führer' grenadiers they could be given no time to rest. Now that the American hold on the crossroads had been broken the enemy had be pursued relentlessly. The 2nd Battalion attacked Malempre village and 3rd Battalion struck up the road and into the woods north-west of Odeigne. No. 7 Panzer Company, which had been attached to 'Der Führer' for its assault, then rejoined the main body of the panzer regiment concentrated around the crossroads north-west of Belle Haye. The 1st Battalion of 'Der Führer' took no part in the day's battle because it had to foot march a great distance to reach the combat area and when it arrived, late in the night, its grenadiers were in no condition to be committed to battle. Corps' orders for 24 December were that the 'Das Reich' was to continue its efforts to capture the Manhay–Grandmenil sector.

The two battalions of 'Der Führer' that had been committed to the fighting in the woods around Malempre were soon locked in bitter battle with the Americans and there, too, the SS casualties brought into the regimental aid posts included not only men with gunshot and shrapnel wounds but others who were suffering from frostbite and the effects of exposure.

'Deutschland' Regiment, which had been ordered to capture another road junction south-east of Odeigne, put 3rd Battalion into a night attack and as the grenadiers stood waiting for the order to advance they experienced the tragedy of taking needless casualties when shells from the Division's artillery barrage fell short. The attack finally rolled with the regimental infantry gun company supporting 3rd Battalion and the pioneers employed on mine-lifting and other duties. The pioneer company commander was a keen diarist and described the operations carried out during Christmas in the following entries.

'24th December. Christmas Eve. The day dawned foggy and damp. The Regiment is to attack during the coming night in collaboration with 1st Battalion of the Panzer regiment. Our objectives: Manhay – Grandmenil and a break through westwards to Erezee. Part of the Company . . . detailed for minesweeping duties and for reconnaissance patrols while the remainder are to be used as circumstances dictate. In the early evening a patrol was sent out to locate crossing places for the panzers across the stream which runs to the north-west of Odeigne. Another patrol is to carry out a recce towards the road ' crossing at Belle Haye.

'The weather changed and became a bright, moonlit night. The patrol reached Odeigne leaving the cover of the woods to the west of Belle Haye and passed across undulating fields and meadows. It was not the nicest way to spend Christmas Eve, moving over open ground and without the protection of white camouflage clothing. The men could be seen as dark spots and were soon under fire . . . The patrol withdrew bringing back three wounded; one of them serious . . . That bloody outcome of the recce patrol dampened our Christmas Eve. Our thoughts were with the mine-lifting group. The ration party arrived and had also brought mail from home – bridges to link us with our loved ones. Our Company HQ was in the same house as regimental TAC HQ. There was a piano in a large room and one of our comrades began to play a carol. There was some half-hearted singing but we had no Christmas spirit in us – our regiment and 1st Battalion of the panzer regiment were in action. Reports flowed in and during the night both Manhay and Grandmenil were reported taken. The enemy's resistance had been bitter and he employed masses of artillery and armour. The Regiment had suffered heavy losses.

'25th December 1944. Christmas Day. The day opened with bright sunshine and a strong frost. Sounds of artillery fire came from both Manhay and Grandmenil. Fighter-bombers and artillery spotting aircraft swooped and attacked any vehicle or movement on the roads or on the open fields. Apart from these detachments which were in action with 2nd Battalion at Grandmenil, the remainder of the Company did not go into action.

'26th December. Second day of Christmas. We marched at dawn and reached TAC HQ of 1st Panzer Battalion. Signs of heavy fighting everywhere. Enemy artillery fire forced us to take cover. At about 08.30 hours we resumed our marched to Grandmenil . . . The road between Manhay and Grandmenil was under fire from both artillery and tank guns. We took cover with some men of the Regiment and a few prisoners, behind an isolated house. Suddenly the enemy's fire stopped. We went on and reached Grandmenil. Some 200 metres south of the place the enemy barrage opened up again. We took cover in the first house but soon moved because Ami phosphorus shells set it alight.

'During a pause in the firing we moved into another house outside which stood a couple of panzers. Inside it we found some forty badly wounded 2nd Battalion comrades. The blast from a massive explosion just outside the house lifted the concrete ceiling of the cellar where the wounded were being treated into the air and settled again without breaking up. That must have been a pretty sight for the badly wounded to see. We rushed out of the cellar to find out what had happened. The partially camouflaged panzers which had been standing on the road had been attacked by fighter-bombers. One bomb had fallen between one of the panzers and our house and had exploded leaving a huge crater. The panzer itself showed no signs of damage. Then about 12.15 the shelling stopped and the Ami infantry began to attack. The enemy advanced with a mainly tank force up the road to Manhay. All hell was let loose to the west of Grandmenil but the enemy's furious attack was halted by our regiment . . . We had to get back to Battalion TAC HQ and jumped over fences and ran across gardens in our haste. As we reached a smithy we were fired at from the right flank. A single enemy tank had broken through . . . and was in a garden about 125 metres away. Its machine-gunner must have seen us for he concentrated his fire on the brick pillar at the smithy entrance. He seemed to have an endless belt of ammunition. The pillar was about 40cms wide and machine-gun bursts tore out whole bricks. Then the tank's main armament opened up. The armour piercing shots passed right through the smithy's rear wall. Each time the gun fired two of my comrades poked their heads out of a door in the farm house and beckoned me join them. That was impossible. Had I done so I would have walked right into the burst of machine-gun fire. I decided to wait until the enemy machine-gunner changed belts. The next shot from the tank's gun was an HE round. There was smoke, dust and then shrapnel whirled around. After that shot the tank's machine-gunner stopped firing. I was unhurt and raced across the yard but in my haste fell into the midden. We three rushed round the corner intending to attack the Ami tank, but the round of HE it had fired had been the last shot it would ever fire. A Corporal from 2nd Battalion had destroyed it with a Panzerfaust.

'We reached 2nd Battalion's TAC HQ and I reported in. The CO told me that the battalion was surrounded, that the Amis had attacked and had captured Manhay. The battalion was practically out of ammunition and supplies. Thank God, the Amis did not attack again although artillery fire continued to fall . . . In view of the shortages of ammunition, fuel and rations our own attack had had to be called off but we still had to fight our way out of the encirclement. The badly wounded were left behind with some medical orderlies. Radios and vehicles were destroyed.

'We made our move, covered by a rear guard, but did not in fact have to fight our way out. Reconnaissance found a gap in the southern part of the enemy's ring and by midnight 2nd Battalion and the attached groups of No. 16 Company were approaching the enemy lines. Silently we filtered through the gap, marched across meadowland, over a small stream and reached at last a large wooded area. It was there we gained touch with our own forces. At dawn we moved north of Odeigne out of the forest and reported to Regiment . . . on 28th the Company moved to a new battle area where it regrouped and was employed as an infantry detachment.'

To record one particular highlight of the five-day battle in the Baraque – Manhay sector, it is necessary to go back again to Christmas Eve – and Oberscharführer Barkmann's panzer raid through the American lines. At 22.00 hours on 24 December, No. 4 Company of 1st Panzer Battalion, in which he was serving, moved out to capture the village of Manhay. As the double column of panzers approached the crossroads at Belle Haye it was overwhelmed by a storm of US artillery fire which knocked out the leading pair of vehicles. For a time it seemed as if that barrage had halted the panzer advance, but then Barkmann ordered his Panther forward and opened a run of victories. His first victim was a Sherman which he mistook in the dark for one of his own Company's vehicles. By the time he realized his mistake he was too close to kill the US vehicle and had to reverse the Panther before he could open fire. Two more US tanks met on the road were attacked and knocked out. Then, as he turned a corner on the serpentine, country road Barkmann saw a line of nine Shermans drawn up in a field. These he approached at normal speed to avert suspicion and quickly manoeuvred his Panther into a position from which only one of the Shermans would be able to fire at him. Before he could attack the US tanks their crews abandoned the machines and fled. Rather than waste ammunition on the deserted vehicles he left them to be destroyed by his comrades following some way behind him and continued his advance.

The Panther then swung on to the main road to Manhay and Barkmann roared past columns of retreating American soldiers none of whom identified his vehicle as an enemy. His good luck did not long endure and on the Liège road Barkmann encountered a mass of vehicles of US 2nd Armored Division whose actions soon made it clear that the Panther had been recognized. The SS panzer commandant ordered smoke to be laid and sought to escape behind the screen. As his Panther rolled forward a jeep charged him with its driver making signs that he should halt. The Panther ignored the signs, struck the jeep and then collided with a Sherman. Both AFVs were then locked together and to add to the tension the Panther's engine cut out. There were several anxious moments before it roared back into life and when it did

Barkmann's driver reversed the vehicle, pulled the heavy Panther away from the American tank and raced up the road. A Sherman took up the pursuit but was fired at, hit and destroyed. Far away in the distance Barkmann could hear the sounds of battle. It was the panzers of his Battalion forcing the Americans back into Grandmenil and Vaux Chavanne. In Manhay itself thirty undamaged Shermans lay abandoned by their crews. Barkmann realized that his run of luck could not last, turned off the main road and drove through deep, snowy woods until he had regained touch with the battalion.

Diary entries, earlier in this chapter, written by a pioneer officer of 'Deutschland' Regiment are complemented by the diary notes of an officer named Freihoffer, who served in a grenadier battalion of that regiment. The factual tone of the entries is sometimes laid aside and replaced by bitterness when Freihoffer compares the American prodigious expenditure of artillery shells with the meagre barrages fired by his own side. As with the other diary extracts Freihoffer's open on 23 December, the Division's first day of battle in Operation 'Watch on the Rhine'.

'Saturday 23rd December, 1944 . . . We can hear the sounds of battle. Machine-guns fire, the flat explosion of hand-grenades and salvoes from the Nebelwerfers are everyday music and when our artillery does open fire then the Americans respond with a hurricane from hundreds of medium and heavy guns . . .

'Tomorrow is Christmas Eve. We stand in the courtyard [of the farm in which his unit was billeted] and strain our ears and eyes trying to penetrate the clinging fog which changes shape and makes it difficult to estimate distance by sound . . . High above our heads there is a monotonous droning as heavy bombers fly eastward to drop their bombs on German cities. Peace on earth, goodwill to all men ?????

'A sudden barrage falls on a road crossing in front of us. Two shells land in the infantry slit trenches killing three men and badly wounding five others. Stretcher-bearers are sent out to take away the dead and wounded. We hope that they will return with food dixies and ammunition which is running very low.

'Sunday 24th December. Once the road block near Belle Haye was removed we set up TAC HQ in Odeigne, a small village. It is cold and there are frequent snow showers. Now and again the skies clear and the sun comes out. But only for short periods, thank God. Not long enough for the Allied fighter-bombers to become active. This sort of weather grounds them because they cannot see in the fog. Strehl, our Company Clerk, has lit a fire in the grate to warm his frozen fingers. The enemy notices the thin column of smoke and opens fire. When the barrage ends we have more fresh air coming through new holes in the roof and the walls. Strehl now warms his fingers by rubbing them between his knees.

'Because of the traffic jams in the Ardennes area fuel and ammunition for the panzers is not coming up, to say nothing of rations. The Quartermaster is disappointed that all he can offer us on Christmas Eve is a meatless stew . . .

After the meal I go with my runner on an inspection of the individual Companies. With a little effort one could imagine that the Very lights and the fiery fountains where shells are exploding could be the lights of Christmas Eve.

'Monday 25th December, 1944. With panzer support we drive the enemy out of his positions. He withdraws slowly towards Manhay and Grandmenil under the cover of a barrage fired by hundreds of guns. There is absolutely no cover. Our guns in a orgy of spendthrift recklessness reply with 8 rounds – and then cease fire. We have to save ammunition. But the order to attack has raised our spirits. It is much better than lying about in slit-trenches in the cold and subject to the enemy's savage bombardments. Some men are brought back suffering from frostbite. There are not enough felt boots to go round. During the evening the enemy is driven out of Manhay and Grandmenil and for tonight at least we have dry billets. We are guarded by only a thin outpost line on the edge of the village . . . An attack has been ordered for tomorrow. The objective is Mormont. This means that we have to be in position in good time. But the tanks and the artillery have almost no fuel or ammunition left.

'Three years ago we would probably have stormed forward during the night in order not to allow the enemy any time to recover. But now after nearly five years of savage fighting things move much more slowly . . . The men are all right but tanks and guns need fuel and shells and it does not matter how much fighting spirit there is, without those two things nothing much can be achieved. "Fuel supplies can be obtained from the enemy petrol point in Dinant"; that or something like that was in the order issued on the eve of the offensive on 16 December. What still gives us hope for a successful outcome of the war are the secret weapons and the determination not to let our country fall into the hands of the Reds. We still have confidence in the inventive genius of our scientists. It is true that in the autumn we often had to take cover from VIs which were landing prematurely, but then we saw the smoke trails of the V2. One of these missiles fell in Hellesheim and the blast effect of the explosion was terrifying. And hadn't we seen, in the days before the offensive opened, jet fighters which roared over our heads flying at unbelievable speeds. Too little and too late, say our pessimists but on one thing we are all agreed. We do not want our country to be under the heel of the Soviets. We have seen the "Soviet Paradise" . . .

'Tuesday 26th December, 1944. The attack by "D" 1st Battalion along the wooded heights is brought to a halt by the enemy's fire. The men press themselves into the ground and wait for the hurricane to pass over them. Here and there figures rise and then sink back. One senses rather than hears the cry for stretcher-bearers, but for the moment no medical orderly can attend to them. Those orderlies who have not themselves been hit are busy with the wounded lying alongside the road. I leave the battalion signals platoon at a point some two kilometres away and go forward on a motor-cycle combination with the driver and my runner. It is a difficult journey because the road is cratered with shell holes and fallen trees.

'In a cellar, 50 metres behind the front line, I interrogate a wounded officer of US 7th Armored Division. His tank fell victim to one of our Panzerfausts. His knee is shattered but the rest of the crew have escaped injury. He is given a morphine injection to kill the pain and answers my questions casually. "Back home they told us the Waffen SS was very cruel and killed prisoners." Now he is astounded that he receives the same treatment as one of our own men and hands round his Chesterfield cigarettes. The motor-cycle combination takes him to the main dressing-station. As Hauptsturm-führer Meisenbacher and I reach the corner of the house to watch the companies going into action, the house seems to explode. A direct hit by a heavy-calibre shell smashes half of it and out of the ruins rises a great cloud of smoke and dust. We are both untouched and start looking through the ruins for survivors. My runner and some stretcher-bearers help us. The next salvo passes over the house and explodes in a field. The American fire moves farther and farther back and we free the wounded from the rubble of the house. The usual type of injuries. I bring the ambulance farther forward to carry the wounded to it in the motor-cycle combo. It is a hairy business in such a barrage but where is there any safe place in such a situation. Our artillery is silent. The guns have run out of ammunition.

'We finally move forward. Hauptsturmführer Stockhammer's No. 2 Company attacks through the woods and opens up enfilade fire against the tanks, the anti-tank guns and the machine-gun posts on the bend in the road. Bastian's No. 1 Company gives covering fire. Prisoners are brought in and so is a Sherman tank. Loose, our Adjutant, looking out of his cellar window sees the outline of the tank with its foreign markings and is seized with a desire to demonstrate his bravery. He snatches a Panzerfaust from one of the runners, races outside and opens fire. Luckily he only hits the track. The curses of the crew accompany Loose back into his cellar . . . There are dead and wounded lying all over the place – our own and American . . . The skies have cleared and the fighter-bombers are back again showering their victims with fragmentation bombs and cannon-fire. We press ourselves to the ground and do not look up. Suddenly Meisenbacher shouts out, "Get forward, get forward. They can't hit us there." He is right. In those places where the pilots and the artillery observers cannot distinguish between friend and foe, there is safety. Towards 16.00 hours the loss of visibility halts the fighter-bomber attacks and eventually the American artillery ceases fire.'

The Americans facing the 2nd SS Panzer Division had, by the end of Christmas Day, regrouped their forces. During the afternoon of the 26th, having absorbed and defeated the attack by 2nd Battalion of 'Deutschland' Regiment, they went over to a counter-offensive which captured Manhay and surrounded the grenadier companies that were holding Grandmenil. The regimental commander authorized 2nd Battalion to break out southwards. Freihoffer's account continues.

'A runner comes forward with a report that enemy tanks have cut the road. We wait in vain for relief. The situation is unclear because our radio has been smashed by shellfire. On the horizon we can see long columns of enemy vehicles moving forward and not being fired at. Perhaps we should attack. It would certainly cause confusion among the Americans, but what could we do after that? A few more dead Americans will not decide the outcome of the War. Elements of "Der Führer" Regiment as well as our 1st Battalion are cut off. Otto Weidinger, the commanding officer of our sister Regiment, is among them. I am ordered to establish how many men we still have and to organize the positions. There are 60 of us armed with carbines, four machine-guns and two Panzerfausts. Well, we will not be able to put up much of a show. There is a short discussion and we decide to rush in one single group across the road which the Americans have cut. As we emerge from the woods we see on the road rows of American tanks. There is no way out of here. In the moonlight we see, half-left of us, two, three steel helmets. Are the wearers Americans or Germans? I am told to lead the column so I will be the first to find out. Before starting I try to make a joke of it. If the Americans take me prisoner I'll send a card from Texas. I slide across to where the group of helmets is. I am quite calm now and begin to count the number of men. In front about forty, behind them more. There is the sound of voices coming out of the woods. Is that the American line? I go a few more paces and suddenly meet a Captain. I can think of nothing else to say but "Are you American?" "Yeah," is his stupid answer to my stupid question. The Americans look at the long line of soldiers behind me, all of them clearly visible in the bright moonlight. The end of the column is still in the woods.

'How easy it would have been for the Americans to mow us down with their machine-guns. Nothing happens. The Americans seem to be paralysed despite their superior numbers. "You want to fight?" I ask the Captain. Once again I could think of nothing better to ask. "No, we don't," and I finish the session with a short "OK" and with a casual salute walk back to my men. I can feel eyes boring into my back as I walk away. Weidinger gives us the order to "weasel" our way past the two enemy tanks. We have about 200 metres to cover before we can get into the next patch of woodland where we will find cover. Then the shells start to land. One killed and four wounded that flight cost us. The enemy guns continue to fire on the spot where we vanished into the dark woods. Towards 4 in the morning we are challenged by the outposts of 560th Volksgrenadier Division. We've made it. Well, that was Christmas. The sixth Christmas of the War.'

Throughout 27 December, American attacks continued to drive the grenadier regiments back towards the Fraiture crossroads. The battle line swung to and fro as the soldiers of both sides attacked or were attacked; advanced or were repulsed. To the grenadiers it was clear that the offensive which had opened with such great expectations, could not now succeed. At senior level it had long been accepted that Sixth SS Panzer Army was no longer the spearhead of 'Watch on the Rhine'. The advance was being carried forward by Fifth Panzer Army. But in an effort to revitalize its sector, Sixth SS Army ordered a regrouping and a concentration of all available units. As part of that action 'Das Reich' was taken from its sector of the line and put in to the south of the L'Oourthe, between 560th Volksgrenadier Division and the Army's 2nd Panzer Division. Once again divisional units were detached to serve with other formations; the panzer recce battalion, an artillery battalion and two grenadier companies with the 12th SS 'Hitler Jugend' Division; 'Der Führer' Regiment, less its 3rd Battalion, was with 560th VG Division and that regiment's 3rd Battalion was attached to 9th SS 'Hohenstaufen' Division.

Towards the end of December the scale of operations on the sector held by 'Das Reich' Division was reduced to patrol activity and those attacks which the divisional units did launch were of a minor nature. Corps still had ideas for a swift offensive operation but this came to naught. This could not be said of the Americans whose assaults were frequent, heavy and well-supported by tank gun fire, artillery barrages and air assault. The US units were clearly building up to a major offensive. An anecdote which one of the gunners in 1st Battalion 'Das Reich' divisional artillery regiment sent in, can be considered today, half a century later, as humorous. It may not have been so funny all those years ago.

'It was no great surprise for us to be told, shortly before the end of the year that we were to change our positions. Thanks to the low cloud and other conditions we were untroubled by American aircraft and from our new positions carried out an attack at midday on 31st December . . . We did not gain much in the way of war booty but the Americans had left behind in their flight tins of food, biscuits and sweets which were a welcome supplement to our rations . . . The enemy artillery fire grew daily in volume and then the extra supplies we had gained from the Americans came to an end. We had to find our own hot food as none was coming forward . . . Well, in the houses around us we found enough potatoes, fat, salt and even a handful of onions. I was appointed chef and chose to cook potato pancakes. The smell was appetising and the comrades gathered round the little stove eating their fill. By that time I, too, had worked up an appetite and had just put on my first pancake when I found that the wood for the stove had all been used up. On the way to the wood shed a sudden barrage of shells forced me into cover. I thought longingly of my potato pancake which must surely be cooked by now and raced back into the kitchen as soon as the barrage stopped. The little room was filled with smoke and plaster dust – not exactly a tasty addition to my meal – because the frying-pan had been deliberately left uncovered to obtain a nice crusty surface on the pancake. I soon found out that a shell had struck the kitchen but had not exploded and was stuck in the wall above the stove. One cannot play the fool around such things and my pancake was, in any case, inedible so we all moved out to another cellar a few streets away. I swore that in future I would eat the first pancakes myself and not wait to be the last.'

The following battle report was written by Obersturmführer Georg Vilzmann, commanding No. 5 Company of the Panzergrenadier Regiment 'Der Führer'.

'On 4th January, the Company lay in defensive positions extending from the northern part of Magoster up to the wooded area around Point 405. Our right-flank neighbour was our No. 7 Company and No. 9 Company of 'Deutschland' Regiment was on our left.

'Apart from artillery fire and reconnaissance patrols there had been little activity over the past few days, but in the grey dawn of the 4th, at about 07.30 hours, a heavy bombardment fell on the woods around Point 405 and upon Magoster. The enemy fired smoke in order to hide his movements and the noise of tracked vehicles and heavy engines indicated that he would be making an attack. When the smoke-screen thinned there were six Shermans and about 150 infantry in front of us. The main force of the enemy attacked No. 7 Company on our right and had soon got into the woods so that by 09.00 hours, as my platoon commander reported, the enemy had already passed through the woods and was in position some 200 yards behind us. Through binoculars I saw fourteen of the Shermans on Point 405, turning towards Magoster. I ordered the Company to withdraw to defensive positions to the east and south-east of Magoster; a move carried out in conjunction with our left-flank neighbour. During the withdrawal the enemy bombarded us with mortars and phosphorous shells but we had taken up our positions in the new front line by 10.00 hours.

'Enemy infantry and tank forces, numbering some twenty-one machines, concentrated their attack upon the northern exit of Magoster and the high ground near Trinal. Despite the fierce barrage and the enemy's attacks, the grenadiers held their positions. At 10.30 hours the enemy opened a tank attack with fourteen machines against the south-eastern side of Magoster. During this attack Grenadier Stephan showed remarkable courage by firing his machine-gun and separating the US infantry from their tanks. He continued to fire his gun even after his No. 2 was killed by a tank shell. The Shermans advanced to within 150 metres of the eastern side of Magoster and suddenly halted. During the fighting I had received a wireless message ordering me to hold out as our own forces were about to open an attack. One of No. 14 Company's anti-tank guns which was supporting us was knocked out at this time.

'At about 11.00 hours the Shermans around Point 405 suddenly began to pull back and I assumed that our counter-attack was going in. Three enemy tanks, supported by enfilade fire from other Shermans near Trinal had, however, advanced into the northern part of Magoster held by No. 9 Company of "Deutschland" Regiment and the enemy infantry on that sector fought from house to house but did not bring their tanks forward in close support. The enemy regrouped and renewed his attack on the woods around Point 405, at the same time blocking the south-western parts of Magoster and the high ground behind it with a furious artillery bombardment. By 11.00 hours the enemy had taken nearly half of the village of Magoster and I distributed the reserve ammunition in the expectation of a fresh assault. I sent a wireless message to battalion, "Sufficient ammunition. Company is defending the road crossing and the south-eastern exits of Magoster. We shall hold out to the last." An attempt by Oberscharführer Glienke and ten men to seize the high ground to the south of Magoster so as to protect my right flank, failed in the fire of the enemy's tank guns.

'By this time my Company had been reduced to only 20 men and these I put into all-round defend of the road crossing on the southern side of Magoster and in the ruined houses there. The Commander of No. 9 Company, Untersturmführer Vicha, was killed by a shot through the head and I put some of his men into my own positions. We were now under fire from all sides and I decided to hold the remaining five houses and the chapel until the last, as I had reported to battalion.

'The enemy advance in the south-east had reached to within 100 metres while from the north-west the enemy was firing with tank guns and machine-guns into the ruins of the houses. Phosphorous grenades set fire to my TAC HQ, and we were then involved in house-to-house fighting of an intensity which I had not met before in all my front-line service. My Grenadiers fought for every house wall and for every pile of rubble. My TAC HQ fell at 13.00 hours and the Shermans, drawn up as if on parade, now supported the infantry advance. Half an hour later and we had to give up the last house and the chapel on the right-hand side of the street. Now only the remnant of the Company, the wireless operators and a few men of No. 9 Company were holding out in the ruins of the last two houses and we used Panzerfausts and hand-grenades in the unequal fight against superior numbers An enemy machine-gunner, setting up his weapon in the house opposite, had a direct hit scored on him by Grenadier Niessen firing a rifle-grenade. Oberscharführer Fenske played a great part in the defence, firing his English automatic rifle at a group of the enemy as they tried to cross the road near the chapel and knocking them all out.

'The enemy brought up a rocket-firing weapon near the chapel and I fired a Panzerfaust at this target but could not establish the result as both of us fired simultaneously and his rocket hit my position. I was not hurt but the man next to me was wounded. Oberscharführer Stroeckl led the fighting in the neighbouring ruin and Rottenführer Knop and his No. 2 on the machine-gun stopped the enemy from outflanking us to the south. The Shermans fired HE and AP at us and then I received a report that there was no more ammunition for the machine-guns or for the personal weapons. Quickly I destroyed all maps and messages, the Company war diary and the ciphers used by the signallers. A final signal was sent to battalion. "Ammunition used up. Documents destroyed. Situation hopeless. No escape possible." I then ordered the set to be blown up with the last hand-grenade. The enemy was now in the front room of the last ruined house. With a Panzerfaust which I found lying about I fired this at the enemy group attacking us and put some of them out of action. The fight put up by my Company then had to end. Together with the rest of my men, some fifteen in number, I got on to a pile of straw but was fired at by a tank from the high ground around Trinal. That attracted the attention of the other enemy groups who joined in the firing. I decided to give up the fight. My runner was wounded as were some of the men of No. 9 Company.

'At this time of our deepest crisis our regiment's Nebelwerfers opened fire. One of my runners, Sturmmann Hausler, carrying a message, had met up with the FOO of the Nebelwerfer Battery. In response to the FOO's inquiry "Have you got a target for me," my runner was able to report that I and fifteen other men were in Magoster and that fire should be laid on the crossroads. As the rockets came in I realized that they would fall on us. When they did the enemy infantry took cover and the tanks were blinded by the smoke of the explosions. Under cover of the smoke and exploiting the shattering effect of the Nebelwerfer shells, I decided to break out. Calling to my men to follow me we rushed down to the road and set off for Beffe, crossing barbed wire fences and hedges until we reached the shelter of a hollow. Two enemy spotter planes flying about 15 metres above our heads tried to stop our retreat by firing at us. Some of my men who had not been able to follow us that far lay out in the open until dark, pretending to be dead. Even some of the wounded found strength enough to escape. Accompanied by two of my NCOs and two men, the signallers and the FOO, I arrived at battalion TAC HQ by 15.30 hours. The remaining men, under the command of Oberscharführer Stroeckl, came in at 22.30 hours on the following night, and another man who had been reported missing, came in on the following day. All the unwounded men of my Company fought their way through to No. 2 Battalion, but the badly wounded fell into enemy hands. Unterscharführer Kopsch, who was suffering from frostbite in the feet and who could hardly move but who had nevertheless stayed with the Company, was reported missing and was probably taken prisoner.

'That same night No. 5 Company, with a total strength of one officer, three NCOs and eight men took part in a counter-attack.'

During the evening of 4 January, SS Panzer Corps sent out a signal ordering all attacks to be broken off and for 'Das Reich' to be taken out of the line and put into Army reserve. This latter order could not be compiled with immediately because divisional elements were serving with other formations. On 9 January 1945 a major American offensive opened and struck both 1st and 2nd Battalions of 'Der Führer' Regiment. The US thrust against 1st Battalion was spearheaded by 50 Sherman tanks and although the grenadiers were able to hold that initial assault and also to inflict heavy casualties on the attacking armour, when another American strike came in from a different direction the companies stood in danger of being cut off and were ordered to withdraw to Dochamps. Losses had so reduced company strengths that the rearguard could not be formed from the weak grenadier detachments and the divisional artillery, deployed on the open fields, fired a succession of barrages to hold back the US forces while the grenadiers of 'Der Führer' carried out a slow-paced withdrawal. One post-battle report stated: '... US troops exploited the situation very quickly. Our own troops, weak in number, held out by forming a "hedgehog" by day and pulling back at night to unprepared positions. Our counter-attacks could only by carried out with panzer support which, in any case, brought only temporary respite . . . '

On 15 January 1945 'Deutschland' Regiment moved into the bunkers and strongpoints of the West Wall, which its units had occupied during the previous autumn and out of which they had gone into the Battle of the Bulge. By the 16th, 'Watch on the Rhine' could be said to be at an end. In the final weeks of January 1945 the Division began to leave the line unit by unit, but it was not until 4 February that that action could be completed. Rumours swept through the Division that it was to leave the Western Front and would, after a period of rest, be returned to front-line service, probably in the east, but the exact location was unknown.

The involvement of 'Das Reich' Division in 'Watch on the Rhine' was at an end. It had fought a series of wasteful actions on one small sector of the front but not as a single unit. From the first day of the offensive to the last, divisional components had been detached to serve with other formations, a situation which 'Das Reich' had often faced in its active service life. Ahead lay new challenges.

1945

Axis territory and general strategic movements

'Das Reich':
1 Hungary, February–April
2 Prague, April–May
(See sketch maps overleaf)

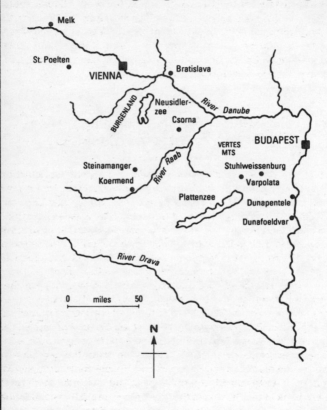

1945

Hungary, February–April

The Third Campaign
on the Eastern Front, 1945

When the offensive in the Ardennes failed to achieve a strategic victory for the German Army in the west, Hitler's attention, which had been concentrated on smashing the Western Allies, returned to the Eastern Front. There, despite the divisions with which he had reinforced the struggling Army Groups, the military situation was deteriorating badly and among the crises which had to be mastered the most urgent priority was in Hungary.

Operation 'Spring Awakening':
The Plattensee Offensive, Hungary

Even before the Ardennes offensive opened in Belgium the situation in Hungary had been serious. At the beginning of December the Red Army had crossed the border and within days its spearheads had reached Ercsi on the Danube, some 30 kilometres south of Budapest. The Russians crossed the river barrier at that point and established a large bridgehead in which they intended to concentrate their forces and out of which they planned to erupt in new offensives. Forced back by numerical superiority the German formations on that sector took up strong positions along a line running from the Plattensee, via Stuhlweissenburg and the Velenczsee to Budapest; the so-called 'Margaret Positions'. Unable to break through the German defences on the sector to the south of Budapest, Stavka changed the point of its main effort to the great bend of the Danube to the north of the Hungarian capital. On 20 December two Red Army Fronts, 2nd and 3rd Ukrainian, opened a major offensive. Success came quickly. Within four days the Russian 18th Tank Corps had cut the road between Budapest and Vienna and shortly thereafter 6th Guards Tank Army and 7th Guards Army of 2nd Ukrainian Front reached the southern bank of the Danube in the area of the Gran estuary and formed a bridgehead there. The town of Gran (in Hungarian Estergom) was captured by troops of 3rd Ukrainian Front but was retaken by a German infantry division on 6 January 1945. On this sector the advantage swung inconclusively between both sides but then the Red Army mounted a major offensive. It failed because the Germans holding the high ground inflicted such terrible losses on the Russians that Stavka was forced to break off the offensive. A series of German operations with limited objectives and mounted along other sectors of the Hungarian battle front then compelled the Russians to give ground, but their hold on the Gran bridgehead could not be broken at that time.

Unable to smash the Gran bridgehead the Germans followed the Russian example and switched their main effort to other areas. They concentrated fresh forces and launched several offensives designed to raise the siege of Budapest, but these failed and on 12 February the city fell, releasing the Russian armies, which had been held down in the siege, to resume their westward advance. This soon precipitated a dangerous crisis in southern Hungary. Germany, lacking indigenous natural resources was, by this stage of the war, totally dependant upon the oilfields and refineries at Nagykanizsa. These were now seriously threatened for the Red Army's advance had brought it to within 50 kilometres of the vital supplies. If the Hungarian oilfields passed into Russian hands the German war machine would stop and the war would come to an end. In order to smash the Russian assault and to build a strong defensive line east of Nagykanizsa, Hitler would have to commit the finest divisions and corps of the German Army.

Acting upon that urgent need, he ordered the withdrawal of the élite Sixth SS Panzer Army from the Western Front. His insistence upon secrecy in military operations had become so total that when Sturmbannführer Günsche, Hitler's personal adjutant, briefed Sepp Dietrich, the orders had not been committed to paper but were verbal. Dietrich was told that Sixth SS Panzer Army was to take the leading part in a major offensive which the Führer was planning to open in Hungary. The decision to employ his Army on that sector of the Eastern Front came as a surprise to its commander who had expected the defence of the River Oder, east of Berlin, to be a more important priority. He was wrong for, as Field Marshal Keitel explained to the Chief of Staff of Sixth Army, it was vital to hold Hungary not only because of the oil, but also for its grain resources. Another of Keitel's imperatives for the new offensive was the need to protect the city of Vienna.

The written movement order, confirming the instructions that had been given verbally by Sturmbannführer Günsche, was issued on 16 January 1945, and directed I SS Panzer Corps with its subordinate units, 1st SS Panzer Division, 'Leibstandarte SS Adolf Hitler' and 12th SS Panzer Division 'Hitler Youth', together with II SS Panzer Corps' 2nd SS Panzer Division 'Das Reich' and 9th SS Panzer Division 'Hohenstaufen', to move into the 'Margaret Positions' in Hungary. In accord with the Führer's insistence upon security the major formations of Sixth Panzer Army were given cover-names. For example, II SS Panzer Corps was redesignated SS Training HQ (South) and its constituent formations were renamed as 'Training Group – North', ('Das Reich' Division) and 'Training Group – South', ('Hohenstaufen' Division). The regiments of the formations of the Panzer Army were also redesignated and all identifying marks had to be taken down before the units headed east. Heid Ruhl of the divisional artillery regiment recalled: 'For our move to Hungary we were ordered to remove every divisional identification, even the monogram on our shoulder-straps.' Hitler's demand for secrecy led to the ridiculous situation that it was not until the end of February 1945 that the headquarters staff of Sixth SS Panzer Army were allowed into the operational area and not until late in the afternoon of D-Day minus 1, that the regimental commanders of 'Das Reich' Division were able to carry out a visual reconnaissance of the ground over which their units were to attack. Even Dietrich himself was not allowed to enter the area until immediately before the opening of the offensive.

The plan which Adolf Hitler had worked out was that in a combined operation by Army Groups South and South East, the Russian forces in the area between the Danube, the Plattensee and the River Drau were to be destroyed. General Wöhler's Army Group South, with Sixth SS Panzer Army, German Sixth and Eighth Armies and Hungarian Third Army on its establishment, was to strike southwards over the land bridge between the Plattensee and the Velenczsee. Second Army of Army Group South East was to advance eastwards. Between those two jaws Tolbukhin's 3rd Ukrainian Front would be crushed.

The Russian formations holding the triangle of land between the Plattensee, the Danube and the Drau, were initially 4th Guards Army, 26th Army, 57th Army and Bulgarian 1st Army. When, by swift assault, I SS Panzer Corps smashed the Gran bridgehead, the Russians, who had been moving methodically through Hungary, became acutely aware that the presence of such an élite formation could only mean an imminent German offensive. Stavka carried out an immediate and massive reinforcement of the troops in the threatened area and ordered the construction in depth of field fortifications. The fearsome combat reputation of the SS formations made such precautions essential. Stavka advised 3rd Ukrainian Front to expect a German assault during the latter half of February or the first week of March and were correct not only in establishing the timing of the assault but also anticipated correctly that the main German effort would be made between the Plattensee and the Velenczsee. This was the area into which the mass of Sixth SS Panzer Army had begun to arrive. On those sectors where panzers might be used Tolbukhin ordered concentrations of anti-tank guns to be deployed, extensive minefields to be laid and anti-tank ditches to be dug. Stavka did not, despite those precautions, halt preparations for its own offensive aimed at wearing down the German attack by a strong defence before launching a counter-offensive aimed at smashing Army Group South.

The operational plan drawn up by the German Army Group directed Sixth SS Panzer Army to attack in a southerly direction on both sides of the Sarviz Canal to cut Russian communications across the Danube. Dietrich placed I Cavalry Corps on the right, I SS Panzer Corps in the centre and II SS Panzer Corps on the left. The canal formed the boundary between the two SS Corps. General Bittrich, commanding II SS Panzer Corps, described his formation's part in the forthcoming offensive. 'From the narrow neck of land between the two lakes II SS Panzer Corps was to begin its attack on 8 March. The I SS Panzer Corps was to the south of us. The plan foresaw that both

Corps, having made a breakthrough of the Russian line, were to move on a broad front south of Budapest to reach the Danube at Dunafoeldvar. If possible, that is to say, if we were strong enough and the situation permitted, we were then to swing north and advance towards Budapest.'

The ground over which Sixth SS Panzer Army was to attack was prone to severe flooding which produced swamp-like conditions. Strong winter frosts freezing the soil would normally have allowed armoured fighting vehicles to be used, but in February and March 1945 there had been an early thaw and the ground was water-logged. Not even tracked vehicles could operate off the roads in such conditions and there were in the operational area very few roads capable of standing up to either the numbers or weight of the traffic which would use them. Thus, panzers could not be expected to move across country and those which tried became bogged down. Under interrogation while he was a prisoner of war, Dietrich was to speak bitterly of Sixth Panzer Army's experiences. 'For reasons of security I had been forbidden to make a reconnaissance of the ground. The marshy terrain, impassable for panzer units, held one hundred and thirty-two of our vehicles fast in the mud and fifteen Royal Tigers sank up to their turrets.' Panzer units which tried to move by road found them congested with wheeled traffic.

Army Group South ordered that D-Day for Operation 'Spring Awakening' was to be 8 March and H-Hour would be 04.30 hours. Few realized that it was to be the German Army's last major offensive on the Eastern Front. It was the final act of the war against Russia which had begun so well in June 1941, but which was now, in March 1945, approaching its end.

This account of the final battles of 'Das Reich' Division or its subordinate units covers Hungary, Austria and Czechoslovakia and the period of time is from March to May 1945. The military events described are the failure of 'Spring Awakening'; the Red Army's counter-offensive which forced back Sixth SS Panzer Army to Vienna and fragmented it there. Finally, there is an account of the mission by 'Der Führer' Regiment to rescue the German population of Prague.

Whatever confident feelings High Command may have had about the outcome of Operation 'Spring Awakening', these were not shared by the senior officers of 'Das Reich', which would have to fight the battle. They considered the plan too ambitious in view of the lack of combat experience of the replacements, the shortage of supplies, the terrain and the weather. Nevertheless, whatever their reservations they had orders to obey and men to lead into battle. They began to prepare for action.

On 2 March the grenadier regiments were put under notice to move and set out towards their concentration areas under a grey and lowering sky. Neither regiment was up to full strength. The 2nd Battalion of 'Deutschland'

Regiment could not be committed to battle as it was not up to its full complement in men or vehicles and a similar shortage affected one of the battalions of 'Der Führer' Regiment. According to Heid Ruehl, the artillery battalions in their battle positions south of Stuhlweissenburg were not allowed to 'shoot themselves in', for security reasons.

Throughout 3 and 4 March snow fell and made worse the already poor road conditions. It was very clear that the drive to the forming-up areas would be long and exhausting and doubt was expressed whether the Division would be able to attack at H-Hour. This concern was deepened by an order which directed that ' . . . as a security measure . . . ' unit transport was not to bring the grenadiers closer than 20 kilometres to the forming-up area. This condemned the grenadiers, who would be carrying full equipment, to a long march along roads which were in places calf-deep in mud.

The Corps Commander, Bittrich, concerned at the effect that this tiring march would have upon his men asked that the attack be postponed. He reported to Army that from the window of his TAC HQ, some 10 kilometres away from the forming-up area, he could see his grenadiers marching through the mud. They would arrive late to battle and be in no condition to undertake an attack. He considered it essential to put back the opening of the operation, but was told that this could not be done. 'On 6 March', wrote Heid Ruehl, 'we fired a heavy barrage behind which our grenadiers should have attacked. They did not because they could not and the barrage served only to warn the enemy. At 05.00 hours on the following day the grenadiers went in behind another, but this time much shorter, barrage. The marshy ground meant that armour could not support the attacks and these suffered heavy loss.' The SS infantry had gone in, storming across open country against an enemy in superior strength and holding prepared positions. The grenadiers were without armoured support but their élan brought them across a succession of enemy trench lines and they went on to capture a number of tactically important pieces of high ground.

Despite these initial successes, the regiments realized within days of the offensive opening, that they could not achieve the Corps tasks of establishing a bridgehead on the Danube, between Dunapentele and Dunafoeldvar. Their bloody assaults were not gaining enough ground against an enemy already strong and being continually reinforced with fresh troops. These points were put to Corps who informed Army, from whom came the uncompromising order that the attacks be continued. On 9 March the divisional commander, Gruppenführer Ostendorff, was wounded while on an inspection tour of the 'Deutschland' positions and was replaced by Standartenführer Kreutz.

Throughout the next few miserable days the grenadier regiments, by repeated effort, were able to make more gains, but it was a slow, wasteful process and by 13 March it was clear, even to Army Group, that the offensive was failing. Not only would the Führer's orders not be carried out, but the threat was growing of a Russian counter-offensive. The War Diary of Army Group South recorded that air observation showed ' . . . motorized columns in the Stuhlweissenburg–Zamoly sector numbering approximately 3,000 vehicles,' and deduced that the enemy's main thrust would be made in the Zamoly sector. If the Russians attacked towards the Plattensee the SS spearheads would be cut off.

The Russian offensive which Army Group had forecast opened on 16 March along the whole front south of the Velenczsee–Plattensee Line and its initial blows were sufficient to bring Operation 'Spring Awakening' to a halt. On 'Das Reich' sector every unit of the Division was engaged in the unequal fight against assaults coming in from three directions, and in a desperate effort to hold them Dietrich was forced to take units from less threatened sectors to bolster the battle line. But in other areas the Russian offensive gained ground and when Sixth Army reeled back under its blows the left flank of Sixth SS Panzer Army was exposed. Russian troops thrust through the gap and when they had flung an armoured pincer around Szekesfehervar Dietrich's Army was encircled. There remained only a narrow corridor through which its units could withdraw. There followed days and nights of almost unceasing combat in which the battle line moved with the direction of attack and counter-attack. The most bitter fighting was in the area of Varpalota and Stuhlweissenburg where 'Das Reich' fought to keep open that narrow escape corridor. There could now be no question of stopping the Russian advance. The best that could be hoped for was to delay it and to achieve this the grenadiers were put in time and again, usually without armour support, for the ground was still too soft to carry the heavy vehicles. Under the enemy's assaults 'Das Reich' was eventually forced back to positions south-east of Raab. There 'Deutschland' found that its 2nd Battalion, which had had to be left out of battle, had now been brought up to strength and had come forward. The 2nd had not only prepared the positions into which the other two battalions moved, but also held the line so that their comrades could rest and recuperate.

This was a time when loyalties began to change and as the war drew to its close the signs of collapse on the part of Germany's ally, Hungary, became more and more obvious. Many men in the Division reported encountering Hungarian units, usually in company strength, marching backwards and forwards across the country. There came the suspicion that Magyar generals were keeping their troops on the move so that they could not be put into the line. The reports also mentioned that the Hungarian detachments were often without arms but were usually outfitted with a complete ration train and always accompanied by a steaming field kitchen. One man who recalled coming across such a phenomenon was Friedrich Huck.

'Towards the end of March we were withdrawing towards Vienna . . . I was starving . . . We passed a Hungarian unit. It was meal time and food was being served. I stopped my truck and poked my nose out. There was a lovely smell. I put a sentry guarding the truck and together with my mates joined the queue of Hungarians standing by the field kitchen. The cook filled our mess tins with potatoes, cabbage, meat and a fiery red sauce. It was made of paprika and pepperoni and burned like fire. We also received a cup of wine. That was the first and last time that I ever ate a real Hungarian goulash. It set me on fire from head to foot and I spent the next three days drinking water wherever I found it. Not until the end of the third day could I breathe properly again.'

The paced withdrawal of II SS Panzer Corps was interrupted when 1st Honved Cavalry Division, on the left flank of 'Deutschland' Regiment disappeared overnight. The Russians exploited this new open gap and the regiment's attempts to disengage from the Russians' grasp were long and wasteful. To make good the grievous losses which all units of 'Das Reich' had suffered, replacements were still coming in – one batch was made up of sailors – but they were too few in number to redress the balance. By a bitter paradox, as battalion and regimental strengths declined, the area of front which the grenadier regiments had to cover increased. Each was expected to hold a sector up to 14 kilometres wide against all the assaults of the enemy.

It was a time when the men in the line realized that there were two military worlds. Theirs was the one of danger, of continual losses, of short rations, numbing tiredness and furious battles with an uncompromising foe. The other world was that of the High Command whose orders took on an increasingly surrealistic nature because the Staff refused to accept the front-line commanders' assessment of the situation and based their orders for attack or counter-attack upon the situation as they thought it to be. How little Führer Headquarters understood of conditions in Hungary was shown in the order which Hitler issued at this critical time. In his opinion Sixth SS Panzer Army had failed to gain the objectives he had set it and had to be made aware of his displeasure. Goebbels' diary entry records. 'The Führer has decided to make an example of the SS formations. He has commissioned Himmler to fly to Hungary to remove their armbands ...' The indignation of the SS commanders in the field can well be imagined and Kraemer, Dietrich's Chief of Staff, suggested asking Führer headquarters whether the armbands of the SS men killed between the Plattensee and the Danube should also be removed ...' Stories have been told of Knight's Crosses being returned to Hitler in chamber-pots or of his being sent the shot off arms of fallen SS men complete with cuff titles, but many such stories are doubtless apocryphal. What is certain is that the cuff title order was not passed down from the senior commanders to their men although knowledge of such a deliberate humiliation could not long be kept hidden.

Within ten days of the Red Army opening its counter-offensive it had smashed its way through the Vertes mountains across three major rivers and had crushed the German formations opposing it. The speed with which 2nd and 3rd Ukrainian Fronts were now moving and the flexibility with which their commanders conducted operations must have reminded the German commanders of the old days of *Blitzkrieg*. Massed armour accompanied by fleets of low-flying fighter-bombers and dense waves of infantry, created and exploited every breach in the lines of Army Group South. To the north of

Stuhlweissenburg SS blocking units, put in to slow the Russian advance, were overrun and destroyed. One of the sub-units smashed in that careering Russian advance was the 'Das Reich' Assault Company. One of its members wrote an account of the fighting in Hungary when 'Spring Awakening' faded and was replaced by the Red Army's counter-offensive.

'We reached Varpalota, north of the Plattensee, at the beginning of March. . . . It was on the 6th or 7th that we first met the Russians. We had been advancing towards Aba, but within days had been forced to pull back under the enemy's crushing weight. By the middle of March we had withdrawn as far as Csorna, but thankfully with little loss. We received replacements on 25th March, so that the strength of the Assault Company was once again 250 men. Unfortunately, those replacements had had little training and were, of course, without any combat experience whatsoever. Three days later, on 28th March, we were forced to give up Csorna and moved to a small village about 4 kilometres to the south-east. Only a short time later Russian infantry and armour struck from the north-west and entered Csorna. At about 15.00 hours we carried out a recce and found that the village directly in front of us had also been occupied by the enemy. The attack which we made to take that village was driven back by Russian infantry backed with armour, artillery and mortars.

'We received orders to pull back and to guard the road leading from Csorna to Esterhazy. A railway line ran to the south of the road. Untersturm-führer Tychsen, Rottenführer Wysz and I, first of all covered the area from positions on top of the railway embankment but then moved into ditches along a country track which ran parallel to the road. The carts and lorries of the Train were in a small village. Suddenly, the Train fled from the village, heading westwards. We saw about 40 T-34s coming along the road. One of our men made a stupid move which drew the attention of the Russians to where we were and they bombarded us from every direction. Waves of Russian soldiers came storming towards us, advancing through their own barrage which increased in intensity. As we had only light infantry weapons and could make no effective reply we moved off at the double, keeping together for protection. The Russians who were in front of us thought that we were making a counter-attack and raised their arms in surrender. When they saw how few we were they started firing at us again.

'We were now being shot at from every type of weapon and the T-34s were hunting us down. Very few of us escaped. After dodging about for between four and five hours, moving often across completely open country, we finally gained touch with No. 2 Company of the panzer recce battalion. Our strength was now only 15 men – among others we had lost Tychsen in the fighting – and after a short rest we were taken on the strength of the recce battalion's No 2 Company, with whom we carried out other missions, including counter-attacks and fighting patrols. But all the time we were withdrawing and always in a westerly direction.'

Under the Red Army's blows the SS were driven out of Stuhlweissenburg, then from Koermend and Steinamanger, across the River Raab and back towards eastern Austria. Burgenland, Austria's easternmost province, has a large shallow lake, the Neusiedlersee. East of this the two corps of Dietrich's panzer army, which had become separated in the fighting, marched separately towards the new line inside Austria. I Panzer Corps went along the southern shore of the lake while II Panzer Corps moved along the eastern bank and then swung in a left-wheeling movement across the border regions of southern Czechoslovakia. Friederich Huck recalled, 'We marched via Gols and Poldersdorf into Burgenland. Here we smashed or blew up all the boats to make it harder for the Soviets to cross the lake'.

Accounts recalling those days mention that the so-called Reichs Defence Positions, which should have been strong enough to protect the eastern borders of the Reich were, in Austria, generally incomplete. In some areas no work had been done at all, while on other sectors, the Russian advance had been so rapid as to reach the uncompleted trenches ahead of the slower-moving German units. On 1 April, during the time that Division was withdrawing out of Hungary, fresh orders were received: first, for its units to take up positions between the Neusiedlersee and the Danube and, later, for them to move into the southern approaches to Vienna and to defend the Austrian capital.

By 4 April Tolbukin's 3rd Ukrainian Front had already surrounded the city on three sides and he was ready to open the attack. His tactical plan was for 1st Guards Motorized Corps to strike from the south-east and for 5th Guards Tank Corps and 9th Guards Motorized Corps to attack from the south-west while a blocking force in the hills to the west of the city prevented the German forces in Vienna from escaping into the Wachau and thence into Salzburg. It was Tolbukin's strategic intention to seize the bridges across the Danube so as to link up with 2nd Ukrainian Front, whose 46th Army, was sweeping down from the north-east towards the capital. The mighty force of 2nd and 3rd Ukrainian Fronts would then strike, irresistibly, westwards across Czechoslovakia's southernmost provinces and into the heart of Austria.

Sixth SS Panzer Army no longer had the power to thwart that Russian strategic intention. All that its weak, depleted divisions might do would be to delay the junction of the Ukrainian Fronts by denying them the Danube bridges for as long as possible. It was the task of 'Das Reich' Division to defend that sector of the Austrian capital in which the principal bridges were located, and the story of the nine-day struggle for Vienna, is of the 2nd SS Panzer Division's battle line being forced back until the last perimeter it held, around the Florisdorf bridge, was only half a kilometre in extent. For the greater part of those nine days the fighting was confused and fragmentary, with little groups of grenadiers fighting from house to house as they pulled back towards the defence perimeter along the line of the Danube Canal. The bitter fighting for the capital was not restricted to ground level. In the extensive and cavernous sewers below the city battle patrols clashed and flame-throwers incinerated soldiers from both sides as Russian Guardsmen sought to bring the advance forward and the SS grenadiers struggled to prevent this.

The battle opened with Russian attacks against 'Der Führer' Regiment which had taken up defensive positions east of Leopoldsdorf with its regimental headquarters in a brickworks. Those first probes, they were little more than that, came in to determine the SS positions and were easily driven off. But they were the harbingers of things to come. There was a brief spell of quiet and then crushing bombardments came down. These were of such intensity and accuracy that both Division and 'Der Führer' headquarters had to be moved to avoid destruction. Regimental headquarters moved from the brickworks in Leopoldsdorf to Vosendorf but its stay was brief. When the barrage ended waves of tanks from a Russian Guards armoured unit roared forward, cutting the Leopoldorf–Voesendorf road, and effectively separating 'Der Führer' from the main body of Division. During the evening of 5 April Regiment was ordered to retreat into a perimeter being set up outside the Ringstrasse which encloses Vienna's inner city.

The co-ordinated and furious attacks of Tolbukin's forces had shattered the Division's front and had separated the grenadier regiments from each other. At Command level it was feared that it would not be possible to close the breach between 'Deutschland' and 'Der Führer' Regiments because no reserve of divisional units existed which could be inserted. Every formation of 'Das Reich' was in the battle line fighting against overwhelming odds. Then, as so often in the past, the flexibility of the German military system was demonstrated. A battle group was created out of remnants of miscellaneous formations and brought forward to close the gap.

The Loss of Vienna

An extract from Otto Weidinger's combat report covering operations during April 1945, contains the words, 'South of Vienna a dangerous gap yawned between "Deutschland" and "Der Führer" Regiments into which the enemy threw strong infantry and armoured forces. "Battle Group Hauser", formed from hastily collected replacements, was assigned to "Das Reich" Division and put in at Münchedorf to plug that gap in our line. Thanks to Hauser's inspired leadership and his tireless personal example the heavy Russian attacks failed. That successful defence had a decisive effect on operations along the whole of the front south of Vienna . . . '

Hans Hauser's account of the events of those days is interesting because it shows, first, that despite a certain amount of confusion as the end of the war approached the German Army's command system still functioned sufficiently well for personnel department to post officers from one unit to another. It shows, secondly, the speed with which battle groups could be created and put into action. Hauser, at that time a Sturmbannführer, begins his account in March 1945.

'I was ordered to entrain the remnant of my own group as well as those of the "Kurmark" Recruit Depot and to bring them to the military training ground at Beneschau, south of Prague. We reached the supposed "fortress" of the Reich, the Protectorate of Bohemia–Moravia, together with the Junker-school "Kienschlag".

'During the time that we were waiting for orders my men were posted away to other units. Then, some time later, I received new movement orders from Berlin. With immediate effect I was to take up the post of regimental commander in the "Handschar" Division. I could not find out where that formation was in action, but using the Field Post number which had been supplied left Prague by train and set off for Vienna. On arriving there I had a surprise. A special "Führer Befehl", had empowered SS General Steiner to take all soldiers from the trains on which they were travelling, irrespective of rank. My movement order was now redundant and I found myself in the motor school in Schoenbrunn. There I was informed that my posting to the "Handschar" Division was cancelled and that in view of the threatening situation in Hungary I was to take command of a new battle group. The military personnel taken from the trains passing through Vienna were brought to Schoenbrunn and the majority of them were either returning from leave, were lightly wounded or were convalescent. In addition there were others who, like me, had been on our way to new postings. Luckily, among those men there was a sprinkling of old soldiers, many with decorations for bravery. Those men were a great help in creating and building the new battle group. Within a few days I had it organized even though our arms consisted only of standard infantry weapons: carbines and bayonets, machine-pistols, grenades and Panzerfaust rocket-projectors.

'A lorried column was created and then, in the first days of April 1945, we received operational orders. These included the instruction that the trucks were to be sent back as soon as we met the enemy, in order that reinforcements could be brought up. En route from Vienna to Burgenland we saw a long column of unarmed Hungarian soldiers heading towards Vienna . . . After a few kilometres the numbers grew fewer and then, suddenly, we were quite alone.

'As a result of years of war service we commanders had developed a sort of sixth sense which warned us of danger, even if none were apparent. I felt this sense warning me and ordered my column to pull up on the autobahn and for the men to dismount. The lorries then drove back to Vienna and I sent out the first patrols to check on Münchedorf, a village which lay directly ahead of us. There seemed to be no enemy about but as we reached the southern end of the village and I was giving orders to secure that flank three Russian T-34s came rolling towards us. They had no infantry protection and it seemed that they had not seen my battle group. Immediately in front of the village was a bridge where we had dug in. My men had orders not to fire without my permission and I gave the order to fire as the first Russian tank began to cross the bridge. One of our Panzerfausts scored a direct hit and the T-34 began to brew up. It was entangled in the wreck of the bridge and thus formed a barricade against any further advance on that sector. Our machine-gun fire forced the other tank to turn away. It disappeared from our sight. We had scored the first victory and while waiting for the next Russian move took the opportunity of strengthening and camouflaging our positions. How important this was we found out towards evening – just before last light. The Russians smothered us with a hail of artillery shells and bombs from the Stalin Organ rocket-launchers that numbed our senses. During the first hours of that bombardment I was forced to evacuate my command post three times and in the third move my aide as well as the adjutant were knocked out. Then followed a short pause in the shelling while other T-34s began to work their way forward towards the village. That attack only began to ebb away at dawn after our Panzerfausts had knocked out some more tanks.

'While it was still dark a liaison officer came down in his Tiger from the unit on the northern flank. He had come to gain touch with my battle group about which he had heard marvellous things. He was full of admiration for our achievements, particularly when he realized that we poor bloody infantry had no heavy weapons or vehicles. What he did tell me was that my battle group was occupying a sensitive area between the two regiments of "Das Reich" Division – "Deutschland" and "Der Führer". The orders which he brought were that we were to hold the village of Münchedorf for at least three to four days, so that a firm front could be knitted together behind us.

'We had just brought in and arranged for our wounded to be evacuated and had set up a wireless link with "Das Reich" Division when another barrage told us what we had to expect. The liaison officer and his Tiger tank left us after assurances that he would be available if we required help.

'Across the open fields to the south of us we could see Russian infantry racing towards us but our machine-guns held them back. Then we knocked out another T-34 using the Panzerfaust, after which there was a short pause, which we welcomed as it gave us a chance to look after the wounded. The houses in the village were mostly single-storey and so many of them had been destroyed by shellfire that it was hard to find a suitable place to set up my command post.

'It was very clear that the Russians had not carried our proper reconnaissance in our sector. It would have been easy for them to have by-passed the village on both sides and to have cut us off. Instead, they persisted in making frontal assaults. By the end of the second day, they had succeeded in gaining a foothold in the village and by the end of the fourth day we held only half the village because casualties had so reduced the strength of the battle group that it was unable to offer the same determined resistance. In the evening of the fourth day the order we had been expecting came from Division. We were to disengage from the enemy during the hours of darkness and report to "Der Führer" Regiment.

'Finally, at the end of four days I could begin the withdrawal operation. Russian numerical strength had increased so greatly that we would certainly have been wiped out during the fifth day. We, the survivors of the battle group, had a number of adventures during our flight, but eventually reached the outpost line of "Der Führer" Regiment. When I reported to the regimental commander, Otto Weidinger, he asked me to take over his 1st Battalion, which had lost its CO. He also took the opportunity to thank me and my men on behalf of the divisional commander for what we had achieved and told me that he had recommended me for the Knight's Cross. I was glad in the turbulent days which followed that I was no longer the commander of "Battle Group Hauser", but that I was serving with a famous Division. As CO of "DF" Regiment's 1st Battalion, I took part in the withdrawal via Moedling and in the house-to-house fighting in Vienna up to the Florisdorf bridge.'

The situation for 'Das Reich' deteriorated rapidly. Communications broke down with the consequence that 2nd battalion 'Der Führer' did not receive the divisional order to pull back, until 22.00 hours; two hours after it had been issued. The battalion, as a result, had to fight its way through masses of the enemy in order to reach its new positions. In the opinion of Dr Manfried Rauchensteiner, the eminent Austrian historian, the final battle for Vienna opened during the evening of 5 April. The attacks of a Guards Mechanized Corps and a Guard Rifle Corps, penetrated the 'Das Reich' divisional perimeter and a withdrawal was ordered to a new line around Vienna's inner city, a movement which Division ordered to be covered by the panzer regiment whose surviving vehicles were in action in the park of Schoenbrunn, the former imperial palace.

Held Ruehl forwarded an account sent to him by a member of the artillery regiment, who fought in the battle for Vienna. That man recalled that the Division's right flank had, at first, been in the Vienna woods, but that the Russians soon penetrated the great forest because it had been so weakly garrisoned. Other Russian units had by-passed the city to the west and others were thrusting towards the western railway station. The SS Division's artillery was positioned south of that station, near Schoenbrunn palace and was deployed to cover the Division's northern sector.

'On each of the north–south roads along the outskirts of the 15th District we positioned a gun and a machine-gun. It required five crew in all to man both weapons. We were fortunate in not having to fire the guns.' The writer goes on to explain that these stood on streets of cobblestones whose surface would have given the trail spade no purchase if the guns had been fired. He recalled that there was a change in organization at that time and that as a result the battalion's remaining guns were formed into one large battery. The signals detachments were similarly grouped; changes which had become necessary because of the serious shortage of commanders within the Division. His narrative continues.

'I was sent out to find maps of Vienna, because I knew the city from my student days. These maps were needed so that the Division's commanders could determine where we would fight the final battle for the city. The journey was an adventurous one and very much in the nature of a reconnaissance in enemy territory because Austrian partisans were now firing on German military vehicles. I located maps in a former cavalry barracks. The barrack square was littered with opened boxes of ammunition which we needed in the firing line, but which were being used here to supply the snipers firing at us from windows. On the top floor of one of the buildings I found an old colonel to whom I reported and in a short time he produced the most excellent maps.

'On the way back to my battery; this would have been about midday on 8th or 9th April, I passed the place where SP guns of the "Grossdeutschland" Panzer Division had destroyed a column of Russian tanks and lorries which had attempted to smash through our Division's left flank. The Russian crews has escaped into nearby houses and this meant that our thin line of grenadiers facing southwards now had the enemy at their backs.'

Russian armoured units, pushing from two directions, threatened to cut off the SS in this sector. The knocked-out Soviet tanks and lorries which the author recalled seeing were less than a kilometre from the enemy's armour spearheads around the West station. The danger to his group had become acute and the corridor along which his battery would have to pass in its withdrawal into the new defensive perimeter was narrowing under successive attacks. It was along this narrowing corridor that the author of the narrative had driven on his map-finding expedition. Not long after returning to his battery orders came that the positions around the Schoenbrunn palace were to be evacuated during the night and a withdrawal made to new positions along the Danube Canal. Once again, the narrator would have to make the perilous journey.

'We marched with the rest of the Division through the "eye of the needle" corridor which the assault guns of "Grossdeutschland" were holding open and reached the Danube Canal. My battery took up positions in the Augarten, which lies between the canal and the river itself, while the Grenadiers held the line of the canal.'

Soviet assaults in the evening of 8 April had threatened to cut off 'Der Führer' Regiment as it conducted its fighting retreat along a narrow escape corridor across the Ringstrasse, the boundary of the inner city, and towards the canal. The inner city, in which fires were now raging uncontrollably, was being given up. Many in 'Das Reich' Division believed that SS General Dietrich wished to save Vienna from total destruction, a fate which faced it if the SS and the Russians fought a long battle in its streets and buildings. During the following day the last panzers of the Division's 2nd Regiment formed the spearhead behind which 'Der Führer' and the divisional artillery withdrew to the canal line. The retreat was a bitter battle as the SS fought their way through a corridor lined with Russian armour, artillery and infantry. But it was not a one-sided battle and the panzers 'killed' a number of enemy AFVs as they pulled back. The canal line afforded only temporary respite. Russian assault troops had forced bridgeheads across it in the sectors held by 4th Panzer Division, and 'Das Reich', now outflanked, was forced to abandon that line of defence. The Grenadier Regiments 'Deutschland' and 'Der Führer', side by side, then battled for every house and for every room in every house as they were forced back towards the Florisdorf bridge, one of only two bridges across the River Danube which had not been blown. That at Florisdorf, in the divisional sector, was the sole remaining escape route and the bridge would have to be held until the last rearguard detachment had evacuated the bridgehead and crossed it.

But on 9 April, four days before the Florisdorf bridge was destroyed, 'Das Reich' still held an extensive perimeter which ran from where the Donau Canal joined the river at the Nordbruecke and extended to the Praterstrasse in the parkland of the Prater. The depleted but still determined grenadier regiments, each now reduced to approximately battalion strength, fortified the houses and dug trenches in the sports arenas and open ground which lay in their sectors. From these slit-trenches and fortified rooms they held and drove back with heavy loss the Red Army attacks which came in during the evening of the 10th and in the morning of 11 April. Nowhere were the Russians able to cross the Danube, but their snipers, as well as intense mortar bombardments and crashing artillery barrages, brought casualties which thinned the SS battle line and placed a heavier burden upon the survivors. Throughout the 11th and 12th, the perimeter held, although 4th Panzer Division had begun to move back across the Danube. The end could not be far away for the SS around the Florisdorf bridge. The divisional panzer recce battalion was taken out of the perimeter and sent across the bridge to confront 2nd Ukrainian Front north of the Danube, to delay its link up with 3rd Ukrainian Front and to protect the northern end of the bridge. At the southern end of that structure it was clear that evacuation was inevitable for Russian pressure had reduced the SS bridgehead to an area no more than 500 metres in extent, which was rocked day and night by continual bombardment. Fragments of accounts have been selected to produce an impression of life in the front line during those last days. It is a bewildering kaleidescope. 'We pulled back north-westwards and took up positions along the Canal. When we reached our positions most houses in the area were still intact. Within four days the Russian artillery and Stalin Organ fire had reduced them to rubble.'

The continual barrage is a feature of every account of those days and yet civilians still went shopping or to work, bars and cafes were open and were working normally. It was observed that most customers were foreigners and others just waiting for the war to pass away. 'They [the civilians] sat leading a *cafe-haus* life, as if it were peace-time, while only hundreds of metres distant soldiers were being killed.' The contrast between the two ways of life was grotesque.

Despite the deteriorating, even hopeless situation morale in the SS Division did not diminish. A Hauptsturmführer recalled: 'The most shameful thing was to leave one's comrades in the lurch. In war there was the risk of being killed. Traitors and cowards were certain to die. The Division had spent weeks in battle but not one man thought of running away. In battle one has many chances of surviving – but no one escaped the execution squads.' The evidence of their vigilance is frequently mentioned in Austrian works and one SS man – Division not given – recalled seeing bodies hanging from lamp-posts, each corpse bearing a placard proclaiming the dead man to have been a traitor or a coward. Not even buildings were spared. In revenge for a white flag flown from the spire of St Stephan's cathedral orders were given to a flak battery positioned on the Bisamberg to reduce the historic building to rubble. The order was rejected but the cathedral was not saved. Flames from houses surrounding it started a fire which burned for five days and nights.

'Our withdrawals from the outer city into the perimeter along the Canal, were carried out by night and were protected by little groups of panzer, SPs or Flak guns. The grenadier outposts used torches to signal to one another. In those streets where there were no burning buildings to lighten the darkness, we fired flares to show us whether the enemy was moving. We fought the Russians on the ground, below ground in the sewers and above ground against the Red Air Force, whose planes swarmed like flies over the city attacking everything indiscriminately.' The fiercest fighting was, of course, in the rapidly shrinking perimeter, an area which was blanketed by intense artillery and mortar fire. The few remaining panzers of the Division's regiment supported the perimeter defence, driving from one threatened sector to another, their gunfire helping to smash the assaults of the Russians. Some sub-units of the panzer regiment were also seconded to neighbouring formations and for the period 11–12 April, the last eight vehicles of No. 6 Company were on detached duty supporting the grenadiers of 4th Panzer Division, a formation which now had no armoured fighting vehicles at all.

The sober, factual account by Karl Heinz Boske, commanding No. 6 Company, deals with the fighting in the Danube Canal perimeter in an objective way and begins with the remark that the Prater area was the scene of bitter fighting.

'The panzers of No. 6 Company knocked out a few enemy tanks but suffered the loss of one vehicle. It was not thought likely that the positions in the Prater could be held much longer than 12 April, and as the Russians – from Malinovski's 2nd Ukrainian Front – were also coming down from north of the Danube towards the Reichsbruecke, the 4th Panzer Division decided to withdraw from their sector and cross the Danube before they were cut off. That Division carried out this retirement throughout the night of 12/13 April and the panzers of my No. 6 Company did not leave the Prater area until dawn on the 13th. For reasons which have never been explained the

Reichsbruecke was not blown up to stop the Russians from using it. The General commanding 4th Panzer then ordered me to return to my own Division which was holding positions in the area of the Florisdorf bridge. I drove through the streets north of the Danube and reached Florisdorf where I found not only units of the panzer regiment but also Regimental HQ. The Workshop Company was busy repairing the regiment's vehicles and also worked on those of my own company which had been battle damaged. Armoured units went out to those parts of Vienna where they were most urgently needed. My No. 6 Company lost a vehicle and crew. No one knows how this happened, but it is believed that the machine was destroyed by a Panzerfaust fired by an Austrian partisan. When the line around Florisdorf had to be pulled back the panzer commanded by Obersacharführer Barkmann of No. 2 Company was hit and knocked out. He himself was wounded but survived the War.

'The withdrawal from the Prater of 4th Panzer Division meant that we had an open eastern flank. I put in two of my panzers; a Mark IV under Oberscharführer Glazer and a Panther commanded by Oberscharführer Schinner, to guard the area. They were not able to take a really active part in the fighting which continued throughout 13 April, as they were in too exposed a position. When I reported wth my company to the regimental commander, I was put in to hold a sector on the north bank of the Danube and somewhat to the west of the Florisdorf bridge. There were already two machines from No. 2 Company on that sector and these were placed under my command.

'The Divisional Commander, Standartenführer Lehmann, ordered the panzer regiment's commanding officer, to send a few panzers across the bridge to support the bridgehead until the time came for it to be evacuated during the coming night. The wounded Standartenführer Lehmann was sheltering under the bridge on my sector of the front and I made the strongest possible protest about that order, telling him that the bridge was narrow and had been badly damaged. Vehicles crossing it would have to do so slowly and under direct enemy observation which would mean their certain loss. My objections were in vain. Neither the Panzer IV nor the Jagdpanther were suitable for such an operation and this meant that Panthers would have to make the crossing. This task was not one which I could ask others to take and I left my own Command vehicle Jagdpanther and took over the Panther and crew of Ubersturmführer Wahlmann. Two other Panthers were selected to accompany me.

'Together with the other two commanders I went forward to the bridge to carry out a close recce as well as to discuss with Barkmann, who had recently crossed the bridge and knew the difficulties, the best way of tackling the problem. There was no movement to be seen at all in the area. Everybody was under cover hiding from the heavy barrage which the Russians in the inner city were bringing down. It was agreed that the three Panthers should cross with long intervals between them. Not until the first vehicle had reached the gaping hole in the centre of the bridge was the second Panther to drive up to the foot of the bridge. That also applied to the third machine. In the event that the leading machine was knocked out on the bridge – which seemed very likely because the enemy could observe the whole – area – the other two Panthers were to pull back. I was in the first Panther and as it passed by the hole in the middle of the bridge the second machine, Ludwig van Hecke's, moved forward. I increased speed and reached the perimeter under intense fire from Russian anti-tank guns and tanks. A hit in the hull on the driver's side set my vehicle alight and mortally wounded both the driver and the radio operator, but we others leapt clear. I fell badly and shattered my right heel. Our Panther burned for several hours. As arranged, the second Panther pulled back and the third did not make the attempt. I reported to the Divisional commander that the mission had failed and during the evening crossed the bridge on foot accompanied by my two survivors and returned to my own company. The bridgehead was evacuated that night. Throughout the following day the units on the northern bank and in the suburbs of Vienna began to pull out, moving westwards. The Russians, on the southern side of the river, had perfect observation of our movements and in the wooded hill country behind the northern bank there were frequent brushes with the infiltrating enemy. Despite those we were able to disengage and to set up a new front.

This retreat took 'Das Reich' Divison towards new concentration areas around Melk and St Poelten; a withdrawal which was made under the protection of rear guards fighting against unrelenting Russian pressure. Heid Ruehl's battery was one of the units supporting the rear guard as the Division drew away from Vienna, marching via the Bisamberg towards the heart of Austria. He wrote of those final days.

'We held the flood of Russian infantry storming from the direction of Deutsch-Wagram and Markgrafensiedl until orders came for us to cross the Bisamberg. Army units which should have used the roads along the Danube bank, had been driven from these by Russian shellfire and crowded on to the poor roads allotted to our Division. These were little more than tracks running through extensive woods and were soon deep in mud and severely rutted. We made very slow progress.

'At one point an armoured personnel carrier completely blocked the road at a point where it was not possible to by-pass it. It took so long for the vehicle's crew to repair the broken track that by the time we emerged from the woods Russian infantry were attacking from the direction of Bisamberg village. Our flank was open because the "Grossdeutschland" panzer unit which should have been guarding the units withdrawing from Vienna had been pulled out of our sector and put in at another place. I was the only officer on the spot to deal with the crisis and stopped any threat from the high ground on our flank by putting out machine-gun detachments, while some half-tracks and my own guns went action. We fired a short barrage, after which our signals detachment carried out an infantry attack against houses from which fire was coming. A great many Russians fled from these. I put machine-gun posts on both flanks to keep the crossroads open while the guns and the vehicles drove off in the direction of Stetten.

'The terrain was flat and devoid of cover. The Russians bombarded us from the Vienna woods, about 6 to 7 kilometres distant and the infantry masses which we had driven back earlier returned and attacked under cover of a mortar barrage. I was helping to direct traffic at the crossroads when a mortar bomb wounded me. I was loaded on the back of a prime mover and wedged between boxes of shells and ammunition. While being evacuated to field hospital I saw the regimental commander, briefed him on what had happened and asked him to ensure that the units surrounded near the Bisamberg, were brought out. The vehicle then took me to hospital in Stockerau.'

Another artilleryman, in No. 11 Battery, also records the events of that retreat.

'On the Bisamberg was the Vienna radio station and one could look down from the summit of the mountain and see, to the right, as far as the Czech border while below us on the left, there was the Danube and the Korneuburg–Stockerau road which the Russians had already cut. One of the guns from our No. 12 Battery had tipped over and blocked the road leading down from the mountain top to the village of Bisamberg. We were isolated and spent a whole night, from Saturday 14 April to Sunday, I think it was, unable to move forward. We hoped that our people would make a counter-attack and get us out.

'From our positions we could see great columns of Russians with *panje* carts marching westwards and saw how the Russian soldiers who had occupied the first houses of the village of Bisamberg forced the villagers, men and women, to do the goose step, backwards and forwards, from quite early in the morning. Meanwhile, our artillery continued to fire shells which landed on the outskirts of Korneuburg where there was a Russian battery in position.

'We were without weapons and moved about on the mountain, in and out of the woods, hoping to find a gap through which we could reach our comrades. Finally some Russian soldiers, probably of the third wave, captured us. They took everything we had, including our military documents, and marched us down the mountain to join a group of prisoners already waiting there.'

The mass of the Division had, meanwhile, reached the new concentration area at Melk and there the grenadiers were able to enjoy a few days out of the line. During that time the regiments absorbed the replacements which had come in. Those for 'Deutschland' Regiment were mainly recruits with little training or combat experience. Some were firemen from Dresden. Then Division received orders that it was to march to Dresden. 'Deutschland' Regiment was not, initially, to accompany the mass of the Division but was to beat back the American attacks against Passau. Once it had cleared up that situation 'Deutschland' was to rejoin the main body. 'Der Führer', the other grenadier regiment, drove into southern Czechoslovakia, and while it awaited orders to join the Division, it learned that this had now gone into action around Dresden. Neither regiment was able to join the other divisional units and as a result 'Das Reich' Division never again fought as a complete unit.

'Deutschland' had, in fact, only a minor role in military operations from 29 April until the end of the war. There were skirmishes with American units but little fighting of any consequence. Orders came from Sixth SS Panzer Army for the Regiment to capitulate and on 8 May, after a final parade at which decorations were presented, it crossed the Enns bridge into captivity. With it went the last three survivors of the divisional assault company, but before that surrender there was one final rear-guard operation demanded of part of 'Das Reich' Panzer Regiment in the St Poelten area.

'As commander of an independent battle group I was with the panzer regiment of "Das Reich" Division when, during April 1945, it made its way from Vienna to St Poelten. We took part in the defensive fighting to the east of St Poelten, taking up our position in Spratzern, a southern suburb of the town. It was there that we lost the last men of the unit to be wounded or killed in action during the war. Towards the end of the month the main body of "Das Reich" Division arrived in our area and an attack was planned for the Traisen sector but that operation was cancelled. Slowly the great machine which was the German Army began to die.

'The mass of the Division, including the panzer regiment, reached Dresden, the last area in which the Division was to see action. "Deutschland" Regiment was fighting at Passau and "Der Führer" Regiment was employed on a rescue operation in Prague. Most of the panzer regiment's units were entrained in Poechlarn on the Danube and were to be transported to Dresden by rail. However, when it was my unit's turn to be loaded the railways were no longer running and we were ordered to cross the Danube and carry out a road march to Dresden, going via Krems, Zwettl, Budweis and Prague.

'I made a quick reconnaissance trip by car to Budweis to establish whether there were fuel supplies for us there. There were not and I returned determined not to move up into Czechoslovakia where my company and I might find ourselves at the end of the war with vehicles but no fuel to move them.'

After being ordered to report on temporary attachment to 'Totenkopf' Division Langanke was told that the Division could not use him and he was to return to the Corps that had sent him out. At that headquarters he was ordered to take his unit to Kirchberg am Wagram (which lies between Krems and Stockerau) and to hold the road open until the last German units had passed through.

'I took my company there and the two last days of the war came and went without my being given any orders or news. The company was quite isolated.

It was odd that at the end of the war we had a full establishment of vehicles. We had twenty-two Panthers, a Tiger II (all completely equipped) and five Panther recovery vehicles. We were all determined that none of these would fall into the hands of the Russians. We blew up the recovery vehicles near the village, and drove the remaining machines to a small stretch of road and positioned them, on the verge, in single file, with their guns pointing eastwards. My own panzer was close to the road and located so that I could shoot at and destroy each of the other vehicles when the time came.

'The unit's wheeled transport, held in the main square of the town, would be used to carry the panzer crews once our mission had been completed. We removed all surplus fittings and equipment from the lorries to give us more space. There was a final pay parade and the last canteen supplies were handed out. When that had been done No. 2 Company of 'Das Reich' Panzer Regiment paraded for the last time. The platoons were in open order and after my favourite marching song had been sung I made a short speech thanking my comrades for their efforts on behalf of our people and for the nation. They were now, I declared, released from military discipline as well as from the oath of allegiance which they had sworn. We sang the national anthem and then I went along the ranks shaking each man by the hand. Loyalty and honour were not empty words in the unit. Some of my men, from Vienna, who must have had the most terrible fears for their families, had to be repeatedly ordered to leave before they would leave the unit and go home.

'I told the parade that as far as I knew the demarcation line in the area was the railway line Linz – Budweis and that the best way of reaching it would be via Zwettl. I then ordered the company to board the lorries and to make for the American zone without delay. I went in my own truck to where our panzers were standing. My No. 1 on the gun, Schulten, and my driver Steinbauer, together with my truck driver had all volunteered to stay with me and carry out the destruction of our vehicles as soon as the last units had passed us. The day was absolutely quiet and my thoughts returned to the events of the past years. Suddenly there was movement on the road. A great number of armoured fighting vehicles was approaching. We could not at first determine whether these were Russian or German. If they were Russian tanks then this was the end for us. At last we could make out the familiar silhouette of a Panther. We breathed out. Several hundred metres away the column halted. It was clear that they could not determine who we were. The turrets on the panzer began to swing menacingly towards us. We waved to them and as they seemed still not to realize that we were Germans, I drove over and reported to the commander of the unit telling him of my mission. His reply was that this was the last detachment. Behind him were the Russians. His unit, the Führer Begleit Brigade, rolled passed us and made an impressive sight. The unit was in good order and the men showed no sign of haste or unrest as they drove past us, the last of our army to have been in action against the enemy. Then it was time for us to begin our work. With a lump in our throats we fired at and destroyed our panzers one after the other. The feeling which this aroused in us cannot be described in words. The Tiger II would not die and we had to fire several rounds into it before it caught alight. As a final act the No. 1 on the gun blew up our own machine. For some time we could not move from the place in which our vehicles were burning. Again and again the wall of flames was split by one mighty detonation after another as the ammunition inside the panzers exploded. The death-throes of vehicles which had become part of ourselves, seemed to be a symbol of our defeat. We loaded a few Panzerfaust in the truck, just in case we had to fight our way past Russian tanks, and then away we went towards Zwettl.

'The closer we came to the demarcation line the greater grew the traffic chaos. On every road and track for as far as one could see, thousands of men were making their way westwards. Nobody wanted to fall into the hands of the Russians. Motorized; on foot; mounted on horseback; individually; in groups or still in organized bodies, all of us were heading for the demarcation line and freedom.'

The Prague Rescue Operation

As previous pages have shown, towards the end of April 1945, 'Das Reich' Division was fragmented as its commanders sought to carry out the conflicting orders being received from Berlin. 'Deutschland' Regiment finished the war fighting the Americans in the St Poelten area of Austria. The panzer regiment, the artillery regiment, the Flak, the engineer battalion and the signals battalion, together with the train detachments, moved to Dresden where they were put into action. 'Der Führer' Regiment, which was in the Budweis area of Czechoslovakia, was first ordered to march to Bruenn. Then, on 30 April, that order was cancelled and Otto Weidinger, the regimental commander, was directed to report to Obergruppenführer Pückler, the SS Supreme Command, in Prague. He set out with an escort and after a longish but uneventful drive entered Prague and drove to Pückler's office.

There he learned, among other things, of the evacuation plans drawn up by Princess Stephanie should the situation in the Czech capital deteriorate to a point which threatened the lives of the German population. The senior officers of the Protectorate took pains to point out to Weidinger how calm the city was. The Obersturmbannführer then drove back to his Regiment in southern Czechoslovakia. An 'O' Group called to brief his officers on the result of the visit to Prague was a conference overshadowed, as Weidinger described in a discussion with me, by the news that Hitler was dead. Over the following three days the regiment moved steadily closer to the Czech capital and although undoubtedly aware of the hostility which lurked just below the surface of Czech civil life, saw only few obvious signs of that unrest. There was, as yet, no major Czech uprising, probably because columns of German troops were still moving through the country. But those who were able to read the signs would have noted that the soldiers of these columns were not keen fighting troops but the dispirited men of a dying army, whose hopes were to get home safely and to avoid being taken prisoner by the Russians. That sense of imminent defeat was not one which affected the Grenadiers of 'Der Führer' Regiment. Even though the man whose title they bore on their cuffs was dead, their allegiance, as Weidinger pointed out, had not died with him. They were still bound by their oath to Germany and it was for her that the Regiment would continue to fight until the war's end.

During the time that the Regiment waited in its concentration area, Weidinger received two messages. The first of these advised him that there was no chance of his unit reaching Dresden where 'Das Reich' was in action and that it was, therefore, placed under the command of Field Marshal Schoerner. The second message was from Schoerner himself, who ordered the regiment to open the road to Prague, put down the insurrection which had broken out within the city, contact General Toussaint, the military commander there, and carry out any orders that he might give. Speed of action was essential.

Weidinger had been in Prague only three days earlier and had been assured the city was calm. Now he was told that revolt of such seriousness had broken out that the German garrison and the government were isolated and almost prisoners. He prepared a battle group for action and in the bright dawn of 6 May, the battalions swung out on to the Prague road, formed column and marched northwards. As the units drove towards the Czech capital the signs of the dissolution of the German Army became more noticeable. One was the increase in the number of Czech flags; signs that power was passing from the German authorities.

A more obvious sign of the loss of authority was the increase in the number of German soldiers, disarmed, so they claimed, by Czech partisans. Another were the roadblocks which were met with greater frequency as the regiment came closer to Prague. In the outer suburbs of the city the column was halted by a huge barricade built of cobbles torn from the streets. It was not possible to by-pass this massive obstruction, nor could it be blown apart. The only solution was to set the grenadiers to dismantling it by hand. The task of creating a gap wide enough for the vehicles to pass through wasted a great many hours. Daylight went and in order that the dismantling work could continue Weidinger had the black-out shields removed from the headlights on the lorries. In the light of the headlamps the grenadiers worked, under fire from partisan snipers. A gap was cleared and the column set off through the night, headlamps blazing and making good speed until at the Troya bridge the advance was again halted, this time by a storm of small-arms fire. Weidinger had a difficult decision to make. Either to force a crossing of the bridge in the dark or of halting his regiment's advance until daylight. He chose to stop. Shortly after dawn on 7 May, the artillery battalion of the battle group began to fire a barrage, under which the grenadiers stormed forward. A Czech officer reached Weidinger's TAC HQ and offered to act as an intermediary between the SS and the partisans if only the battle group would break off the fire-fight and withdraw to Leitmeritz. That condition was rejected out of hand but the Obersturmbannführer agreed to a ceasefire only if the partisans did the same.

Hours passed and it was clear that the Czechs were playing for time. Weidinger, furious at the delay, ordered an attack which secured a small perimeter on the far side of the bridge. The battle group, formed up and ready to drive into the city, was delayed by a second Czech officer who offered to negotiate between the partisans and General Toussaint, the German Army commandant of Prague. Weidinger told the new officer of the orders he had received and very firmly expressed his intention of carrying them out. He would prefer to make the advance without interference from the partisans, but, he insisted, his men were willing and ready to fight their way through. An officer of the German Army offered to go with the Czech. Weidinger set a time limit upon the negotiations. If the German officer had not returned by 15.00 hours, he would consider the truce at an end and his artillery would reopen fire. When neither officer arrived back at the appointed time Weidinger, anxious to avoid bloodshed, extended the deadline by another hour. The two officers returned at last with news that an armistice had been agreed between the partisans and the German commanders in the Hradschin palace. During the period that they had been absent patrols from the regiment had collected stores, ammunition and, more importantly, fuel from nearby depots. Also welcome were the reinforcements, German servicemen, who came streaming in from all parts of the city to join the well-armed and resolute battalions.

At a regimental 'O' Group it was realized that there were insufficient lorries to carry the numbers of German civilians who were already waiting. Determined that not one person would be left behind it was decided that if necessary the lorries would be overloaded. The destination was Pilsen, where there were units of the American Army. In accordance with the terms of the armistice Czech partisans removed the roadblocks and erected signs to guide the SS convoy through the night. Weidinger's control of his men was tight and his orders were promptly obeyed. His superiors showed no such understanding of their position. Frank, the Viceroy, was so out of touch with the true situation in the Protectorate that he thought German rule to be still firm, while Toussaint tried to change the destination and to make the convoy head for Austria. Weidinger forced through his plans.

Shortly before the lorried convoy set out a new crisis arose. In the Prague railway sidings there were ambulance trains of wounded German soldiers. The Czech engine drivers had abandoned them. Those men could not be left behind. They would have to be rescued and place found for them in the trucks. Then a group of female SS signallers reported in. They, too, were accommodated. At last, and considerably overdue, the thousand-vehicle convoy left Prague heading for Pilsen, but this was not the end of the problems. During the morning of 9 May, a German general accompanied by a Czech colonel halted the column and demanded that all arms be surrendered.

Weidinger ordered the weapons to be rendered useless before they were thrown away. After a final pay parade and a distribution of canteen goods to the men of the regiment, the column set out again and reached its objective. The civilians and the wounded were unloaded and the column, now wholly military again, set off to drive into captivity. At about 10.00 hours on the morning of 9 May 1945, Weidinger's battle group made contact with the 2nd US Infantry Division at Rokiczany. In a field in Bohemia the fighting life of 'Der Führer' Regiment came to an end. Its last mission had not been a mighty clash of arms but a mercy mission to bring out of danger women and children who would have not survived the insurrection which then flamed throughout the Czech lands.

An account of the last days of German occupation in Prague and of the rescue mission carried out by 'Der Führer' Regiment, were written by Her Highness Ingeborg Alix, Princess Stephanie of Schaumburg-Lippe, who was posted to the Czech capital in the last weeks of the war.

'During the middle weeks of April I was posted to Prague to take up an appointment on the staff of Count Pückler, the SS commander there. A peace-time atmosphere still reigned in that lovely city, a feeling which moved me deeply for I had come from embattled Thuringia. But events were soon to prove that the peace in Prague was a false one. Rumours spread that there was to be an uprising aimed at making the Red Army's conquest of Prague an easy one. There were also reports of treks of refugees, heading for the Czech capital, coming both from Silesia and from the south. The core of that movement was made up of 48 treks with innumerable columns of lorries, horse-drawn carts and other cattle; a situation typical of those days. Other treks moving to join the main body were coming from Saxony, Thuringia and Austria; all of them fleeing in front of the Americans. This vast movement threatened to choke the roads needed by our own troops for the advances or withdrawals.

'No action had yet been taken to bring the German women and children of the Prague garrison to a place of safety, although the Russians were dangerously close and approaching from both the north and the east. We all expected and hoped that the Americans would reach and occupy the capital. They had already reached Pilsen and had taken up positions there.

'After all that I had seen and experienced in the west, my advice to the Brigadeführer, when I discussed the question of evacuation with him, was that a start should be made as a matter of urgency. The next day, Standartenführer Dr Voss, President of the Skoda works, told me that because of my experience in organization the Brigadeführer had delegated to me the task of arranging the evacuation. I had formerly been the leader of the SS Women's Auxiliary Corps in Oberehenheim. Dr Voss told me that office space and personnel would both be made available.

'Acutely aware of the heavy responsibility which had been placed on my shoulders, I took a deep breath and set off to the Hradschin Palace. There I intended to establish the true situation and to discuss co-ordination on the measures to be taken with both the civilian and the military authorities. It transpired that, first, the rumours about the streams of refugees had considerably under-estimated the size of the problem. Secondly; no order for the evacuation of the civilian Ministries had been issued. On the contrary, in order to "avoid a panic", nothing had been undertaken. Further discussion brought to light the fact that the SS commander had made arrangements for the evacuation of the families of his own officials. Count Pückler intended that his ministries would continue to function.

'I was given an office in the building in which he worked. An Untersturmführer and his wife, both of them hard workers, were seconded to me and then a third person was added to my staff. The first thing we had to establish was the number of those who were to be evacuated. We needed this information in order that we could submit an indent to the Quartermaster, Obersturmbannführer Harzig, specifying the number and size of the lorries required. The next problem was to choose an area to which the families would be evacuated as well as to establish who would furnish the escort and how strong this would have to be to bring the lorried convoys safely through partisan infested areas.

'Throughout the following days the landing in front of my office was filled with men of every rank – each of them with a family – who gave the number and composition of those of their dependants who were to be evacuated. It was astonishing how quickly the news of our activity circulated because the number of pleas for help from every branch of the Services grew hourly. The telephone rang without stop.

'That year Prague had had a beautiful spring and the glorious weather showed off the lovely buildings of the city to their best advantage. The lilac was in full bloom, the River Moldau flowed peacefully under the Charles bridge and past our office. Everything seemed to be in order.

'On 29 April the fine weather encouraged Major Knebel, the IA, and me to walk from our billets in Count Pückler's house to the Hradschin Palace. Near the Charles Bridge we met a column of motorized SS, from 'Das Reich' Division. Presently a DR came racing up and skidded his motor cycle to a halt in front of us. "The commanding officer of "Der Führer" Regiment requests that Sturmbannführer Knebel salute him according to regulations," was his message. Knebel was taken aback for a few moments but then shouted a greeting when he noticed Obersturmbannführer Weidinger seated in a Kubelwagen. The two had served together in the Junkerschule in Brunswick. We climbed into Weidinger's car and he brought us to our office building. Knebel invited him for a quick snack and over this we discussed the situation in Prague. Striking while the iron was hot I asked Obersturmbannführer Weidinger where his regiment was headed. He replied that he was on his way to Dresden, where divisional headquarters was located, to collect ammunition. The thought ran through my head, "You will never fire those rounds – but you can be of help if we need it, to bring the families out of Prague and into safety."

'I asked the CO of 'Der Führer' Regiment to keep in touch with me so that when news reached him of the uprising in Prague, he would fight his way through to us. Weidinger promised to do his best. We had, by this time, evacuated about five hundred mothers and children and had them safely under military protection in the Bavarian Forest. They were quartered in a temporary camp. But in Prague there were more than three times that number of dependants waiting, impatiently, to be brought out. They were impatient because the situation in the city had begun to deteriorate. There was a growing number of reports of clashes between Czechs and Germans in pubs as well as on the open street. A general nervousness was evident and the first shots were heard.

'The SS commander had a number of heated discussions with Toussaint, the Supreme Commander, as well as with representatives from the office of the Viceroy Frank. Pückler did not want the safe evacuation of the civilian population to be prejudiced by a premature departure of military units or civil servants and he wanted to maintain a firm front. It was also thanks to his initiative that demolitions using explosive were avoided and that, as a result, the unique and beautiful Charles bridge was left intact.

'Soon the passage of events had overtaken us. News of the fighting in and around Berlin, of the Führer's death, of the rapid advance of the Russians through the Protectorate and the inexplicable halt to the American advance west of Pilsen, filled us all with the gravest worries and caused us to speed up the pace of our work. The last convoy was dispatched only 24 hours before the uprising began. Travelling with it was one of the SS NCOs and his wife who had been working on the "family evacuations". They had been sent because reports reaching us indicated that conditions in the reception camp were deteriorating and that food was running short. Our pair went to bring order into the camp. Acting upon the advice we had been given the SS NCO was told to change out of his uniform and to wear civilian clothes for the journey. This he did most unwillingly.

'Then the storm broke. It was May 5th. It began with a completely unexpected but deliberate act. A Czech traffic policeman on duty in Wehrmacht Square fired his pistol at Obergruppenführer Kammler as the latter drove past acknowledging the policeman's salute. Kammler had been on his way to Berlin for he considered that his place should be at the Führer's side and not stuck in Prague. The Obergruppenführer's reactions were lightning fast and his bullet struck home. What then happened turned Prague into an arena of unimaginable horrors, in which murder and beatings took place. These have been described in other places and I will not repeat them here. A fresh transport of women and children had already been brought together in one of the buildings in Wehrmacht Square. I had already advised one of my staff, a female SS auxiliary who lived in the old quarter of Prague, to leave her flat and move to the Wehrmacht Square office if no accommodation could be found for her in her own office. By this time our evacuation action had been extended to cover any German families who asked for our help and our building had begun to take on the appearance of a large camp.

'6th May 1945. Absolute chaos reigned in Prague and we were at its centre. Czech partisans hiding in the houses opposite us, on the far side of the Moldau, fired at the windows of our building. Thank God most of their bullets flew high and struck the ceilings, but one or two of our people were lightly wounded. They cursed like mad when they were hit but then carried on with their work. Other units quartered in the building sent out fighting patrols to clear the streets round about and to recapture the Luftwaffe hospital close by. Their assaults were supported by an SP gun positioned in the main doorway. Our four-storey building was built of concrete and all its floors had open staircases. As you can imagine the noise was indescribable and often we had to shout in order to pass a message. The building began to look more and more like a beleaguered fortress. Then I received a telephone report from our SS NCO that the convoy had arrived safely. He wanted to know what was happening in Prague so I told him and underscored my words by letting him hear the rifle fire. Although I warned him not to return his reply was, "I am not going into captivity without my uniform, so I'll come back and collect it." This he did.

'More and more civilians, overtaken by the events on the streets outside, collected in the cellar of our building. Not surprisingly, worry and fear were printed on their faces because outside on the pavements lay dead and wounded people, including several women. I myself witnessed how one woman with a shopping basket, walking along a relatively quiet street during a pause in the fighting, was shot dead. And the bullet which killed her certainly did not come from a German weapon.

'The wounded were brought in and treated in a first aid post which we had set up. Many of these were the very young but very brave soldiers of the Hitler Youth Division. It was my task to deal with the civilians. They had to be quietened down and fed. To calm this anxious group was an almost impossible task. Prague had not suffered from air raids and many families from Germany had been evacuated to the city. The mothers of these families, separated from their children by the uprising, were desperately worried and made efforts to reach home, only to be driven back by the conditions in the streets.

'Towards nightfall it became quieter and only the sound of isolated shots could be heard. Slowly the cellar began to empty until only a few Germans remained together with some Czechs who were afraid of their own countrymen. Throughout those difficult days I pinned my hope on "Der Führer" Regiment coming to rescue us. That we were in Obersturmbann-führer Weidinger's thoughts was certain, but it was uncertain whether he would be able to reach us in time. Or had he indeed received orders which would prevent him from coming to our rescue and if that were indeed the case, then would he be able to organize help from another quarter in time?

'On 7th May, aircraft dropped bombs, but we did not know at first whether these were our own or Russian machines. It turned out that these were our fighter-bombers which had been brought in to blast a way through for other pockets of trapped troops. There was little firing on the 8th or 9th May, and only isolated shots were heard. Rumours that relief was coming let me breathe again and, indeed, rumours grew and the relief which had been only a rumour became a fact. My own authority would have been insufficient to achieve very much but that of the commander of 'Der Führer' Regiment enabled nearly one thousand vehicles to be assembled and used to rescue the German women and children trapped in Prague. Thereby, thousands escaped from a hell of Czech terror, torture, death and deportation.

'It had been no easy task to leave Prague and Count Pückler spent a long time negotiating with Czech representatives. On 9th May, our headquarters group moved out preceded by Czech representatives carrying white flags. These were not respected and despite the ceasefire which had been proclaimed, we were involved in street fighting. Our group spent some time picking up wounded and after three unsuccessful attempts finally left Prague by using side roads. The vast jams we encountered on the main roads were created by the vehicles of Field Marshal Schoerner's army which was withdrawing in front of the Russians. Some time after midday we crossed the Moldau which, until 11.30 hours, formed the boundary between the Americans and the Russians. We arrived one hour too late. On 11th May, together with 40,000 German soldiers gathered in an American camp near Pisek, we were handed over to the Russians. Obergruppenführer Kammler, Count Pückler the commander of the Waffen SS, and Obersturmbannführer Knebel did not survive.'

Czechoslovakia was the country in which the SS 'V' Division had been raised. It was perhaps, fitting that it should be the country in which it died.

While Sturmbannführer Weidinger and his regiment were fighting their way towards and into Prague, another unit of the Division, the replacement battalion of 'Deutschland' Regiment, was holding out in one of the city's suburbs. A replacement battalion is, by definition, one which sends out drafts of men to units in the field. Most of those replacements were recruits but their numbers were leavened by experienced soldiers, convalescents, determined to return to 'the old mob'. The recruits and veterans of 'Deutschland's replacement battalions were quartered in the Rusin barracks, some five or six kilometres outside the Czech capital and adjacent to the aerodrome.

In May 1945 the unit, with an establishment of eight companies, had a total strength of some 1,300 men. The demands upon the battalion's clothing and weapons stores, to outfit earlier drafts, had been such that by March 1945 there were insufficient uniforms to clothe all the soldiers. More seriously, a shortage of weapons meant that the recruits could be armed only with carbines and 30 rounds of ammunition.

Rumours of Czech uprisings, together with an increase in partisan activity were not unexpected by Sturmbannführer Oettinger, the battalion commander, and his concern must have deepened with the news that General Buntyaschenkov's Division, about 18,000 strong, had switched allegiance. That formation, part of General Vlassov's army, which had been raised to serve on the side of the Germans, had now changed sides and had made common caused with the Czechs against the Germans. On 2 May Oettinger's battalion was ordered to block the roads to the south-west of Prague so as to halt the advance of the turncoat Russians. Before undertaking this task the Sturmbannführer decided to concentrate inside Rusin airfield all those units that had been billeted in the neighbouring villages. That done, the next step was to provide fresh meat in the event of a siege and he ordered cattle to be driven on to the aerodrome. The third step was to organize its defence so as to create a firm base for the battalion's efforts. This accomplished he was ready to march his men out on their blocking mission – but events overtook him. Insurrection broke out in Prague and spread throughout the whole of Czechoslovakia. The under-armed replacement battalion now had to hold and defend the aerodrome against Czech partisans as well as against the renegade Russian Division.

The Luftwaffe colonel commanding the airfield learned of the uprising, entered into negotiations with the Czechs and agreed that partisans should take over guard on the airfield. Oettinger replaced him with another Luftwaffe officer, a highly decorated lieutenant-colonel, who was as determined to defend the area as was the SS commander. Oettinger deployed two hundred of his men to undertake the defence of the airfield. He also increased his battalion's fire-power with several 88mm guns and a four-barrelled anti-aircraft cannon. With its defences in order and with an adequate supply of food, the replacement battalion stood to arms awaiting the onslaught of the Russians and the partisans.

The SS did not have long to wait. Within a day Buntyaschenkov's men reached the airfield perimeter and opened fire with mortars and machine-guns. Their snipers soon dominated the 500-yard-wide strip of ground between the barracks and the airfield. Despite the danger Oettinger made frequent trips across the strip to keep up his men's spirits. Morale suffered a loss when the telephone lines between the airfield and Pückler, the senior commander of the SS in Prague, were cut, leaving the airfield's wireless set as the garrison's only remaining link with the outside world.

Over that set the Luftwaffe officer learned of Germany's imminent capitulation and informed Oettinger, advising him of the High Command directive that all German units were to make best possible speed so as to reach the American lines. The two commanders decided that their units would make separate attempts to break through the Vlassov troops to reach the west. The Luftwaffe had transport which the SS did not. Outside the Russian ring the Luftwaffe had a great vehicle park of coaches and omnibuses which would carry them to safety. To help evacuate the replacement battalion's wounded, the Luftwaffe commander promised that the coaches would be brought back and turned over to the SS. Oettinger then set about organizing his unit's breakout. Chief among his problems was the need to find sufficient volunteers to form a rearguard which would hold the enemy at bay while the main body of the battalion escaped. This problem was resolved when Obersturmführer Wagner, commanding the battalion's Convalescent Company, volunteered his 120 experienced soldiers so that the desperate, almost suicidal task would not fall upon untrained recruits. Oettinger accepted Wagner's offer but stressed that once the main body of the battalion had broken through the enemy ring, Wagner was to bring his group out.

In the early hours of the morning of 8 May, the replacement battalion set out to smash its way through to reach Laun. At the head of the column was a self-propelled vehicle mounting an anti-aircraft heavy machine-gun. Behind this came the lorries carrying the men of the grenadier companies, armed with just their carbines and a few rounds of ammunition. Dispersed among the companies were the badly wounded men laid on horse-drawn carts. Another self-propelled vehicle mounting a heavy machine-gun brought up the rear of the column. When Wagner realized that the main body of the battalion was nearing the Russian positions he and the rearguard fired off one last volley and stormed forward in a charge. They smashed through the encircling ring and by striking southwards hoped to draw the attention of the Cossack troops away from the main breakout attempt. It was unnecessary. The mass of the battalion broke through without incident and sped along the road to Saaz.

At about 10.00 hours Oettinger's battalion reached the area where it had been arranged that the Luftwaffe coaches would be waiting. Neither transports nor Luftwaffe personnel were there and the commander decided to waste no time waiting for them to arrive. Every minute was precious for the battalion was halted in what was now enemy territory. The column set out again and after hours of travelling finally reached Zlonice where it was decided to make camp for the night. Hardly had the tired grenadiers settled down when they were awakened again. The time was just after midnight and the report which had been brought in by dispatch rider announced the end of the war and the urgent need to gain the American lines at Pilsen. The column reformed ready to continue the march, but reports which came in from motor-cycle reconnaissance patrols told that the roads to Saaz were blocked by Russian tanks. The battalion could now no longer move as a single, cohesive body but would have to fragment into small groups which would filter through the enemy line. At Oettinger's final conference group leaders were selected. Then, parties each about 120-strong, began their escape attempts, plunging into the dark forests, moving noiselessly and skirting paths or crossroads on which the enemy would have guards.

Little has been learned of what subsequently happened to these groups, nor are the names known of all the men who constituted them. What is known for certain is that the greatest number did not escape. Whether as groups or as individuals most were captured, although there were others who fell in battle against Russians units or partisan detachments, firing their last rounds of ammunition as they made a hopeless charge against an enemy superior in numbers and fire power. In a sense those who fell in battle were the fortunate ones, for the end of many of those who surrendered was a brutal one at the hands of a murder squad. Of those held in a barn at Zlonice, for example, only seven managed to get away. The remainder were beaten to death or shot. After making one escape Oettinger and his group were recaptured near Saaz and held in a gymnasium from which only he and an NCO managed to break out. All the other prisoners-of-war held in the gymnasium were slaughtered.

What happened to the rearguard under Wagner is not known. It is assumed that he and his men fell in battle fighting against the numerically superior Russian division, but there is nothing known for certain for nothing more has ever been heard of them.

All that is certain is that the replacement battalion of 'Deutschland' Regiment died in the pine woods of Bohemia.

The End of the War

With the end of the war in Europe, the SS divisions laid down their trophies and passed into captivity. There had been concern expressed among the Western Allies that the SS would ignore the order to surrender and continue the armed struggle, but that fear proved groundless. Obedient to the orders issued by Admiral Dönitz, who had succeeded Hitler as Head of State, the survivors of the proud divisions entered makeshift prison camps. Most tried to surrender to the soldiers of the Western Powers for they knew that to be taken by the Red Army, or by Tito's partisans, was a sentence of death which might be quick – a bullet in the back of the head – or long-drawn-out, working as a beast of burden in the carcinogenic and poisonous atmosphere of a uranium mine.

Some elements of 'Das Reich' Division capitulated to the Russian forces in or around Dresden. Another major grouping finished the war fighting against the American Army in Austria while a third group, which had been involved in the Prague rescue mission, surrendered to other US units in the border region of western Czechoslovakia.

The veterans of 2nd SS Panzer Division 'Das Reich' were proud men; men whose boast it had been that the articles of their faith were inscribed on the cuff titles they wore. Many had served in the pre-war 'V-T' where any slight physical defect had been a bar to being accepted into the ranks of that élite unit. Those men had fought Germany's first campaigns and had then criss-crossed the continent of Europe from the Atlantic coast to the suburbs of Moscow. They had endured the killing cold of a Russian winter and the suffocating heat of that country's summer season. They had survived the fury of enemy barrages on the ground and fighter-bomber attacks from the air. Now, although they did not feel themselves to be defeated, they had been ordered to surrender and obedient to that humiliating order, prepared themselves for the ordeal. What, they asked themselves, were they like, these Americans, whose prisoners they would shortly become? The soldiers of 'Das Reich' were very soon to find out.

Hans Hauser, commanding officer of 1st Battalion 'Der Führer' Regiment, spent a year as a prisoner-of-war in American hands. From his book covering the period from May 1945 to May 1946, I have selected the account of his first two days in captivity.

'Early morning on 10th May 1945. Thousands of us from the Army and from the Waffen SS are lying in a meadow on the left side of the Prague–Pilsen road. In the early morning light we can see the American tanks which surround our field are covering us with their guns. American sentries tramp to and fro as they guard the sleeping camp. Without a blanket but wrapped in my overcoat, I lie on the bare earth and shiver with cold. Slowly the memories of what happened yesterday come back to me.'

Hauser recalled that the regimental commander, Otto Weidinger, was determined that his formation would not be taken as a rabble but would surrender in correct military fashion. 'Der Führer' Regiment, therefore, marched into captivity as an organized body and Hauser, whose battalion formed the Regiment's rearguard wondered, too, about the Americans.

'Suddenly, we saw American soldiers on both sides of the road. My car was stopped, the door was torn open and before I could grasp what was happening the watch was snatched from my wrist and a negro hand tore off all the medals and decorations on my jacket. The car door was slammed shut and we were ordered to drive on. I noticed that all the following vehicles were dealt with in the same fashion. Then we were halted again. This time I was dragged out of my seat and on to the pavement. The car was ordered to drive off without me. An American soldier gestured that I should carry a huge black suitcase but before I could obey his order another American came, took one look at me and told the first man, "He is an officer." I was ordered to join the column marching along the edge of a road lined with American soldiers and Czech civilians who spat at us and felt our wrists to see whether we still had watches or jewellery. This gauntlet was about 1 kilometre long, but then a sentry pointed to an empty field on the left of the road. I could see men of my regiment there and after undergoing a body search joined my comrades who had been waiting for some time in this field. Among them was my regimental commander, Otto Weidinger, to whom I reported in the standard formal fashion, that 1st Battalion had arrived. Suddenly I was grabbed violently by a tall American who stuck a pistol into my chest and asked whether I had given the "German salute". Truthfully, I replied that I had, because it seemed pointless to explain that a military salute and a "German" salute were one and the same thing. The American asked whether or not I knew that the use of the "German salute" was forbidden. He kept his pistol pressed to my chest while I explained to him that I had only just arrived and did not know that that salute was not allowed. He then left threatening to shoot me at the first opportunity. My comrades and I slowly began to understand that although the Geneva Convention did exist – on paper – how it was applied by the victors to the vanquished was another thing; particularly when those vanquished were members of the Waffen SS.

'The same American came and ordered me to march the prisoners to another field some 500 metres distant and to make camp there. When the men had fallen in I pointed out to the American that my superior officer was present and that he should take the parade. At this he shook his head and said, "No! You must carry out the order." I duly marched the column across to the new place and found my driver who had had the presence of mind to take my overcoat before being forced out of the car. Those comrades who had blankets began to make camp on the field. Others opened their rucksacks and began to eat. I noted that the number of sentries guarding us was being increased and saw a long column of German soldiers marching along the road accompanied by the insults of Czech civilians and sometimes those of American soldiers. Slowly it began to get darker and quieter, except for the unusual noise made by the American tanks. We were more accustomed to the sound of Russian ones. Searchlights began to sweep across us, but whether this was to protect us from the plundering Czechs or whether the Americans were afraid that we might escape, I cannot say.

'I was woken from sleep by the bitter cold. The pale light of dawn on 10th May, showed me that those around me were beginning to wake up . . . An American soldier came up to me and showed great interest in my cap. Before I could understand what interested him he had seized it and removed the motoring goggles, which he obviously considered valuable. He flung the cap back to me and left. Another American appeared and he too looked at my field cap. He then pointed to his head and I understood. He wanted the death's head cap badge. He thanked me – as if it would have been possible for me to refuse his request – and left saying "Souvenir". These little episodes showed the whole stupidity of war. I had spent years fighting on the Eastern Front, never knowing whether I would ever see my family again, and these American boys had come across the Atlantic and would take home as trophies a pair of motoring goggles and a death's head badge.

'Otto Weidinger had had his 'Oak Leaves' torn from his throat and other comrades had their epaulettes and collar patches ripped off. Rings, cash and other things were taken and always accompanied by a mocking smile, the word "souvenir" and a pointed pistol. I had nothing more to fear. I had nothing left, except my silver death's head ring and my wedding ring, both of which I had concealed in the heels of my jack boots during the night. The sun came up and there was more traffic on the road, including more long columns of prisoners all with empty, tragic faces.

'In the full light of day we could see one POW camping place after another. The road was still packed with tired, marching German soldiers and around the camp Czech civilians who came steadily nearer and nearer to us, until at last an American officer ordered them to be driven back . . . Our questions about food were not answered directly. It seemed that our Ration Train had been sent to another camp. Suddenly my driver arrived bringing with him my rucksack with tooth brush, shaving kit and other necessary items. There was even something to eat and a number of cigarettes. My driver's thoughtfulness and care were deeply touching, especially because I had not asked him for help. Little incidents showed us that life was returning. We drew water from a nearby stream; some men began to wash and to shave. We must not let others see how deeply the catastrophe had hit us. Slowly the 10th May drew to a close and I noted with a certain satisfaction that things began to be organized. We talked about missing comrades, but none of us spoke of the capitulation or of the future. Fires were lit and quiet descended upon our camp.'

Another group of units belonging to 'Das Reich' Division were among the great mass of German soldiers which surrendered in Ober-Haid, north of Freistadt, in the Waldviertel of Bohemia. The local civil population was busy swapping things with the soldiers, things which the military would have had to abandon anyway. Straw stacks in the area were practically cleared out as the soldiers tried to find something to put between them and the cold earth. 'The Americans were not much in evidence – a few lorries and a jeep patrol. The "Chewing Gum men" were creatures from another world for us. Not bad types but to be handled with care. There was no fence around the camp, but there was a demarcation line, which was enough. The thought that had gone through all our heads as our lorries had driven into the camp area was "We've survived".'

In captivity the SS sought to hide their identity by wearing the uniform of other branches of service, by destroying their identity documents or, in extreme cases, by being operated on. Understanding doctors of the German Army helped to disguise the SS tattoo mark under the left armpit by operating on the area and writing on the medical notes that the wound had been caused by a gunshot or by shrapnel. Rumours are the currency in prisoner-of-war camps and those in western Czechoslovakia were no exception. The greatest number of rumours dealt with discharge – a quick discharge, just in case the Allies decided that this mass of men should be handed over to the Red Army. If that were to happen no one from 'Das Reich' Division would ever return from Russia. Rumours swept the camps – that discharge must soon take place because the Americans could not feed such a great number of prisoners; because there were no camp facilities and because plague and pestilence would soon sweep the camps. Indeed a start was made in the US camps to sort out from the great mass of prisoners those who would be of greatest help in the reconstruction of Germany.

'I was employed as a clerk in a commission that was set up to release prisoners and my friend Rudi was one of the first to be seen by a group of people who called themselves doctors. They checked the inside of his left arm and asked him stupid questions. His answers were a tissue of lies but were accepted. Rudi was soon out. A quarter of an hour later that commission was broken up because a stupid Viennese boy admitted not only that he had been an SS man but more seriously that a lot of his comrades were also in the camp. This 15-year-old boy who had been evacuated with the Division when both his parents were killed in the fighting for the city, had let the cat out of the bag. What were we to do?

'I sat thinking and suddenly a man crawled into my tent. "We need another man to play cards," he said as an introduction, and took me back to his own place. This was almost a feudal palace – a field kitchen with chairs and a table. Then he introduced himself as a Sturmbannführer. How did he know that I was an SS man? "From Rudi," he answered. We ended the evening with cognac. It was something which he had brought and which had to be consumed quickly before the enemy seized it. Two days later I was ordered to report to the Demobilization Commission. I was interrogated for half an hour but was then discharged to become a farmhand, and with papers made out for my home town. I waited for my card-playing partner, but he took his time. His home was in the east and he was in no hurry to return there. When he came at last he had a man with him. "He has two artillery horses," he said, "and I have the limber. He wants to get to Mainz and I to Wiesbaden. We need someone on this trip to act as ballast. Do you want to come?"

'We set out next morning and when we reached Aigen were given a roomy cart and a tarpaulin cover, but before we had even left the village two pretty girls from the Signals and a 16-year-old anti-aircraft gunner asked to come with us. They all wanted to get to Cologne – away from the Russians – even though they lived in Silesia. We had enough space and enough food and moved slowly resting the horses which grazed on the clover that was beginning to ripen. We underwent checks in nearly every village and in one we had an unpleasant experience. We had halted to buy bread using the coupons which were issued when we left the camp. An American sentry stopped us and brought his sergeant who told us that we would have to give up the horses as a new order had been issued. I pretended not to understand him but then he lost his temper and spoke in perfect German. Now I had to understand and I said that we had so much luggage that we would have to unload it outside the village. He warned us against trying to escape with the cart but one of the girls gave us directions and we drove down a path on the left-hand side of the road and made our getaway.'

Despite its sinking up to its axles in swamp and having to be dragged out backwards from the clinging slime, the wagon and its occupants soon found firm going, drove along a forest path across a ford at the River Ilz and headed westwards into the American zone of Germany.

Another survivor of those days told how he wandered through the bombed-out streets of Würzburg not knowing where to go until an old woman told him that he was not allowed to be on the street after curfew and took him home with the explanation that she had a son in the Services and hoped that some mother would look after him if he needed it. "For the first time for years I sleep the whole night through; a deep and dreamless sleep, without the feeling of constant danger or the pressure of unending watchfulness . . . On the roads there are many making the same sort of journey as me . . . an army of millions going home, searching for peace. I did not dare go to our home because if someone recognized me then I would be certain to be arrested. And so I worked as a labourer in a farm near my father's birth place. I now had a roof over my head and enough to eat, even if it was only simple fare. Displaced persons had stolen all the farmer's supplies. The Americans allowed the DPs to steal what they liked until the farmers organized patrols and fought against the thieves. After that the raids stopped. When harvesting was finished I received news from my wife. We arranged to meet in Munich and en route I gained employment as a joiner's apprentice in a little village. Another piece of luck came my way. I found a furnished room in the village and my wife came to join me. Learning to live with her was another lesson I had to learn because we had married in 1942 during convalescent leave and had only spent a few months together.

'There were also a few anxious times. The Communist authorities in eastern Germany confiscated my father-in-law's property. Another piece of the past had been lost; another hope of better times had vanished. Then my wife worried because a jeep-load of American soldiers had arrested a neighbour who had been in the police force, but nothing happened to us and we celebrated our first peace-time Christmas. In February there was a new form which had to be filled out and as a result of the details which I had to give became aware that the time of reckoning was close. My wife and I went to our old home town even though we knew we would certainly be denounced by those who wanted to be rewarded with Chesterfield cigarettes and chewing gum.' [At this time there was a de-Nazification programme in Germany. All those who had been in proscribed organizations, such as the SS, were interned, then tried and imprisoned until they had been 're-educated to learn about Peace . . . '] 'Those who tried and condemned us were quite ignorant. The counsel who prosecuted me stated I must have been a war criminal because within the space of three years I had reached officer rank, whereas he (who had served in the German Army) had only risen as high as a lance-corporal despite the fact that he had a matriculation certificate. I learned, later, that he had been discharged from his post for corruption and immorality with a number of women. And we were supposed to be re-educated by people like that.'

Although the greatest number of men from 'Das Reich' Division surrendered to the Americans there were others who endured captivity at the hands of the Russians. One of these had been wounded and was in a hospital in Budapest when the Russians captured the city. He was taken to a prison camp near Cegled, 100 kilometres to the east of Budapest and experienced there the method of selecting prisoners for discharge or for transportation to Russia. The prisoners, all stripped to the waist, were first thumped on the chest and then stamped on the buttocks and the chest with a number – 1 to 4. All groups lower than four went sent to the Soviet Union. The No. 4 Group was made up almost exclusively of amputees. One morning the cripples were ordered to parade and were addressed by a Russian officer who told them that they were now free to go home. Each man had to leave his boots behind but none was given a discharge certificate.

Within two days the German group, numbering some 400 men and including some from the SS, had organized carts to carry their more seriously crippled comrades and set out on their westward march. In Hungarian villages the locals had lost almost everything but still managed to give the hungry ex-prisoners something to eat and advised them to avoid Budapest where they might be attacked by Hungarian Communists and Russians. The group, still barefoot, then marched to the border town of Vecses. To the north lay Saxony and Silesia, to the west was Austria and to the north-west the road to Salzburg and to southern Germany. Three of the group, including the author of the above account, set out to reach Salzburg. A Hungarian fisherman ferried them across the Danube and advised them to head for Erd where a number of Volksdeutsche families lived. These fed the group and gave them old shoes to cover their bare feet. The railway lines had, by this time, been repaired and a service of sorts was running. On the platform at Erd there were some hundred men from the Cegled camp waiting patiently for a train to take them westwards. The Russian railway transport officer was all for shooting the ex-prisoners until he was told that they were all amputees. He telephoned the Cegled camp commander who assured him that the men were not escaped prisoners and he then put them on a train as far as the frontier town of Hegyeshalom (Gran). The frontier was crossed and an Austrian village entered. There the men were welcomed as the first ex-prisoners to come from the east. They reached Vienna at curfew and escorted by policemen, the group of shaven-headed, mostly shoeless, amputees reached Vienna's West Station. The next step was to pass through the Russian zone of Austria and to try to reach Salzburg, which lay in the American zone. The group was advised not to try to cross the frontier at the town of Steyr and were ferried across the Danube again. On its southern bank the three comrades infiltrated past the Russian patrols but once inside the American zone were betrayed by civilians to some drunken American soldiers who took them to the concentration camp at Mauthausen. The four-week period in that camp was marked by several types of torture inflicted by those who had formerly been inmates of the concentration camp. One former inmate took great delight in beating the SS men on the stumps of their legs and arms. The American guards made no effort to halt the brutality and torture.

Then came the night when the SS men were ordered to move into the punishment block on the edge of the camp. Two days later the American sentries were withdrawn and replaced by Red Army men. To the prisoners it seemed that they were about to be taken to Russia and to avoid that some men cut the veins in their wrists. Their suicide attempts proved to be unnecessary; the SS group was taken first to Linz, in the American zone, and then moved to a new camp. For the author this was the start of a 14-month-long journey through a number of US camps. Some were hell-holes in which the GI guards acted with incredible brutality, but in others the American guards treated their captives as soldiers. Harder to understand was the attitude of a great many Germans. The Archbishop of Munich visited the camp and announced, 'We Germans are all responsible for the war. You are all guilty of crimes. Every unborn German child in its mother's womb is guilty of this war.' That accusation, as the same author stated sarcastically, was a very fine greeting from the Catholic Church. The last stage of the road was when the author reached a British camp and was discharged with his 'certificate'. He could go home again.

The final story of the life and conditions experienced by former SS men in the immediate post-war period is by Heinz Waechtler who began his anecdote with the words:

'It was in the days when engine drivers were being arrested because the German word for engine driver was "Lokomotiveführer" and anybody who had been a Führer was automatically arrested. Just before the Americans reached our area I was discharged from hospital, some 3 kilometres from my home town where my wife and child were living. Under the "automatic arrest" regulations I was soon under lock and key. One day an American lieutenant leading a group of heavily armed soldiers, stormed into the workshop of the little electrical company in which I had found employment and declared I was under arrest. I must admit he was embarrassed at seeing what a fine catch he had made – a one-legged, badly wounded cripple.

'In the county gaol I was interrogated by a US officer of the CID who spoke excellent German. After taking down my details he asked for those of my family. When I gave him these he asked where my wife came from and then asked whether I had married Lina or her sister Ida. He then dismissed me and I expected to be transferred to a prison camp. Instead a few days later I was put into a jeep and taken home. I entered the small room we had been given because we were "refugees" and in which the only pieces of furniture were two beds, one of them a child's bed, a cupboard, table and two chairs. There was also an old-fashioned stove which looked just about good enough to warm up a cup of coffee. In the doorway I could smell goulash (probably made from corned beef), real coffee, cigarettes, etc. My wife had prepared a fine meal for my homecoming and in the corner was a box filled with tins of every sort.

'I stood there with my rucksack on my back wondering where the food had come from. My feelings can be understood when it is remembered what women were prepared to do in those days for a tin of food. The explanation was more improbable than any piece of fiction. It appeared that my wife, uncertain of what had happened to me, had gone to the CID, taking our baby with her. She saw the head of the Section and in the course of their talk it came out that he and my wife had gone to the same school. Also their parents had been neighbours before his had emigrated to America. He had, therefore, filled our baby's pram with food and had sent my wife and child home.'

Epilogue

Shortly before he died in 1972, Paul Hausser, the SS-'V-T' Division's first commander, wrote the foreword to *Wenn alle Brüder schweigen*, an illustrated history of the Waffen SS. In that foreword he stated that the role of the German Army during the Second World War was no longer 'problematical', but went on to say that there were still differences of opinion concerning the part played by the Waffen SS in the Second World War.

Hausser was restating the thesis advanced in his book, *Soldaten wie andere auch*, which claimed that, 'Never before in the history of warfare had the soldiers of any formation carved for themselves a reputation like that of the Waffen SS.' He went on to cite the battles which the SS units had fought, out of which had grown a legendary reputation acknowledged by both friends and foe, ' . . . positioned', as he claims, 'between envious admiration and superstitious fear. There was agreement on this point, that a warrior spirit was to be found in the Waffen SS which was never equalled or ever surpassed by any other formation. The Waffen SS became the embodiment of military reliability [in defence] and joy of combat [in attack] . . . '

This brief history of 'Das Reich' Division, has I think, proved that in the case of 2nd SS Panzer Division Hausser's claim was no exaggeration but rather a sober appraisal of the fighting ability of that formation and the men who were part of it.

Appendixes

Divisional Commanders

If one excepts the pre-war creations and amalgamations of the Politische Bereitschaften into SS Standarten and accepts 1939 as the birth year of the SS 'V' Division, the life-span of the formation which became 2nd SS Panzer Division 'Das Reich' lasted less than six years. That 'Das Reich' gained an imperishable fighting record in that brief period is due to the calibre of the men who were its commanders. In many cases they had only a brief tenure of office, for some had been appointed when wounds or illness removed the incumbent, while others were posted to take up new, more senior posts. Hausser, was a case in point. He went from divisional commander to become a Corps commander and then to lead Seventh Army in north-west Europe during 1945, before taking up post as commander of Army Group 'C' in 1945.

Hausser, the first commander of 'Das Reich' Division, was wounded on 14 October 1941 and his place was taken by Bittrich, who was posted away after only a few months and promoted to command, at first a fresh division and then a Corps. The brief period in office of Mathias Kleinheisterkamp was followed by a longer period enjoyed by Georg Keppler. He led the Division until a brain haemorrhage removed him from command and he was succeeded by Herbert Vahl, who had until then led the divisional panzer regiment. When Vahl was wounded Hausser, commanding the SS Corps, appointed Kurt Brasack of the artillery regiment to fill the post temporarily, until Walter Krüger was able to take over. It is not known for certain when Krüger ceased to be in command because the dates given in official documents do not agree, but when the Division was posted to the Western Front the general officer commanding 'Das Reich' was Heinz Lammerding. On 26 July 1944 Christian Tychsen of the panzer regiment, became GOC, but was mortally wounded only two days later. Otto Baum took over the post and held it until November, when he was posted away to command another SS division. Lammerding, who had commanded 'Das Reich' at the beginning of 1944, led it again in November and held the post until 20 January 1945 when he handed over to Karl Kreutz, the CO of the artillery regiment. During the second week of February 1945 Kreutz was replaced by Ostendorff, who was mortally wounded in the fighting in Hungary and was succeeded by Rudolf Lehmann. When, during the fighting in Vienna, he too was wounded, leadership of the Division passed back again to Karl Kreutz, under whom 'Das Reich' passed into captivity.

HAUSSER, Paul. Born 7 October 1890. Served during the Great War and in the post-war Reichswehr, from which he retired in 1932 with the rank of Lieutenant-General. He was then invited to join the SS and rose to become Inspector of the SS Verfügungstruppen in 1935. Hausser raised the SS 'V' Division and was its first commander, serving from 19 October 1939 to 14 October 1941, when he was wounded in action. From 1942 to 1944 Hausser served as General Officer commanding the SS Panzer Corps (later II SS Panzer Corps), and took over command of Seventh Army in Normandy until he was badly wounded in the Falaise fighting. After convalescence he took up the post of commander of Army Group

'C'. His decorations included the Knight's Cross with Oakleaves and Swords.

BITTRICH, Willi. Born 26 February 1894, Bittrich saw service during the Great War as a pilot in the Air Force. He joined the Verfügungstruppen and by 1938 had become commander of 1st Battalion 'Der Führer' Regiment. Within two years he was commanding officer of 'Deutschland' Regiment. He took over command of the Division when Hausser was wounded and led it until 31 December 1941. He then went on to lead the SS Panzer Corps during the Battle of Arnhem in the autumn of 1944. Bittrich's decorations included the Knight's Cross with Oakleaves and Swords.

KLEINHEISTERKAMP, Matthias. Born 22 June 1893, Kleinheisterkamp saw service during the Great War. He joined the Verfügungstruppen in 1934, and led a battle group during the Polish campaign of 1939. He then commanded the 3rd Battalion of 'Deutschland' Regiment and became the Division's third commander, succeeding Bittrich on 9 January 1942. He led Das Reich until 1 April 1942. He was posted 'missing believed killed in action' on 8 May 1945. His decorations included the Knight's Cross with Oakleaves.

KEPPLER, Georg. Born 7 May 1894, Keppler served with the German Army on the Western Front throughout the Great War. In the post-war years he served in the police force between 1920 and 1935. He then joined the Verfügungstruppen and was promoted to command 1st Battalion 'Deutschland' Regiment. By 1938 he was commanding 'Der Führer' Regiment which he led until promoted to command the Division on 1 April 1942. He held the post until 15 February 1943, when he suffered a brain haemorrhage. His decorations included the Knight's Cross.

VAHL, Herbert. Born 9 October 1896, Vahl served in the Great War, taking part in the battles of Verdun and the Somme. It was not until 1 August 1942, that Vahl transferred to the Waffen SS and he led 'Das Reich' Division from 15 February to 18 March 1943. He was killed in an accident in Greece on 22 July 1944. His

decorations included the Knight's Cross.

BRASACK, Kurt. Born 6 April 1892, he was commanding the divisional artillery regiment when Herbert Vahl was wounded in action on 18 March 1943. Brasack led the Division until 3 April 1943, when he was replaced by Walter Krüger. His decorations included the German Cross in Gold.

KRUGER, Walter. Born 27 February 1890, Krüger served in the Alpenkorps during the Great War and was badly wounded. He joined the SS in May 1935 and rose to command a battalion of 'Germania' Regiment. He took over command of the Division during March 1943 and held the post until 23 December 1943. He is reported to have been killed in action on 22 May 1945, in Courland, but since the war had already ended, he either died or was executed by the Soviets. Among his decorations was the Knight's Cross with Oakleaves and Swords.

LAMMERDING, Heinz. Born 1905, Lammerding commanded the Division on two occasions. First from 7 March to 24 July 1944, and then from 23 October 1944 to 2 February 1945. His decorations included the Knight's Cross.

TYCHSEN, Christian. Born 3 December 1910, he served in the Division, chiefly in the panzer regiment. He was called upon to lead 'Das Reich' on 26 July 1944, and was posted 'missing, believed killed in action' only two days later. His decorations included the Knight's Cross with Oakleaves.

BAUM, Otto. Born 15 November 1911, he was commissioned in April 1939 and served with the Division throughout the war. He led the Division after Christian Tychsen was posted missing in Normandy on 28 July 1944. Baum commanded 'Das Reich' during the Falaise battles and was succeeded by Lammerding on 23 October 1944. His decorations included the Knight's Cross with Oak eaves and Swords.

OSTENDORFF, Werner. Born 15 August 1903. He served in the pre-war SS. He was commissioned in 1934 and rose to command the divisional battle group which stayed on the Eastern Front after the mass of 'Das Reich' was withdrawn to Germany. He took over as divisional commander on 4 February 1945 and held the post until 9 March 1945, when he was wounded in action and died as a result of those wounds on 1 May 1945. Among his decorations were the Oakleaves to the Knight's Cross which were awarded posthumously on 6 May 1945.

LEHMANN, Rudolf. Born 30 January 1914, Lehmann was commissioned Untersturmführer on 20 April 1936, and had risen to the rank of Standartenführer by 30 January 1945. He succeeded to command of the Division upon the wounding of Werner Ostendorff, and led the Division in the battle of Vienna. He was wounded during the fighting and handed over command on 13 April 1945.

KREUTZ, Karl. Born 20 September 1909, Karl Kreutz entered the SS and was commissioned as an Untersturmführer during November 1935. He too served twice as divisional commander. The first period was from 2 to 4 February, when he succeeded Lammerding, and then from 13 April to 8 May 1945, when the Division ceased to exist as a fighting formation. The decorations which Kreutz won included the Oakleaves to the Knight's Cross.

SS Ranks

It must be appreciated that it is not possible to give exact equivalents of certain ranks. There is, for example, no equivalent rank of General Oberst in the British Army. Similarly, the subtle distinctions found in the German Services, between an NCO with portepee and one without portepee, are not found in the British Army. SS ranks are usually given in German books accompanied by their Army equivalents, i.e., SS Brigadeführer und Generalmajor der Waffen SS; SS Gruppenführer und Generalleutnant der Waffen SS, etc.

Grenadier/Panzergrenadier, etc.	Private soldier
Obergrenadier, etc.	Lance-Corporal
Sturmmann/Rottenführer	Corporal
Unterscharführer	Lance-Sergeant
Scharführer	Sergeant
Oberscharführer	Colour-Sergeant
Hauptscharführer	Warrant Officer 2nd class
Sturmscharführer	Warrant Officer 1st class
Untersturmführer	2nd Lieutenant
Obersturmführer	1st Lieutenant
Hauptsturmführer	Captain
Sturmbannführer	Major
Obersturmbannführer	Lieutenant-Colonel
Standartenführer	Colonel
Oberführer	Brigadier
Brigadeführer	Major-General
Gruppenführer	Lieutenant-General
Obergruppenführer	General
Oberstgruppenführer	('Colonel-General')

Glossary

It is self-evident that a difference exists between certain terms used in the British and German armies. If one excepts military ranks, a comparative table of which is given above, there are German words which need explanation.

Freikorps At the end of the First World War various countries attempted to seize and to occupy parts of eastern Germany. Groups of former German soldiers fought against those foreign invasions, and in time those irregular formations were formally organized and titled the 'Frei Korps'. Much of the organization of the Storm Troops was taken over from the Freikorps, as were certain items of insignia.

HIWI This acronym describes Russian soldiers taken prisoner by the Germans who volunteered to work for the German Army, often (though not always) in a menial capacity.

Politische Bereitschaften The need for bodies of men to put down any attempt at a counter-revolution in Germany led to the creation of Politische Bereitschaften of SS men. In time, the Bereitschaften were organized into battalions and eventually Standarten.

Spiess There is no direct equivalent in the British Army to the Spiess, who was in one sense in charge of unit welfare and who held Warrant Officer rank.

SPW The abbreviation for the German compound noun 'Schuetzen Panzer Wagen' (armoured personnel carrier).

Standarten A Standarte approximated to a German Army infantry regiment and was created out of the combination of several SS battalions which had them-

selves grown out of the Politische Bereitschaften organization.

Tross This is translated as 'Train' or 'B' Echelon. In either case, what is meant is that part of a formation other than its fighting units. 'A' Echelon, in the British Army was where ammunition was issued during battle. 'B' Echelon was where the cooks and clerks worked.

VB This is the abbreviation for Vorgeschobene Beobachter, known in the British Army as the FOO or the artillery forward observation officer.

SS – Allgemeine The Allgemeine, or, General, branch of the SS was a bureaucratic hierarchy which infiltrated every strata of German society.

SS – Verfuegungstruppen The Nazi government's dependence upon a politically reliable armed police force (the Politische Bereitschaften) led to the creation of Verfuegungs units. These were located in the principal cities of the Reich and were eventually grouped regimentally. When those regiments (Standarten), were divisionally grouped the Verfuegungs Division was created.

SS – Waffen When the decision was taken to create an SS Division to serve in the German Army, the logical step was to arm the existing SS Standarten of the Verfuegungs troops and to organize these along correct military lines. They then became the Armed SS – *die Waffen SS*.

Bibliography

German titles

Bundesverband der Soldaten der ehem. Waffen SS. Befehl des Gewissens

Hauser, H. *Regiment 'DF' vom 9ten Mai 1945 bis 17ten Mai 1946*

Hausser, P. *Soldaten wie andere auch*

Klietmann, K. *Die Waffen SS: Eine Dokumentation*

Kraetschmer, E. *Ritterkreuztraeger der Waffen SS*

Kurowski, F. *Die Schlacht um Deutschland*

Lehmann, R. *Die Leibstandarte SS Adolf Hitler* (all volumes)

Maier, G. *Drama zwischen Budapest und Wien*

Meyer, H. *Die 12te SS Panzer Division 'HJ'* (both volumes)

OKW. *Tagesbuch*

Regts Kameradschaft. *Das Regiment 'D' 1934–1945*

Schulze-Kossens R. *Die Junkerschulen*

Schwinke, W. *Errinerungen an meine Dienstzeit in der Waffen SS*

Stadler, S. *Die Offensive gegen Kursk*

Steiner, M. *Die Freiwilligen*

Tessin, G. *Verbaende und Truppen der deutsch. Wehrmacht und Waaffen SS, 1939–1945*

Weidinger, O. *Oradour*

— *Kamerad bis zu Ende: Die Geschichte des Pz. Gr. Regiment 'DF'*

— *Division 'Das Reich'* (all volumes)

Woltersdorf, A. *Picknick zwischen Zhitomir und Biarritz*

Additionally, the magazine of the Waffen SS, *Der Freiwillige*, post-battle reports, private correspondence, interviews and other material supplied by former members of the Division.

English Language

HMSO. *The War in France and Flanders*

— *The Campaign in North West Europe*

Keegan, J. *Six Armies in Normandy*

Lamb, R. *Montgomery in Normandy*

Lucas, J. and Barker, A. J. *The Killing Ground: The Falaise Gap*

Index

Index